Managing Information Communication Technology Investments in Successful Enterprises

Sam Lubbe, University of KwaZulu-Natal, South Africa

T0321986

IDEA GROUP PUBLISHING
Hershey • London • Melbourne • Singapore

Acquisition Editor:	Kristin Klinger
Senior Managing Editor:	Jennifer Neidig
Managing Editor:	Sara Reed
Assistant Managing Editor:	Sharon Berger
Development Editor:	Kristin Roth
Copy Editor:	Larissa Vinci
Typesetter:	Jamie Snavely
Cover Design:	Lisa Tosheff
Printed at:	Yurchak Printing Inc.

Published in the United States of America by
    Idea Group Publishing (an imprint of Idea Group Inc.)
    701 E. Chocolate Avenue
    Hershey PA 17033
    Tel: 717-533-8845
    Fax: 717-533-8661
    E-mail: cust@idea-group.com
    Web site: http://www.idea-group.com

and in the United Kingdom by
    Idea Group Publishing (an imprint of Idea Group Inc.)
    3 Henrietta Street
    Covent Garden
    London WC2E 8LU
    Tel: 44 20 7240 0856
    Fax: 44 20 7379 0609
    Web site: http://www.eurospanonline.com

Library of Congress Cataloging-in-Publication Data

Managing information communication technology investments in successful enterprises / Sam Lubbe, editor.
    p. cm.
  Summary: "This book reports accounting and other information about business processes to assess performance. It discusses the impact of the IT revolution on the accounting function, and indicates the process of IT investment, its advantages and limitations. It is a revolutionary explanation of the purpose of IT investment and its role in organizations"--Provided by publisher.
  Includes bibliographical references and index.
  ISBN 1-59140-802-4 (hbk.) -- ISBN 1-59140-803-2 (softcover) -- ISBN 1-59140-804-0 (ebook)
  1. Information technology--Economic aspects--Africa. 2. Information technology--Africa--Management. I. Lubbe, Sam, 1952-
  HC800.Z9I5558 2007
  658.4'038--dc22
                 2006033749

British Cataloguing in Publication Data
A Cataloguing in Publication record for this book is available from the British Library.

All work contributed to this book is new, previously-unpublished material. The views expressed in this book are those of the authors, but not necessarily of the publisher.

Managing Information Communication Technology Investments in Successful Enterprises

Table of Contents

Foreword

This book addresses the need to corral some of the works on IT investment, even if in a condensed format. A daunting task indeed as there is a multitude of works that all deserve a place. A monograph on this task of IT investment could possibly be the end result and a fitting tribute to all the researchers who are still contributing to this subject. The editor (Prof. Lubbe) did a splendid job in ensuring that a wide spectrum of topics is addressed and as many authors as possible participated in this book. It is hoped that this work can be used by managers, teachers, and researchers.

Some of the chapters repeat the same idea but stated and explored in a different way. This deliberate strategy aims to unravel clarity since ideas can be viewed from different perspectives and we can therefore weigh and consider various alternatives. The careful reader must therefore be patient and trust the experience of the editor.

This book is an abbreviated explanation of this important topic. All possible areas are not covered and the book should be regarded as an introduction to this area of study encouraging further research. The list of references for each chapter indicates the multitude of related works and can help give direction to follow-up research. It must also be cautioned that there are many works available on each topic and each could be a study on its own. Much of the work presented in this book will add value if the reader expands the circle of focus and comparison, using Kipling's timeless advice:

> "It had six stalwart men;
> They taught me all I knew
> Their names were What? And Where? And When?
> And Why? And How? And Who?"

Prof. Brian McArthur
University of KwaZulu-Natal, South Africa

Professor Brian McArthur lectures information systems and technology at the University of KwaZulu-Natal in South Africa. His special areas of interest include research methodologies in IST, software engineering, knowledge and change management, critical reasoning, contemporary topics in IS, and their systemic relationships with systems analysis and design. He would describe himself as a generalist, combining varied experience in industry and education with academic qualifications spanning information systems, computer science, psychology, business leadership, mathematics, and English literature.

Preface

IT investment has made significant progress even in the short space of time since the first chapter was published. The importance of this subject has been widely appreciated. I have tried to incorporate illustrations of the types of research likely to draw attention to the formulation of management policy in this field. The field has been extended to include as many chapters as possible.

The book follows the normal procedure and tries to address some of the questions raised on the Internet. My acknowledgment is due to those who have written chapters and offered suggestions for improvement. I would also like to express my thanks to Idea Group Publishing for their patience with me and for suggestions on improving the book.

Organization of the Book

The book is organized into XVI chapters. A brief description of each of the chapters follows:

Chapter I: In the first half, the author focuses on what information communication technology (ICT) could be implemented in Africa in order to integrate the continent into the emerging global culture and associated economy. He also assesses the state of ICT implementation (investment) in Africa.

Chapter II evaluates the effective use of telecentres by small business owners. The world has changed and new ways of accessing information and obtaining knowledge is around. Telecentres can therefore play an effective role in facilitating communication between customers and small business owners. The study makes some recommendations that can be used by small business owners to improve their use of ICTs and Telecentres.

Chapter III notes that organisations are being forced to invest heavily in the deployment of information systems (IS) to obtain value and benefit in the new knowledge-based environment. He argues that organisational Intranets are being used as the platform for developing and deploying critical business applications to support business operations and managerial decision-making across the Internet-worked enterprise and this impact on IT investment decisions.

Chapter IV reviews the revolutionary advancement in information and communication technology (ICT) with strengthening of economic and social aspects that transforms global communities. A new kind of dynamism—the information dynamics—is emerging where communities are not restricted within boundaries and becoming competent with information, knowledge, networking, and versatility on a global basis.

Chapter V reviews the possibility of a link between organisational performance and information technology (IT) investment intensity in SME organisations practising e-commerce for 2001/2002. The answers to the research questions note that in top performing organisations (i) IT costs as proportions of operating costs were higher, (ii) IT costs as a proportion of turnover were lower than in weak performing organisations, and (iii) that a positive correlation exists between the computerisation index (CI) and the operating costs ratio. The investigation also reveals that Chief Executive Officers (CEO) expect additional output while planning e-commerce operations and keeping IT budgets constant.

Chapter VI addresses the effective use of information technology (IT) in small businesses. Worldwide it is regarded as a problem as was illustrated in the literature review. Small Business owners need to calculate and plan proper use of IT in their businesses by aligning their strategic IT planning to the business plan. A computing grid is proposed with a proper structure and guideline to help the owners.

Chapter VII demonstrates that SDC provides financial services knowledge with cross-industry technical skill capabilities. Their emphasis is on advanced development techniques and tools. The model they used is proving to be successful for all parties and the growth process had provided them with invaluable experience and expertise in the HR transformation. The lesson they have is that they need to ensure that they have a strong presence in the market to ensure that they are part of the IT investment process.

Chapter VIII considers if a link exists between company performance and information technology (IT) investment intensity in selected South African companies. The study covered the period 1989-1991.

Chapter IX reviews the present methodology and come to the conclusion that there is a solution for the predicament of the managers. The author is convinced that the ITIEM methodology is the solution.

Chapter X: Assessing extreme opinions, how does a small business Web site operator determine a feasible and responsible course of action for handling personally identifiable information collected in the course of business? Theoretical and practical frameworks must reinforce privacy treatment. Mishandling of the privacy issue can disrupt both the reputation and success of an e-commerce or other Web site, threatening the return on investment for the business. This chapter explores the current developments in privacy legislation in South Africa and examines the practical issues faced by a B2C (Business to Consumer) small business Web site owner implementing an online privacy policyt.

Chapter XI: Despite the technological progress made by organisations in Namibia, the impact of IT has not been studied. The existing definition of IT is not comprehensive enough to include all relevant IT expenditure. No return calculations are made, though managers are showing growing concern at the increasing IT costs. The purpose of this chapter is to determine what organisations in Namibia use as basis for investing in IT. In interviews with six organisations in Namibia, it was determined how they define and manage their investment in IT. Some conclusions can be drawn, the first being that organisations need to look at their definition of IT to include all aspects of IT like communication systems, maintenance, etc. The second implication is that somebody must be appointed to take responsibility for managing the IT investment.

Chapter XII: The author conducted research to determine whether IT managers, IT auditors, users, management, etc. use a certain evaluation and selection process to acquire software to meet business objectives and the requirement of users. An argument was used that the more thorough the software evaluation and selection process, the more likely it would be that the organisation will chose software that meets these targets. The results confirmed that Media24 uses suggested protocol as noted in the theory for software acquisition correctly during most stages

Chapter XIII examines the impact of the Internet (as part of IT investment) on a student society by investigating the effective use of the Internet at tertiary education. The main objectives of the studies were to determine whether the Internet is being optimally utilized at tertiary education, and to evaluate the level of utilization of the Internet.

Chapter XIV reviews the impact of security in small and medium enterprises. It views the development of a security policy in serious light and comes up with some recommendations on how this can be handled.

Chapter XV: Constructivist theories and modern pedagogical concepts emphasize that an activation of students is one of the most influential factors for learning effectiveness. The focus is on student's demographics in order to analyze their reaction towards e-learning. Solving tasks and observing and critiquing this solution process, instead of merely assessing the end product of e-learning processes. A sample of 105 students from the University was drawn and the findings suggest that e-learning investment can help address a need for this type of support

Chapter XVI addresses the needs for a community computer centre (Telecentre) for the community of Emkhambathini. This study was part of the information systems research exercise that was conducted by students. The problem that the researchers experienced was that Emkhambathini has no access to information and a need exists to ensure that this community joins the 21st century. The Telecentre will also serve as a community upliftment tool. The data was collected using a questionnaire, it was collated and analysed using SPSS. The conclusion was that gender or employment does not play a role when there is a real need to access information.

Sam Lubbe

Acknowledgments

The editor would like to acknowledge the help of all involved in the collation and review process of the book, without whose support the project could not have been satisfactorily completed. Also, a special word of thanks to Prof. Rembrandt Klopper who helped to ensure that the papers are on the same level and that they flow into each other. Deep appreciation and gratitude is due to Prof. Klopper for other editorial support services for coordination of this yearlong project.

Some of the authors of chapters included in this book also served as referees for articles written by other authors. Thanks go to all those who provided constructive and comprehensive reviews. Support of the School of Information Systems and Technology at the University of KwaZulu-Natal is acknowledged for archival server space in the completely virtual online review process.

Special thanks also go to all the staff at Idea Group Inc., whose contributions throughout the whole process from inception of the initial idea to final publication have been invaluable. In particular to Kristin Roth, who continuously prodded via e-mail for keeping the project on schedule.

In closing, I wish to thank all of the authors for their insights and excellent contributions to this book. I also want to thank all of the people who assisted me in the reviewing process. Finally, I want to thank my wife and son for their love and support throughout this project.

Sam Lubbe, PhD
Durban, South Africa

Chapter I

What Kinds of Organisations do We Want to Build in Africa with Information Communication Technology?

Rembrandt Klopper, University of Zululand, South Africa

Abstract

In the first half of this contribution, the author focuses on what information communication technology (ICT) could be implemented in Africa in order to integrate the continent into the emerging global culture and associated economy. In the second half, he assesses the state of ICT implementation in Africa. The emergence of worldwide information and communications technology (ICT) networks in the last quarter of the 20th century has steadily effected vast and permanent changes with regard to how people in free market open societies communicate, work, do business, and spend their leisure time. In spite of the recent bursting of the dot com bubble and increasing strains experienced in the ICT manufacturing sector, advances in information technology and telecommunications (ICT) will continue to reshape the major institutions of society in the 21ˢᵗ century. This ought to lead to a more efficient way of life for at least some people. However, it is not clear whether this "progress" will actually be satisfactory for all. There are many more facets to the application of ICT than simple business efficiency. This chapter asks, "after 50 years of ICT, what kind of society do we want to create for ourselves, and what level of choices are available to individuals and corporate entities?" As was pointed out at the EU meeting in Lisbon in 2000, we need to be particularly aware of the potential for ICT to improve the lives of those who are disadvantaged.

Introduction

It has increasingly become clear that ICT plays an important role in how society develops. This is apparent from the plethora of initiatives we have seen in the past few years ranging from computer applications in business, education, transport, government, and medicine—to mention only a few areas of application. This relentless application of information and communications technology (ICT) has developed a momentum during the past 50 years during which personal computing has developed and grown in the workplace, and at home to an extent that could not have been envisaged when the first business computers went on sale in 1952. Despite the obvious importance of this technology in shaping the way we live, work, and play, we hardly ever hear the question asked, *"What kind of society do we want to build with our ICT?"* We seem content to have the providers of ICT shape the institutions that will ultimately determine the quality of our lives.

IT: The Shape of Things to Come

The central role of technology in shaping our society is not disputed by many. In fact, there is the argument that technology is a primary driver of history (Smith & Marx, 1994). This type of notion implies that we are on a technological treadmill, which gives us very little option, but to adopt technological innovations as soon as possible. This view suggests that we cannot escape from racing after each new wave of technology. And although in a number of ways this view is clearly true, we suggest that we are actually in a position as individuals to make important decisions about the society we actually want or believe to be appropriate. We may not have complete control over how technology influences our society, but at the same time neither do we have no control at all.

The first step in deciding how we might like to see ICT implemented in the future is to have a view of how the technology will develop in the medium term. To look into the future and suggest what we can and perhaps should be achieving with the help of ICT is no mean task. There is an old quip sometimes made by stand-up comic entertainers (which has also been attributed to the quantum physicist Niels Bohr); "Prediction is always difficult; especially prediction about the future." And when it comes to the application of ICT, the ability to predict is especially daunting. Furthermore, there is also an interesting admonition against prediction in Dante Alighieri's Inferno where he suggests that the 8th level of hell—the second worst out of nine levels—is reserved for futurists and fortune tellers (Jacoff, 1993). It is also very sobering to remember the famous remark of Lincoln Steffens upon his return from the Soviet Union in 1919, "I have seen the future, and it works." It is just as well that Steffens wasn't attempting even a rudimentary course in prediction or forecasting.

Therefore, from fear of the fires of hell or just simple embarrassment about being wrong, this author will not attempt to foretell the future of ICT, but will instead identify potential trends based on the technological options presently available to us. The options are of course many and it can be very difficult to see which are real and which are just figments of the imagination of technicians, the digitrati, and others. It is always interesting to remember how wrong important people have been when they spoke about how computers might develop in the future. For example, Thomas Watson Sr., the founding father of IBM said, "There is a world market for five computers!" Ken Olsen, the founder of Digital Computer Corporation said rather to his regret one supposes, "Who would ever want a computer in their home?" Also, let us remind ourselves of Bill Gates' contribution to these faux pas "Who could ever need more than 640K of memory?" Furthermore, in this chapter we are not just interested in the technology but rather in how it will be used in our society, which actually makes forecasting even more problematical.

However, we need to start with a view on how the technology will develop in the short and medium terms. From a pure technological point of view, there is every prospect that computers and telecommunications technologies—the bedrock of the IT revolution—will continue to improve in leaps and bounds. Computers will no doubt relentlessly continue to become more and more powerful. Moore's Law is alive and well and living in Silicon Valley and other parts of the world. At the current time, no foreseen limit is envisaged to this law. Our capacity to process and store data seems virtually limitless. It is now being said that we are producing some one to two exabytes[1] of data per year. This will no doubt continue to grow. In the next five to ten years, even greater advances in computing and memory power may be derived from the suggested amalgamation of biotechnology and electronics. Telecommunications will continue to become faster and faster. This will be done while the price of the equipment and facilities will continue to fall. This does not necessarily mean that computers will become cheaper as such, but rather that the price will probably stay at about the same level with much more power being provided for the same amount of money.

A more fundamental problem with IT adoption relates not to whether communications technologies will improve, but to human problems around IT adoption in Africa. The real question is whether the potential users of ICT in urban and rural communities of Africa would be willing to incorporate ICTs into their daily lives. The answer probably is that regardless whether they live in urban or rural communities, most Africans would adopt ICTs if they consider them to provide a cost effective and sustainable way of solving a range of problems that beset their daily lives. Those problems are formidable: all-consuming poverty fuelled by unemployment, drought, diminishing land resources, poorly developed health care and educational resources, rudimentary transport infrastructures, local political and global economic exploitation, and so on.

As economies of scale make established technologies evermore affordable and because conscious efforts are presently being made to develop a new generation of light, affordable, and ergonomically efficient ICT, increasing numbers of African consumers will be willing to invest in ICT—provided that they even faintly believe these instruments will enable them to break the grip of poverty and isolation on their lives.

On the telecommunications front we will see bandwidth increase and prices fall dramatically, provided that governments deregulate telecommunications to ensure that the monopolistic stranglehold of telecommunications providers is broken through competition in the market place. In deregulated economies, international phone calls are charged in pennies an hour.[2] This will completely open up communications in a way hard to currently envisage. Technology changes such as this will impact Telco's and their employees as traditional pricing models break down video-on-demand will become a reality as will domestic and mobile video conferencing, probably even from wristwatch type devices as envisaged in the Dick Tracey stories, will eventually become ubiquitous.

It appears that nearly everyone on the planet (at least in the more developed countries) actually wants mobile teleconferencing in some form or another. The mobile phone has become a very much superior version of the security blanket by which those who are lonely and who need to feel connected to others anywhere in the world can do so instantly. The mobile telephone has changed the focus of communication to the individual rather than a particular location.

It also seems that many people want to be able to talk using the most modern and fashionable handset and in this respect, a piece of telecommunication equipment has become a personal fashion accessory. As a result of this attitude towards these hand sets, it is estimated that there are more than 100 million discarded mobile phones in the United Kingdom alone, awaiting ecologically clean disposal. Furthermore, it is interesting to note that the race for new features accompanying these handsets and the corresponding generation of additional revenue streams can have interesting consequence. The advent of mobile phones capable of taking and sending pictures or video clips has led to a variety of enterprises banning their use. Banks, schools, gyms, and exclusive nightclubs[3] for example have all barred the taking of pictures or video footage on their premises.

Not only do we put computers and telecommunications abilities into many in all kinds of domestic devices, we also install tracking chips into our pets and our children's clothes. Sooner or later, someone may even propose that we put a microprocessor and a telecommunication device into a diagnostic toothbrush, enabling it to report problems to the dentist and to schedule an appointment, and in between even doubling as a telephone!

Remotely operated electronics is increasingly being used by the authorities for crime control. Great Britain already uses thousands of closed circuit television cameras (CCTVs) in urban communities, linked to computer networks and other telecommunication devices to detect criminal activities, to enhance private and public security, and to serve as evidence by helping to identify perpetrators. On the other side of the Atlantic, there is disagreement between the president of the USA and Congress about the legitimacy of co-opting Internet service providers to enable the Federal Government to monitor the communications of American citizens as part of ongoing an anti-terrorist campaign.

The recent upsurge of phishing e-mail messages and the successful swindling of banks and governments are examples of evasive criminal behaviours, as are evermore innovative ways trading in pornography over the Internet. There is little doubt that in the next ten years smart computers and telecommunications devices will exist, many of which have not yet been invented at this stage as a ubiquitous part of a global fully wired society. The jury is still out on where citizens will eventually draw the line between being willing to be under constant surveillance for safety's sake, and insisting on the right of individual privacy.

Where communication networks with proper bandwidth permit fast electronic communication, we are beginning to integrate intelligent decision making protocols in networked appliances that form part of smart kitchens and other intelligent devices throughout our homes (Herper, 2001, Levinson, 2003). Ovens, kettles, and climate control devices can already be operated remotely, curtains drawn and TVs or audio devices activated via cell phones, or baths filled to just the right level and temperature as we approach our homes at the end of the day. During the day, our fridges will have placed orders for us with our grocers, supermarkets, or fast food vendors, to be delivered just in time as we arrive at our homes, kept clean by roving bots.

Fault detection will be incorporated into many of our domestic appliances, which will alert us about worn out equipment. We will use the technology in an attempt to remove as many domestic chores as we can as we become more efficient in our home life. Hopefully, not many of us will buy these fully wired homes as they will take away much of the familiar routine that actually constitutes human life. But they will be on the market for those who want them and who have a lot of spare cash to buy them, as they will not come cheap—at least initially. Of course, it will also be necessary to be trained in how to use one of these at home. Perhaps one day some entrepreneurial university will offer a master's degree: *Mastering your fully wired home.* In a similar vein, smart communication devices are disappearing off our desktops into our clothes and bodies, soon to be followed by companion robots (Cowley & Kanda, 2005; Klopper, 2005).

Generally, software use will become more user-friendly and intuitive. This will allow computers to undertake many more tasks for us. On the advanced software side, we will make progress with artificial intelligence (Kehal & Khurshid, 2001). Computers will not only dominate chess tournaments, but will take on and eventually become champions in the game of Go. We will produce more intelligent programs, which will increasingly help us in many different situations from medicine to banking, and travel selection to cooking. The computer will indeed help us make smarter decisions. It is however worth noting that sometimes smart decisions are at the expense of wise decisions, which generally need a broad and long term perspective and which often have to cope with paradoxes—one aspect of human thought that will remain a challenge to computers and companion robots for a while yet. It is thought that in the next 5 to 10 years we will make some progress towards a robotic or silicon brain. However, in all probability the quintessential essence and extreme complexity of human intelligent decision-making will elude us for the foreseeable future. Until we understand natural intelligence it is not likely that we will be able to fully master artificial intelligence. Given the reality that human cognition is a continent of which we have only begun to explore the beach on which we landed, Arthur C Clarke's estimate that by 2001 there would be mature artificial intelligence (AI) that could interact with human intelligence, represented by HAL in Clarke's visionary film *2001: A Space Odyssey* was clearly quite overoptimistic. Sophisticated and mature AI will almost certainly be only realized by the middle of the 21st century, if not in hundreds of years' time. Gene Roddenberry's fictional portrayal of the android *Data* in the Star Trek series, set about three hundred years in the future, is probably a more reasonable estimate of when mature AI could be available.

On the business front, ICT has been well established and should grow in leaps and bounds, making organisations more efficient. There will of course always be computer project failures with the concomitant lost of money. But on the whole information technology investment will continue at an increasing rate and it will turn out to be successful. DotComs and e-business will probably play a lesser role (Remenyi, 2001) while applications such as knowledge management (Depres & Chauvel, 2001) will become increasingly important.

Computers will interface with the public more and more. As a consumer, it will become harder and harder to find a human assistant to talk to. We will buy increasingly either on the Web or through a telephone or via some sort of electronic interface.

It will become hard to find a bank staffed by people rather than ATM type devices. Companies will continue to increase their fees to those of us who want to deal with human assistants. Furthermore, we will buy just about every type of ticket from a machine, or download prepaid tickets remotely onto our cell phones or credit card size cash cards. Train tickets, bus tickets, airline tickets, theatre tickets, and meal tickets will be dispensed by machines 24 hours per day and seven days a week. This could be seen as the siliconization of relationships between entrepreneurs and clients. Many companies see this as an improvement in efficiency. But for some people, siliconization is simply a synonym for depersonalisation and for many depersonalisation means a reduction in service. As the application of information technology and telecommunications continues to show good returns for their organizations the so-called productivity paradox (Brynjolfsson, 1993; Willcocks & Lester 1998) will be seen for the misunderstanding that it was. Computers will insinuate themselves into every aspect of the organisation whereby these machines will automatically reorder inventory, plan production, redesign products and reschedule vehicles, and so forth. Customer relationship management (CRM) will come into its own and will ultimately play a significant role in driving the day-to-day affairs of the business (Leavitt & Whistler, 1958).

In fact, with regard to corporate entities, the pervasive nature of ICT is pushing business organisations towards embedding technology deeper and deeper within their business models. For competitive reasons, there is increasing pressure to be more cost effective and ICT is seen as a central way of achieving this. The application of this technology can be with little or no concern for the individuals whose jobs are either lost or dumbed down. Seeing this through the technologic determinism lens, we could say that at present it seems that businesses do not have much choice as to whether or not they embrace this technology. If a particular business refused to "modernise" and its competitors so do then it could be forced out of the market place. It can be seen that the logic of the market has now begun to drive the logic of technological determinism.

To add to this situation, it is important to note that to prosper, businesses will increasingly need to have the capacity to interact seamlessly with other enterprises and dynamically create and dissolve relationships (Kalakota, 1998). This is most effectively facilitated by ICT. There are many examples of enterprises extending beyond their boundaries and acting as a virtual enterprise using ICT as the primary facilitator. Thus, the pressure to use ICT is nothing less than enormous and this has been reflected in the sales figures of this industry sector over the past decade.

When this trend is examined in detail, the concerns of business with generating a demand for their product or service, selling, and delivering their product to the customer, getting paid, managing the relationship with the customer, conforming to regulatory requirements, and managing the relationship with the shareholders, all lend themselves greatly to facilitation by ICT. If we look at each of these generic areas in a business, we can see an almost endless list of possibilities for ICT applications. Even if the enterprise has reservations about the use of this technology and does not want to continually chase after and adopt the latest ICT, the technological determinist argue that they may have no choice due to inevitable disruption of the traditional business paradigm by ICT. It is relatively clear that in order to survive, enterprises have to and will have continue adopting new technology hat gives them a temporary advantage over their competitors.

Given the reality of this determinist approach, the choice facing the corporate sector is how ICT can be introduced and how these systems will be put in place, and how sound policies for their use and governance will be developed. This concern is reflected in the current focus within large enterprises on project and program governance, enterprise architecture, and program office concepts This emphasis allows the enterprise to manage the application of the technology within the context of the corporate strategy, processes, rewards systems, organisation, technology, and measures. In addition, while a lot of research indicates that the technology should be put in to support of business change, a number of organisations appear to be forcing change through the organisation using the technology. Of course, this sometimes leads to poor systems or even to outright failure of ICT projects.

A hard line technological determinist would say that given these circumstances, there is no choice but to chase after the technology and that individual employees need to enthusiastically embrace the new systems by becoming an early adopter of technology, and make full use of it. But this a rather simplistic and incomplete view of the issues involved. Given the above, it is clearly hard to argue against the fact that ICT is rapidly becoming ubiquitous to the point at which it will be a central facilitator to virtually every aspect of our lives. But there are still real choices as to how we implement ICT. For example, as business continues to siliconise,[4] so relationships change. The human-machine interface changes attitudes as well as work practices. As mentioned before, the highly impersonal ATMs, ticket vending machines, and Web sites become the client interface. Telephone systems with multiple menu options may well be efficient from the company's point of view, but we have never heard one single phrase from a client in praise of them. It is hard to find any discussion on this type of issue. In general, this debate is simply avoided. Many corporate systems are either not ergonomic or simply downright user-unfriendly. Repetitive strain syndrome has now become an accepted complaint for office workers. Fortunately, the use of computers to monitor too closely individual work practices is unacceptable. But despite these issues, there seems to be an unquestioned implicit assumption that ICT leading to efficiency is simply good. But this is clearly not always the case. It is not at all clear that the users of ICT always obtain more satisfaction from their work or deliver a better level of service to the organisation.

Furthermore, large swathes of people are almost automatically left out of this ICT driven type of world (Morino, 2001). In general, those who are in any way traditionally disadvantaged have reduced access to ICT. One important group that is paid very little attention is people with disabilities. Virtually no accommodation is currently made for such individuals. Examples of this abound. Few Web sites have facilities for the visually impaired. Few ATMs are placed at a convenient level for those in wheelchairs. Few organisations make braille or voice recognition systems available for blind individuals.

Yet, for people with disabilities, ICT can radically change their lives through emerging neuro-informatics, the melding of electronic, and neurological signalling (Klopper, 2005). In the case of the blind or visually impaired, it is now possible to facilitate their reading of computer screen using various high-tech assistive technologies. Speech input, screen readers have changed the way people communicate. Furthermore predictive text, typing aids, and alternative input devices are available.

If accessibility is not taken into account during the design of technology, it becomes very difficult and expensive to retro-fit it. Clearly, it is desirable that all individuals can obtain the maximum benefit from the developments in ICT and this was recognised by The European Commission when it stated that "It is accepted that in today's Information Society 'learning to use technology' and 'learning to learn' with technology is necessary" (EU, 2000a). In the European context, national government in member countries is expected to encourage this by ensuring that teachers can provide the necessary skills training and by encouraging teachers to teach using technology. Furthermore, the EU has recognised the importance of the issue of inclusion. The EU commission has examined the opportunities, which an ITC empowered society could bring "the information society promises new digital opportunities for the socially disadvantaged" (EU, 2001). For the socially marginalized, technology could educate and inform, bring people closer together and provide them with new services—of course basic computer literacy and access to technology would be necessary. These issues were highlighted at the Lisbon Summit in March 2000 where the challenges of the Information Society and the actions needed to address them were defined in the eEurope Action Plan (EU, 2000b).

So the application of ICT opens up a lot of important issues and we will be forced to face a number of choices. We will need to think hard about our basic values and what sort of society we really want or need to create. We could create a highly siliconised society where the only issue is how to be more efficient in the market place. We could ignore personal preferences as to how people want to work and we can just pay for redundancies and repetitive strain syndrome cases. We can disregard our customer's dislike of telephone menus etc. This is the sort of world where we chase after technology for technology's sake not caring for the human impact of what we are doing.

On the other hand, we could be much more sensitive to individual preferences and also we could create a society where we use technology to enable people to overcome difficulties, to provide high-tech assistive technologies to people with disabilities, to provide support and education and to minimise exclusion. Furthermore ICT can be used to inform those who are struggling for freedom. In this world, we actually face the question of whether we get a better feeling from buying from a machine or drawing cash from an ATM or obtaining information from the Web than we do from having real live people help us. We also face up to the fact that although machines are generally more reliable than mere people, when they breakdown they can have a greater and more catastrophic effect than an inadequate people based service. Remember the last time your credit card was swallowed by an ATM in a far away town leaving you on a Saturday night without cash and without your credit card. Of course, most of us know about having back up arrangements or business continuity plans to use the modern parlance. But even that doesn't always work! Perhaps we will need to cultivate a culture that understands there is more to life than efficiency. Therefore, we need to seriously ask the question and face the implications of its answer: *Do we actually want to deal with machines rather than people?* We can withhold our business from those who want as much siliconisation as possible just to maximise their profit.

It is beyond the scope of this chapter to definitively state what kind of society we want to create for ourselves globally. However, it is clear from the information provided above that we feel that ICT should be used in a sensitive way that bears in mind the preferences and aspirations of the individual. It is also clear that ICT could play a very significant role in improving the circumstances of disadvantaged people including those with disabilities. We argue that not enough attention has been given to this and that it is now necessary to move quickly on this front. It is hoped that this article will generate a more debate and discussion as to how this may be achieved.

The State of Information Communications Technology in Africa

Introduction

As the deal with the Second Network Operator in South Africa takes shape, many questions will remain in the minds of the consumers of information communications technology (ICT), be they private individuals or business, about what benefits may be realised from the deal. However, at the same time we must not ignore the ICT trends unfolding in Africa and in particular within South Africa. There has been significant increase in the consumption of mobile telephony over the last 3 years, throughout Africa. BMI-TechKnowledge estimated in 2003 that the mobile content component of the ICT market was the second largest market segment—estimated then at about R150million a year. The main source of this revenue was from SMS content downloads such as ring-tones and icons [1].

Despite the growing appetite for connectivity, there is still a large portion of the African population that does not have a consistent means of access to connectivity. In a publication on www.bridges.org, one of the definitions given for this digital divide is "*a lost opportunity, with disadvantaged groups being unable to effectively take advantage of ICT to improve their lives*—what really matters is how the technology is used, and its incredible potential to improve quality of life for disadvantaged groups; effective use requires computers, connections, training, locally relevant content, and real applications of the technology to fit immediate needs."

Understanding the consumption patterns and drivers of ICT, as well as the appetite for ICT, will in the future play a key role in the quest to close the Digital Divide within Africa. In this context, it is believed to be pertinent to first examine ICT in Africa, what is driving it, and where the energy currently resides. With this in mind, a fine balance must be maintained in developing First World Business Systems to service a Third World Market.

A View of ICT in Africa

Intent

There is a need to address the knowledge economy in Africa if there is to be any progress in closing the Digital Divide. While there is acceptance and recognition by bodies such as New Partnership for Africa's Development (NEPAD) to accelerate broad-based growth and development, Africa generally lacks the resources, policies, and institutions to draw benefit from the knowledge economy.

The developed world provides the majority of theory and understanding of the information age whereas very little comes from Africa in terms of primary research which can be used to develop ICT policy formulation and strategy.

From this background, Research ICT Africa (RIA) was formed as an initiative of the Learning Information Network and Knowledge Centre of the University of Witwatersrand (LINK). The quoted definition of what RIA is, is extracted from their March 2004 ICT Sector Performance in Africa publication as being "An ICT policy and regulatory resource base for decision-makers in the public and private sectors and civil society, developing public-interest research findings through the networking of researchers at African universities."

General Findings

These initial findings have revealed that although there has been a growth in the access to telephony within the majority of African countries, this has been via mobile technology rather than the conventional more affordable fixed-line telephony.

Data available from the International Telecommunication Union regarding fixed line and mobile telephony trends in Africa between 1995 and 2003 (accessible at http://www.itu.int/ITU-D/ict/publications/world/world.html), reveal that of 43 African countries surveyed by 2003, 78% of them had more mobile than fixed subscribers, that almost 70% of African telephone subscribers used mobile telephony, that by 2001 mobile subscription overtook fixed line subscription, and that by 2003 for every 100 inhabitants there were 3 fixed line subscribers, compared with 6.2 mobile subscribers.

Two clear examples of this are Kenya and South Africa where there has been a decrease in fixed-line subscribers of 0.61% and 10% respectively over the period of exclusivity protecting the Public Switched Telephone Network (PSTN). Both Kenya and South Africa have experienced dramatic local-call tariff increases, which has been mirrored by fixed-line disconnections. Cameroon is likewise experiencing similar trends with a decrease in income of over 40% for the fixed-line operator over a three-year period. However, in the case of South Africa, the decrease in fixed-line subscriptions has been accompanied by continuing profitability by the semi-privatised national fixed-line operator. It appears that this may be partly ascribed to their focussing more on the lucrative business market than on investing in network roll-out.

In Africa, although there are reform models in place in terms of ICT and fixed-line policy in particular, the cost of access remains extraordinarily high. Whereas in the Northern hemisphere, the communications cost is on average 3-5% of per capita income, in Africa it reaches highs of 36% of per capita income.

The result of this is to restrict access to the Internet in an extreme manner. Although there is a very large mobile footprint, the cost effectiveness of Internet via this mode is still prohibitive. Information provided by the International Telecommunication Union (at http://www.itu.int/ITU-D/ict/publications/world/ world.html) correlates Internet access costs, stated in US$, with the number of Internet users for Cameroon,

Figure 1. Growth in mobile subscription in Africa between 1995 and 2003

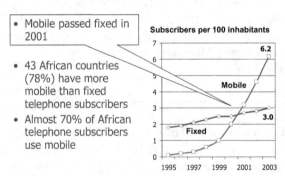

Figure 2. A comparison of Internet usage and Internet costs in seven African coutnries in 2002

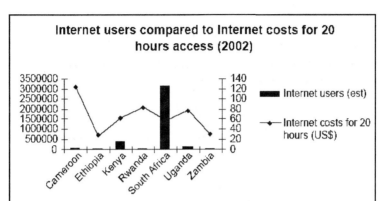

Ethiopia, Kenya, Rwanda, South Africa, Uganda, and Zambia for 2002. From the data provided, one can infer that there is no direct correlation between Internet access costs and number of users because Ethiopia and Zambia respectively have hardly any users (below 20,000), in spite of having of the lowest access costs per 20 hours of access, and conversely South Africa has by far the largest group of Internet users (round about 130,000), in spite of having relatively high Internet access costs.

In countries such as Cameroon and Rwanda, Internet access via Internet Cafe's remains the preserve of the fixed-line operator and it is estimated that there are some 450 cyber cafes in major centres of Cameroon.

Ethiopia on the other hand has adopted a strong monopoly model when they created the Ethiopian Telecommunications Company and the Ethiopian Telecommunications Agency. Despite having a population of some 70 million, there is still an extremely low network development with a waiting list, which represents nearly 85% of capacity. There is a fixed phone teledensity of only 0.6% and an Internet penetration rate of only 0.0001%, possibly the lowest in the world.

A Perspective of ICT Penetration in South Africa

On the following pages is a perspective of what the ICT penetration picture in South Africa looks like. As can be seen from the tables below, the information was produced in the main to include 2003. The 2004 data has as yet not been made available by the ITU. The extent of the impact of the Second Network Operator is as yet unknown and whether or not there will be real saving achieved by the average man in the street remains to be seen. There are hopes that there will be some

Table 1. Main line telephone subscriptions in South Africa and the rest of Africa between 1996 and 2003

Main Line Subscriptions						
	1996	1997	1998	2001	2002	2003
SA	4258.6	4645.1	5075.4	4924.5	4844.0	4895.0
Africa	13411.4	14775.9	16442.3	21015.5	22706.9	24711.9
	31.75%	31.44%	30.87%	23.43%	21.33%	19.81%
Lines per 100 People						
	1996	1997	1998	2001	2002	2003
SA	10.56	11.27	12.05	11.05	10.66	10.55
Africa	1.92	2.07	2.26	2.66	2.81	3.01

form of financial benefit realised by the consumer and that as voice over Internet protocol (VoIP) becomes a reality that further connectivity benefits both in terms of bandwidth and cost will be experienced.

Main Line Subscriptions

Main line subscriptions, the conventional copper landline subscriptions, have traditionally been provided by the semi-privatised Telkom. Information provided by the International Telecommunication Union (available at http://www.itu.int/ITU-D/ict/publications/world/world.html) shows that in South Africa, main line subscriptions peaked in 1998 at 5075.4k subscriptions and that the average number of lines per 100 people has remained the same as in 1996, suggesting that the increased subscription rate has remained in line with the growth of the population.

Cellular Subscriptions

Cellular subscription is a wireless service offered by three service providers in South Africa, Vodacom, MTN, and Cell-C. Although these three ostensibly offer an

Table 2. Cellular subscriptions in South Africa and the rest of Africa between 1996 and 2006

Cellular / Mobile Subscriptions						
	1996	1997	1998	2001	2002	2003
SA	953.0	1836.0	3337.0	10787.0	13702.0	16860.0
Africa	1150.8	2262.6	4156.9	25330.7	36970.0	50803.2
	82.81%	81.15%	80.28%	42.58%	37.06%	33.19%

Figure 3. Comparision of number of SMS messages per subscriber per month in eight African countries in 2002

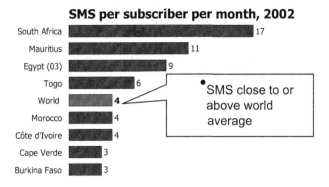

independent telecommunications service, they all three have licensing agreements with Telkom in terms of legislation and infrastructure. They rely on Telkom in terms of infrastructure and other licensing agreements. International Telecommunication Union data (available at http://www.itu.int/ITU-D/ict/publications/world/world. html), show persistent strong growth in South African mobile subscriptions between 1996 and 2003, growing from 953K to 16860k subscribers over that time period.

Along with these impressive growth statistics, we see that there is a very high rate of SMS usage in the mobile world. In 2002, South African mobile subscribers on average sent 17 SMS messages per month, in comparison with a world average of only 4 SMS messages per month.

Table 3. Aspects of Internet density in South Africa and the rest of Africa in 2001 and 2002

Internet Density				
2001	**Hosts**	**Users**	**PC's**	**per 100**
SA	238462.0	2890.0	3100.0	7.0
Africa	273836.0	6118.7	7849.0	1.1
	87.1%	47.2%	39.5%	
2002	**Hosts**	**Users**	**PC's**	**per 100**
SA	198853.0	3100.0	3300.0	7.3
Africa	243171.0	9988.2	9453.0	1.3
	81.8%	31.0%	34.9%	

Internet and PCs

Data provided by the International Telecommunication Union (available at http://www.
itu.int/ITU-D/ict/publications/world/world.html) reveal that there is no differentia-
tion between privately owned PCs and non-privately (business, government, NGOs
etc.) owned PCs. This applies equally for Internet subscription and usage. The data
shows that South Africa has a higher Internet density than the rest of Africa. The
major reason for this seems to be the lack of fixed line infrastructure in the rest of
Africa in comparison to South Africa.

*Figure 4. Comparision of main line subscription between South Africa and the rest
of Africa between 1996-2003*

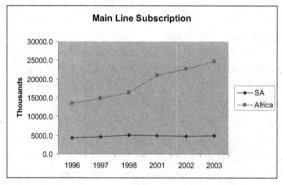

*Figure 5. Comparision of cellular subscriptions between South Africa and the rest
of Africa between 1996 and 2003*

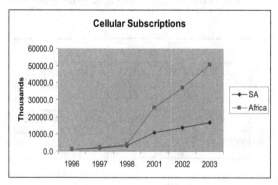

Table 4. Comparision between South African main line and cellular descriptions between 1996 and 2003

South African Main Line vs Cellular Subsrciptions						
	1996	1997	1998	2001	2002	2003
Main Line	4258.6	4645.1	5075.4	4924.5	4844.0	4895.0
Cell	953.0	1836.0	3337.0	10787.0	13702.0	16860.0
	446.86%	253.00%	152.09%	45.65%	35.35%	29.03%

Analysis of Reflected Data

Data obtained from International Telecommunication Union's subscription Web site is summarised by means of two graphs below. The first graph shows that between 1996 and 2003, main line subscriptions in South Africa remained flat in South Africa while at the same time having grown in the rest of Africa. Compared to Africa as a whole, South Africa shows an increase of nearly 184%, this suggesting that the SA market is behaving differently to the continental trend.

In contrast to this, as shown on the second graph, there has been a substantial up-swing in the take-up rate of cellular or mobile telephony in South Africa as well as in the rest of Africa, with Africa's rate being substantially higher. This implies that there is an escalation in African consumption rate, but that this does not imply that the SA market has necessarily levelled out. If one compares the two graphs, the results could be interpreted to indicate that Africa is playing catch-up. With SA only having 36.36 cellular units per 100 people in 2003 and a decreasing Main Line consumption, it would indicate that there is both the appetite and scope for further market growth.

Comparing the two means of telephony, it becomes clear that the appetite in South Africa is definitely in the mobile environment and not the fixed line environment and as such. Investment focus should be accordingly aligned.

With reference to Internet and the ownership of personal computers, there appears to be a large market opportunity for ICT growth both from an Internet and from a PC perspective. Firstly, what we see is that there are more PC's than there are Internet users, implying that the market has not been fully tapped from that per-spective. However, the penetration of the PC into the market as a communications device is lagging far behind that of the fixed lines and mobile telephony. At this stage, the reason for this may very well be a question of affordability rather than one of appetite.

Again, it is interesting to note that in excess of 80% of Internet hosts in Africa are in South Africa. But, the same trend displayed in the mobile environment may well be playing out in the Internet environment, where between 2001 and 2002, there

Figure 6. Increase in community access centers in South Africa between 1994 and 2002

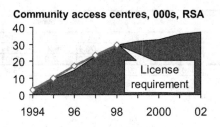

has been a significant change in the ratios of South African hosts and users relative to the rest of Africa, suggesting that Africa is playing catch-up in this environment as well.

With Internet access costs being effectively determined by the monopolistic Telkom as infrastructure provider, and with the South African government showing little inclination to deregulate the local telecommunications market, as can be seen from the fact that Internet access costs are twenty times higher in South Africa than in Europe and the USA, affordability is an important issue in Africa and South Africa. Where there is an economic as well as a digital divide, there have been significant steps taken in providing communication technology to these less privileged markets, as can be seen in the graph below.

Using 2002 as the cut-off period for this exercise, between fixed lines, mobiles, PCs, and CA (Community Access Centres), there were some 21.881 million ICT devices for a population of some 45.45 million, which could imply that only 48% of the population had access to ICT. From the perspective of a developing nation, this may look impressive, but more than that, it illustrates the immense opportunity for further growth and acceleration in the field of ICT in South Africa.

Conclusion

Two main points emerge from this analysis. Firstly, mobile communications will continue to exceed fixed line growth in Africa. Secondly, there is very little chance of Internet growth if it is based on fixed line deployment in Africa.

The conclusion that Internet growth in Africa will depend on non-fixed-line infrastructure has significance in two dimensions. Firstly, the Digital Divide focuses attention on bringing connectivity to the masses, but is mobile connectivity sufficient to fully close this gap? The cost of bringing connectivity and information to the masses via mobile is prohibitive for a third world country so in reality it is not about availability but about the ability to provide access cost effectively. Secondly, given that this scenario seems set to play out into the foreseeable future, it must have implications for financial institutions like Absa (Amalgamated Banks of South Africa). Consideration must be given to the extent of market reach via the Internet vs. the market reach via mobile. Accordingly, planning for the future and investment in the appropriate technologies should be carefully considered. This is not only from a back-office view when rolling out into Africa, but also from a user interface view.

Alliances with key stakeholders remains critical in order to ensure that the developments in African ICT are brought into business strategy on an ongoing basis to ensure that we remain at the forefront of banking in Africa.

References

Brynjolfsson, E. (1993). The productivity paradox of information technology. *Communications of the ACM, 36*(12), 67-77.

Cowley, S. J., & Kanda, T. (2005). *Friendly machines: Interaction-oriented robots today and tomorrow.* Alternation 12.1a of 2005, 79-105

Depres, C., & Chauvel, D. (2001, November 8-9). *The thinking behind the action in knowledge management.* The 2nd European Conference on Knowledge Management, Bled (pp. 133-154).

EU. (2000a, February), Communication from the Commission *"Strategies for jobs in the Information Society."*

EU. (2000b, June), eEurope 2000, *An Information Society for all,* Action Plan.

Herper, M. (2001). *Smart kitchens: A long way off. Forbes.comTM.* Retrieved from http://www.forbes.com/2001/12/21/1221networking.html

International Telecommunication Union Sector Performance in Africa. (2004, March). *International telecommunications union; Free statistics.* Retrieved from http://www.itu.int

Jacoff, R. (1993). *The Cambridge companion to Dante: Introduction to the inferno.* New York: University of Cambridge Press.

Jackson, P., & Curthoys, N. (2001, September 27-28). E-Government: A theory of public sector reform. In *Proceedings of the European Conference on E-Government,* Trinity College Dublin (pp. 209-216).

Kehal, M., & Khurshid, A. (2001, November 8-9). Artificial intelligence applications and implications in knowledge management. In *Proceedings of the 2nd European Conference on Knowledge Management,* Bled (pp. 255-268).

Klopper, R. (2005). Future communications: Mobile communications. *Cybernetics, Neuro-Informatics and Beyond,* Alternation 12.1a of 2005, 121-144

Leavitt, H., & Whistler, T. (1958, November-December). Management in the 1980's (HBR No 58605).

Levinson, M. (2003). Smart appliances, really slow networks. *CIO Magazine*, Ideas 2003, *Future Technology*, January 1, 2003. Retrieved from http://www.cio.com/archive/010103/46.html

Morino, M. (2001). *From access to outcomes: Raising the aspirations for technology initiatives in low-income communities.* Retrieved from www.morino.org/divides/execsum_report.htm

Mach, M., & Sabol, T. (2001, September 27-28). Knowledge-based systems for support of e-democracy. In *Proceedings of the European Conference on E-Government*, Trinity College Dublin (pp. 269-278).

McGovern, G. (1999). *The caring economy.* Dublin: Blackhall Publishing.

Pellissier, R. (2001). *Searching for the quantum organisation.* Cape Town: Juta.

Remenyi, D. (2001). *Business models for e-business.* Working Paper Series, Henley Management College, UK

Smith, M., & Marx, L. (1994). *Does technology drive history?* Cambridge MA: The MIT Press.

Telkom. (2003). Delivering on strategy (EU, 2001) Commission Staff working paper "*E-inclusion—the information society's. Potential for social inclusion in Europe,*" Brussels, September 2001

Willcocks, L., & Lester, S. (1998). *Beyond the IT productivity paradox: Assessment issues.* Maidenhead: McGraw Hill.

Endnotes

[1]   The term *exa* denotes 10^{18}. It is truly quite hard to imagine the implications of anything this size. The volume of data represented by this is truly quite impressive.

[2]   Telephone calls between the United Kingdom, the United States of America and Australia to mention only three such distant countries, now cost only one penny a minute if callers use special cost reducing services.

[3]   Clearly, the rich and famous do not want to be photographed in the leotards or on the dance floor.

[4]   Perhaps a more descriptive word for the ubiquitously use ICT?

Chapter II

Telecentres and Their Impact on Information Technology Investment for Small Business

Maxwell Mdumiseni Buthelezi, KwaZulu-Natal Financial Services,
South Africa

Marcus Sikhakhane, SDT Financial Software Solutions (Pty) Ltd.,
South Africa

Abstract

This study is evaluating the effective use of telecentres by small business owners. The world has changed and new ways of accessing information and obtaining knowledge is around. Telecentres can therefore play an effective role in facilitating communication between customers and small business owners. Telecentres will enable customers to access information such as services, prices, statements, information regarding a product, missed payments, history of credit supplied, etc. The study used a questionnaire to collect data. The study comes up with some recommendations that can be used by small business owners to improve their use of ICTs and telecentres.

Introduction

Telecentres have been hailed as a solution to small business development problems because of their ability to provide access to ICTs (Gómez & Hunt, 1999). It will also be a solution to the IT investment problems experienced by their bigger brothers. Telecentres can therefore play a role by providing small business owners access to information and communication. It will be a tool to communicate with their customers, suppliers, and administration.

The researchers have identified the following problems:

- Small business owners are unable to access help after hours or weekends.
- Most of the normal support is not able to offer similar telecentre support unless they appoint somebody to do so.
- The costs of owning infrastructures (i.e., telephone and Internet cost) are high and might be reduced by the use of telecentres.

An Introduction to Telecentres

IDRC (2003) notes that the information and knowledge age has been characterized by economic globalisation and a new approach to ICTs. Telecentres are a response to this globalisation aiming to provide access to ICTs where people do not have access (e.g., rural areas, etc.). A number of such centres have been implemented by various government and development agencies across the globe (Oestmann & Dymond, 2001).

Telecentres have been initiated in at least 21 developing countries (Gómez & Hunt, 1999b) and may be defined as a shared site providing access to ICTs for everybody. The primary goal of a telecentre is the provision of tools and skills to enhance communication and the sharing of information (IDRC, 2003).

According to the IDRC, the telecentre movement on the African continent is young (the earliest telecentres opened their doors in 1998). The nature and functions of African telecentres vary slightly but they are becoming the fastest tool for the delivery of information, knowledge, and education. Telecentres also have the potential to narrow the "digital divide" in remote, rural, and otherwise disadvantaged communities. They can also be useful in helping developing countries to increase access to the information, education, government information, healthcare, and other services and help develop communities socially and economically.

History of Telecentres in South Africa

There has been a proliferation of a number of variants of telecentres, some of which have proved to be successful (CommunitySA, 2001). The 1997 October Household Survey in SA stated that only 32.2% out of 8.8 million dwellings had access to a phone. Sixty-eight percent had access to a phone through their work, their homes, neighbours, or a communal phone. These figures have increased amongst Africans and coloureds, but are still short of achieving total access (CommunitySA, 2001).

CommunitySA cited Stavrou and Mkhize who suggested that telephones should cost a household not more than 2% of their total income. The results show that households spend on average between R21-R30 pm on telephones. Any notions of ensuring universal service in SA cannot be considered because affordability of usage and delivery do not match (CommunitySA, 2001). Recent work undertaken in KwaZulu-Natal shows that up to 40% of telephone traffic originated from a non-metropolitan host. Should this trend be true for SA, then this has implications for the investment in rural telecommunications (CommunitySA, 2001). A proportion (in some cases over 60%) of all new lines provided in households is cut off for non-payment within six months (CommunitySA, 2001).

The Status Quo of Telecentres in South Africa

Currently the targets for telecommunication operators come from license conditions of the operators (e.g., Telkom is obliged to supply 1.7 million lines in disadvantaged areas during their 5-year obligation period). Telkom also had to provide 120,000 payphones in villages by 2002 (CommunitySA, 2001). It is estimated that an additional 15,000 phone points will enable almost every person in SA to be within reach of a phone. This would not be an easy task, for these 15,000 phones points are in the remote areas of SA and if it could be accomplished, SA would achieve universal access (CommunitySA, 2001).

The Universal Service Agency has established 18 telecentres, 10 mini-telecentres, and had signed contracts for another 30 to be set up by December 1999. Some of the telecentres are successful (e.g., GaSaleka's telecentre offering telephones, copying, small business services, and computing, and their turnover is about R8000 pm). Other successful telecentres are in townships (e.g., Mamelodi Community Information Service who also has a Web page). Not all telecentres have been successful however, with general technical, billing, or organisational problems (CommunitySA, 2001).

Most of the Vodacom phone shops (a Universal Service Obligation of 22 000 lines in disadvantaged areas) are successful, the majority of these are in township areas. These are franchised, while most franchisees had to take up loans to establish their venture. Part of the success can be attributed to the fact that individual entrepreneurs run them. Some of these are starting to expanding into fax and photocopying services. The combined monthly turnover of these phone shops was reported to be about R8 million (IDRC, 2003).

SA has committed itself to provide access to information using telecentres because of a better developed ICT in Africa, and has the resources to aim for universal access. Early in 2005, all communities in SA should have telephones and telecentres, but are a small portion of what is required to fulfil the demand for telephones (IDRC, 2003).

Technology and Infrastructure

As stated before, telecentres provide connectivity and quality-assured portals to the global network. They are typically equipped with networked computers linked to the Internet and software (e.g., word-processing, spreadsheets, databases, etc.). Common accessories include printers, photocopiers, binders, laminators, telephones, fax machines, radios, videocassette players, and television monitors. Some are also equipped with CD-writers, scanners, data projectors, and mobile phones (The Commonwealth of Learning, 2001).

To access the Internet, telecentres need (The Commonwealth of Learning, 2001):

- Computers or computer networks with modems.
- Dial-up public switched telephone network or faster public data network connection, or a leased line with a higher bandwidth.
- An account with an Internet service provider, preferably one offering a point to point protocol account for Internet access by multiple PC users; a Unix to Unix Copy account; domain name registration (to give the centre its own unique Web address), and Web hosting (storing the telecentre's Web site on a server connected to the Internet, 24/7/365).

Telecentres provide affordable PC/Internet-based audio-conferencing, audio-graphics (computer conferencing combined with sound), and desktop videoconferencing. Where the infrastructure exists and the higher investment and connection costs can be justified, centres can be equipped for higher speed and performance ISDN videoconferencing or one-way/two-way satellite television. In choosing technologies, it is important to carefully consider (The Commonwealth of Learning, 2001):

- Communication requirements (e.g., small business owners needs like specialised software, etc.).

- Costs of acquiring, servicing, and repairing the equipment.
- Charges for the phone calls and Internet access (high costs will deter use).
- Quality of the power supply (UPS is highly recommended).
- Compatibility with existing systems and security.

Where small businesses, colleges, schools, hospitals, and government and other community organizations require similar services, it may be possible to share facilities and costs (The Commonwealth of Learning, 2001).

Structure and Types of Telecentres

There are many types of telecentres and they aim to respond to the demand for ICT services. Each telecentre is likely to match the needs of the community and the degree to which it becomes a part of the community. Telecentres start out small and expand their services in response to demand (Jensen & Esterhuysen, 2001).

Small business owners need access to telephones, faxes, photocopying machines, e-mail, and Internet services, as well as community development. If they are involved in the set-up and running of a successful telecentre, their confidence will be boosted. Negativity about effecting change will be banished and benefits for the community will be a result (Jensen et al., 2001). Gómez et al. (1999b) state that there are many types of telecentres (Jensen et al., 2001).

Telecentres can be found all over (e.g., universities, schools, cultural centres, local government offices, communities, etc.). They are funded, owned, and operated in the way they serve different kinds of users, and utilize technology to provide service (Jensen et al., 2001). Gómez et al. (1999b) identified some types of telecentres. These are not exclusive, since some are hybrid versions of previous types.

Micro Telecentres

Micro telecentres (MT) are housed in a shop or other business. They provide pay phones with a built-in Web browser and possibly a smart card reader and a receipt printer (some units are outdoor kiosks in South Africa). They are becoming common in public places worldwide (e.g., such as airports and train stations) (Jensen et al., 2001). The plain kind of MT may be a cell phone and the owner of the telecentre selling user-time to small businesses in smaller communities where there are no telephones. This worked in countries such as Bangladesh. Other examples include public internet terminals (PIT) developed by the SA Post Office (Jensen et al., 2001).

Mini Telecentres

A mini telecentre will offer a single phone line (possibly GSM cellular) with a three-in-one scanner/printer/copier, a fax machine, and PC with a printer, Internet, and a call meter. In SA, the Universal Service Agency commissioned the design of such a unit housed in a lockable wooden cabinet with wheels (Jensen et al., 2001).

Basic Telecentres

Basic telecentres is located in rural or marginalized areas, where there is limited access to services in general, and high rates of illiteracy. Civic telecentres are found in public libraries, school, universities, community organizations, and so forth (Gómez & Hunt, 1999c).

Cyber or Internet Cafés

Cyber or Internet cafés are profit businesses that sell services to the public (e.g., small business owners). MPCC facilities offer more than basic ICT services, focusing on specialized applications such as Tele-medicine and Tele-business. In West Africa, the word "telecentre" is used to refer to what is also known as a "phone shop" (Gómez & Hunt, 1999a).

Full Service Telecentres

A full service telecentre will offer phones, multi-media PCs with Internet, a TV set, a colour printer, a scanner, a digital camera, a video camera, an overhead projector, a photocopier, a laminator, meeting rooms, and a telediagnostic and video conferencing room (Jensen et al., 2001).

Sustainability

Telecentres have the potential for sustainability because of their social and economic utility and their capacity to respond to the ICT needs of the population. Some of the telecentres located in disadvantaged neighbourhoods had become popular meeting places for community members (IDRC, 2003). Telecentres are an integral part of the community's social infrastructure because they are accepted by the people, and the community is involved in their management. It seems that conceptual validity and institutional validity are logically linked to the extent that an idea has found acceptance, value, and concrete expression among the population (Etta, 2000; Jensen, 1999).

The existence and validity of MPCCs are guaranteed but the nature and form of future mutations of the institutions and indeed the idea may not necessarily follow those of the initial conception. The point was repeatedly made that conceptual validity confers on telecentre institutional sustainability (IDRC, 2003).

According to the IDRC (2003), financial sustainability for community telecentres remains elusive given the amount of revenues generated by the telecentres (a few could barely cover their running expenses). Despite steadily increasing incomes (50-70% spent on salaries), this situation does not generate financial confidence, stability, or sustainability. The funds provided by IDRC and other donors ensured that telecentres survive as long as the funding of the projects last.

It is important that telecentres develop strategies to generate income and raise funds from local partners. Short-term resources in the form of working capital, combined with guarantees of resources in the medium and long term, are needed to ensure the continuation of telecentres (Jensen & Walker, 2000).

Common Problems of Telecentres

Service delivery in the telecentres in Senegal was affected by common technical and infrastructure problems (Computer failures, printer breakdowns, and corrupted software) (IDRC 2003). On the other hand, bringing technicians meant appreciable disruptions to user timetables, electricity problems, principally power failures, or interruptions. Telephone and connection problems were also listed but users were not disturbed as they were used to this problem. The cost of use did not surface as an impediment, except among disadvantaged groups, such as small business owners and women (IDRC, 2003).

The Telephone System

A MPCC has at least three lines to start with—a voice line, a fax line, and a modem connection for PCs. If the MPCC is small and phone services are not an essential part of the planned operation, then it is possible to start by sharing a single phone line for all services (Gómez et al., 1999a).

It is possible for some PCs to share a single phone connection for Internet access. E-mail can be provided off-line via a batched service mode such as UUCP; the phone needs to be used for short periods to send and receive mail (Gómez et al., 1999c). If a telecentre intends to offer telephone conferencing facilities, hands-free and speakerphone facilities are useful. A combined telephone/answering machine is an asset to a telecentre, especially if the telecentre is only open certain times. An additional long-distance cordless phone (2.4GHz) can be made available. With a range of 2-3 km over open ground, these phones can be collected from the telecentre and taken to a business for the call. This would be popular among small businesses, the old, and the sick (Gómez et al., 1999a).

If cell coverage is available, a mobile cell phone can be used in a similar way using prepaid time. Because of the high cost of phone calls, cellular use should be avoided unless a special tariff can be negotiated. In some cases where no landlines are available, cell phones may be the only option to provide communication services (Jensen, 1999). The telecommunications operators have targets for providing access in disadvantaged areas as stated before (Benjamin, 2003).

A study was conducted looking at categories of small business owners and needy people that could benefit from subsidy (CommunitySA, 2001, cited Stavrou and Mkhize). The study indicates that in SA, 36% of all households fall under the minimum household subsistence level (Benjamin, 2003). Thus, on current available data, only 3.7 million households and some small businesses (42%) can afford to install and maintain a telephone without assistance. In South Africa, there are approximately 9 million households (Statistics SA, 1996). Around 3 million of these have a telephone, and 6 million do not. From the projections in Stavrou and Mkhize's paper, many households and small businesses would not be able to afford to run a phone (at current prices) even if there was coverage (Benjamin, 2003).

Services Offered by Telecentres

Telecentres aim to provide some of these services (Oestmann et al., 2001): Access to telephones and faxes, e-mail, Internet, Other information services, other developmental support to meet basic needs, and business in "information age" skills. Oestmann et al. (2001) argue that services provided by telecentres vary according to the degree of development of a country. Telecentre services were used for business and government information and for computer training, project hosting, typing services, and news (see also Amicas telecentres, 2002, and Oestmann et al., 2000).

The main reason for using telecentres was to obtain or send information (e.g., social interactions, contacting friends and family, preparing documents for social events (e.g., weddings and funerals), and personal entertainment such as watching television and videos, listening to radio, or reading newspapers). Professional and economic motives (e.g., seeking information) came second on the list of reasons for telecentres use (Etta, 2000).

Oestmann et al. (2000) state that although telecentres are praised as a development tool and have potential; the data available on rural demand and usage of the Internet in such centres suggest that this is not. These reasons are:

- Illiteracy in general and computer illiteracy
- Lack of awareness and culture about the use and benefits of ICT
- Language problems because the Internet is mostly in English

It would appear that computer training has increased Internet and personal computer usage in SA telecentres minimally (Oestmann et al., 2000).

Management, Ownership, Maintenance and Expenses

A telecentre will cost around R200 000 (i.e., five phones, four computers, a photocopier, fax machine, printer, scanner, overhead projector, TV and video, and modem). The building is fitted out with furniture and security. A mini-telecentre follows a model developed by the CSIR—a computer in a moveable cabinet with a printer, copier, scanner with phone lines, and a modem—costing around R15 000 (Benjamin, 2003). Some of the existing telecentres are successful (Benjamin, 2003).

According to the IDRC (2003), most telecentres experience management problems ranging from poor attitudes to weak management and technical skills (see also Etta, 2002). Amicas telecentre (2002) notes that operating costs for the telecentres vary. It depends on the type of connection and number of users (e.g., dedicated connections cost more that dial-up connectivity per mouth). The costs of software are expensive because they need the latest versions of software for users to ensure they are exposed to current technology.

Types of telecentre ownership models were private owned and trusteeship. The franchise model used in SA is regarded as a variant of private ownership. Most of the community telecentres ownership is trusteeship. This is an arrangement where the project is being held in trust by the executing agency for a period of time until the final owner is ready. None of the models was consistently related to good management although private ownership models left authority in the hands of managers (Etta, 2002). Financial sustainability for community telecentres remains indefinable (an example of a sustainable community telecentre was found in Phalala (SA) (Etta, 2002).

Security of Telecentres

Care must be taken to ensure the security of the telecentre equipment and money. Telecentres are public places and internal security measures should include constant vigilance, marking the equipment with identification marks, taking note of serial numbers to detect stolen items and possibly securing equipment to desks and benches (Jenson & Walker, 2000). Locks, window bars, and alarm systems may be necessary in high-risk areas. Some centres even find it necessary to employ guards' fulltime (Jenson et al., 2000). Security alarm systems and video cameras should form part of securing the equipment from being stolen or abused. The equipment needs to be insured as well.

Telecentres are seen as a means of providing affordable access to the Internet for the poor. The Commonwealth of Learning (2001) argues that telecentres should be open 20 hours a week to qualify for grants towards salaries, but actual hours are determined by local committees and community needs. Many centres offer 24 hours access, with individuals using security number or swipe card. The guards also clean, run errands and attend to the public, and so forth.

Telecentre Facilities

Telecentres are located in premises that belong to communities, associations, or chambers of commerce (IDRC, 2003). Telecentres therefore look cramped because premises are narrow and not comfortable (IDRC, 2003). Most telecentres do not guarantee privacy and quality of the furniture and equipment. However, the computer hardware was less impressive in terms of quality and quantity (IDRC, 2003). The management have to ensure that the equipment is in good condition (Commonwealth of Learning, 2001). Users on the other hand have to use the resources responsibly and report all faulty equipment to management (Commonwealth of Learning, 2000).

Global Small Business Communities and Telecentres

Increased small business expansions have been the result of some factors: increased access to training and ICT. The probability of a person participating in business activities at some point in their life has increased from 39% in 1989 to 47% in 2000. Over the same period, the expected duration of small business exposure has also increased, from 3.0 years in 1989 to 3.4 years. It was also noted that people are heavy users of the Internet compared to the general population (use of the Internet should be part of small business owners).

About 20% of people today began using computers between the ages of 5 and 8. By the time they were 16 to 18, all of the people in the USA had been using computers highlighting Africa's problems that support by telephone has a tradition in open and distance learning, but recent research (e.g., CommunitySA, 2001) has concentrated on support by electronic means. Some recent findings however provide evidence that the telephone is still a particularly effective medium for student support (EDEN Research Workshop, 2004).

Telephone contacts can help small business owners and is perceived as particularly encouraging by them. The use of the mobile phone for contact, particularly in countries without reliable landlines, also has potential. Text messaging can also be used by owners and support (EDEN Research Workshop, 2004).

Conclusion Regarding South African Telecentres

Telecentres can play a role in small business owners lives due to the growth of technology because the world is becoming a global village where business, individuals, and organizations are able to communicate effectively through the use of e-mail, telephones, and so forth. Telecentres is a facility that allows people to access information through out the world. Telecentres will therefore enable small business to effectively communicate with their customers and the suppliers. The next section will deal with the research methodology.

Research Questions

The theory has dealt with some issues of the problem statement but some issues remain unanswered:

- How can telecentres be utilized in the small business environment?
- Is there a need by small business owners for such a facility and what services should be provided?
- Is there a difference between normal and academic telecentres?

Research Methodology

Much of the literature and the research reviewed by the author in this study focused on a calculation of the total impact of telecentres without commenting, or providing guidelines for small business who use telecentres. The theoretical and philosophical basis of this study is empirical research. The research strategy employed was based on the approach described by Lubbe (1997). A literature survey of telecentre investment and evaluation issues was completed in two stages. After the preliminary stage, the literature review was written up and became the basis of the research. Subsequently the literature review was extended, a critique was developed, and research questions established.

The author then collected data using questionnaires which were develops to answer the research questions concerning the formulation, adaptation, and usage of a telecentres and its benefits. Thus, the research employed a combination of both qualitative and quantitative methodologies in order to ensure that it complied with scientific principles.

On the issue of bias, it is naive to assert that any form of research, or perhaps human activity generally, is without bias. Even in the physical and life sciences, the researchers' bias is reflected in the subject researched, the experiments chosen, as well as the way the experiment is conducted. Thus, bias cannot be totally eliminated but should be recognized and its implications acknowledged and accepted. The data was entered onto a spreadsheet; some statistics were calculated using EXCEL.

Analysis of the Data

This section deals with the analysis of data obtained from the questionnaires collected from the respondents. The researcher has collected 81 completed questionnaires. The questionnaires were distributed without targeting a specific sample small business population. Out of a total of 81 completed questionnaires, most of the respondents were females (49 respondents). According to the gender statistics, the ratio between females and males in KwaZulu-Natal equals 1:4. Most of the respondents are African. The main reason for the ethnic compilation of the sample is due to the geographical location in the Westville area (Indian) and its surrounding areas are black dominated locations (e.g., Umlazi, Kwa-Mashu, Ntuzuma, etc.).

In the eighties, most small business owners were school leavers. Today, the student population has grown and has seen an ageing of some sections of the student body while other sections have become younger. Young people are the ones who have a desire empower themselves with knowledge and tend to be more study orientated. Small business owners were in the category 30 to 49 and more independent.

A large number of people have enrolled for commerce related degrees and this would impact on small businesses as they would bet better trained and might make better IT investment decisions. Other degrees such as Law, BA, and BSc are also in demand. Increased small business expansion have been the result of two underlying factors: increased access to education and increased duration of support. The probability of a person participating in business activities at some point in their life has increased from 39% in 1989 to 47% in 2000. Over the same period, the expected duration of study for students has also increased, from 3.0 years in 1989 to 3.4 years and will probably impact on the ownership and further expansion. There is an increase in women small business owners.

Americans view the use of the Internet is a part of their daily routine because they are used to computers. It is integrated into their daily habits and has become as ordinary to them as the telephone or television. Support by telephone has a long tradition in but recent research and discussion has concentrated on support by electronic means. Some recent findings however provide evidence that the telephone is still a particularly effective medium for business support (EDEN Research Workshop, 2004).

The majority of the respondents (90%) make effective use of the telephones and the Internet to get information. Seventy-three respondents were making use of the facilities and eight were not using it at all. Telephones are a traditional way of contacting someone although new and effective technologies have been introduced (i.e., Internet and e-mail).

How Regularly Small Business Owners Use Telephones to Obtain Information

The use of mobile phones for contact, particularly in countries without reliable landlines, also has potential and can be used by both business and customer for support (EDEN Research Workshop, 2004). Telephones are still used largely by small businesses and have only recently become the subject of research in the context of mobile phones and "mobile learning." It is useful to differentiate between some types of telephone support, in addition to reactive contact between business and customer (EDEN Research Workshop, 2004):

- Proactive contact between customer and individual
- Proactive contact between supplier and small business owner
- Responsive contact between small business and individual customer
- Planned support by phone, whether with a group or an individual

Table 1. Use of telephones

Rating	Respondents	Percentage
0	20	25%
1	12	15%
2	14	17%
3	9	11%
Above 4	26	32%

Small business owners make use of telephones to get information that they seek from both their customers and suppliers. They also phone to enquire on items such as fees, prices, and confirmation of orders. The majority of the respondents (75%) make use of the telephone to get information.

Most of the respondents do not phone to enquire about the information they need, as they prefer to inquire directly. Another reason for not using the phone is that it is more understandable when the person explains information face-to-face. A little more than 30% of the respondents demonstrated that they, however, effectively make use of telephones. They noted that it saves them time and inconvenience instead of going to the offices or standing in long queues.

According to Table 1, most of the respondents still use telephones to get the information they require. The type of work that they perform over the phone varies. A number of respondents call to enquire about products or services.

Researchers are also contributing to the use of telephones. Small business owners doing research can make phone calls to the respondents that they are dealing with (i.e., calling companies to enquire about specific information such as gross incomes, etc). Other work done over the phone includes issues such as calling friends, to inquire about specific products.

Small business owners are not always available, they often supply their personal cell phone number, and it is sometimes hard to find them. A large number (69%) of respondents are dissatisfied with the availability of owners by telephone. Respon-

Table 2. Type of work done over the phone

Type of Work	Respondents	Percentage
Services	5	6%
Product	18	22%
Other	42	52%
Don't use phone	15	19%
No response	1	1%

Table 3. Hours of accessing small businesses

Response	Respondents	Percentage
Yes	18	22%
No	56	69%
Don't use phone	7	9%

dents stated that it is frustrating to make an inquiry and you cannot get through. Respondents have also suggested that small business owners group together and create a telecentre that will be available 24/7. Customers and small business owners should call somebody that will assist with their problems.

Problems Associated with Making Phone Calls

Most of the problems that small business owners experienced were with regard to the cost of making calls. It is expensive for customers to use the telephone. Many are from a disadvantaged background and waiting on the phone before somebody help them were listed as a problem.

Small business owners are not always reachable by the phone. Also, if people leave messages on the voice mail, they do not return calls. Sometimes people find the line busy. It is inconvenient and time consuming for people to keep on trying. It is not easy to hear what the person is saying when the line is not clear and information can be misleading. Other problems were those of being put through a wrong department by the switchboard, the time, and effort of making a phone call, etc.

Turok cites evidence from Sweden that 77% of people found telephonic support "very helpful"; and Davies (1976) at the University of Linkping (also in Sweden), had used individual telephone calls to teach English at a distance, reported that 91% of students gave telephone teaching the highest rating (5 point scale) (EDEN Research Workshop, 2004). The quality of information obtained over the phone is satisfying for many respondents because they obtain fair and good information over the phone compared to the information that they get over the Internet. The majority stated that it's acceptable. About a third of the respondents noted that they are happy with the information received on the phone, which is different from the results previously mentioned.

Figure 1. Telephone problems

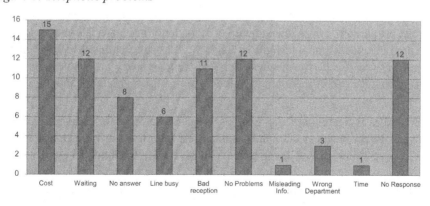

The quality telephones in SA are satisfying for most of the respondents. Six respondents were dissatisfied with the South African telephone service. Only 25% reflected that the telephones are fair. A total of 68% of the responses are satisfied with the quality and service of telephones in SA. A large number of respondents (96%) have access to telephone and cell phone.

Effective Use of Computers by Small Business Owners

Computers are important for small business owners to help do the work. Computers have changed their way of doing their work as well as providing a new environment of entertainment. Computers are part of university students' educational experience. They should use the Internet to communicate, to do research, and to access business contacts. For small business owners the Internet is a functional tool, one that has changed the way they interact with others and with information as they go about their work.

Nearly four-fifths of respondents (79%) agree that Internet use has had a positive impact on their experience. Almost half (46%) of respondents agree that email enables them to express ideas that they would not have expressed in person, but, some interactions are still primarily face-to-face. Only 19% of the respondents stated that they communicate more with their suppliers via email than face-to-face. Nearly three-quarters (73%) of respondents stated that they use the Internet more than the library, while only 9% stated they use the library more than the Internet for information searching. Respondents use computers to do different tasks such as word processing, business processes, presentations, spreadsheets, Internet surfing, etc. The time that each respondent spends in front of a computer depends on the nature of work they are doing.

Respondents may require access to computers to complete work or some might use the Internet (Laird, 2004). Small business owners, staff, and administrative people are using computers and the Internet for various purposes. A recent national survey found that 84% of respondents owned a computer and that 99% used the Internet, with 66% doing so daily (Student Monitor, 2004). Respondents appear to use the Internet primarily to communicate with others and to find materials and assistance with their business (Student Monitor, 2004). Studies suggest that there are benefits for people who use IT for business purposes (e.g., a study on business redesign suggests that the use of technology in redesign results in greater benefits) (Twigg, 2004).

Other studies indicate that small business owners use of IT for business purposes positively affect business outcomes such as self-reported gains in general as well as personal and intellectual development (Laird, 2004). Respondents usually spend an average of three to more hours on computers. Some respondents (42%) are dissatisfied with the access time of computer time offered by telecentres.

Internet addiction can affect anyone who has access to the plethora of online services. As people increasingly use the Internet, psychologists have noticed those spending larger amounts of time online, sometimes to the detriment of their social lives and studies. Some people argue that television or reading also cut into social lives. The Internet is addictive because it offers interaction with people that ostensibly fills a social void. Many stories run around about addicts who lose families and friends.

Small businesses owners tend to seek the same escapist feelings from the Internet that they seek from drugs, gambling, or alcohol. Just as people struggle to keep from taking a drink or popping a pill, they struggle to turn their computer off, she said. Most of the respondents stated that computer related applications such as Internet surfing, playing games, research but doing practical work does not have an effect on their daily life's.

Assistance on Computer Related Work by Experts

Seventy two percent of respondents are satisfied with the assistance that they get with computer related work. More than 70% of respondents were satisfied with the assistance that they get on their computer related work. However not all people are doing their duties effectively, as noted by some respondents. The number of dissatisfied respondents needs to be investigated in a future study. Respondents have further stated that people were doing their duties effectively they wouldn't have problems on their computers. However, computer related work is challenging and small business owners need assistance.

Respondents encountered different types of problems when using computers. More than 10% of the respondents reported that they don't experience any problems. The most common problem that respondents experience was the slow processing speed of the computer.

Other problems:

- **Server:** The server is sometimes down and people are unable to login and access the computer (14%).
- **Cost:** The Internet is an expensive resource, when accessed on other sources such as Internet cafés, telecentres, etc.
- **Page can't display:** Only some of the pages on the Internet does display (11%).
- **Pop-ups:** It is a form or Internet advertisement that appears or pops up on the screen when using the Internet (1%).

- **Getting confidential information:** Small business owners are having a problem with the transparency of the Internet.

- **Fewer computers:** Telecentres have fewer computers to cater all for all the small businesses in its regions.

- Twenty percent of the respondents did not respond to the question regarding problems with computers.

- Quality of information obtained on the Internet compared to telephone.

Information obtained on the Internet has been rated highly by most of the respondents. Only 7% of the respondents were not happy with the quality of information offered by the Internet and 11% of the respondents rated it to be a fair provider of information. These respondents stated that search engines are not a good tool to use when searching for information. This is because it provides a lot of unrelated "hits." The Internet is also slow and it is time consuming to click through every link that has been found. They have further stated that some of the links don't open. The respondents stated that the Internet saves them time because they do not have to go to the library if they can find relevant information with just a click of a button.

Small business owners are not always relaying on the facilities to gain access to information. They can obtain these facilities from different places such as home, Internet cafés, MPCC, etc. Table 4 shows that most of the respondents are gaining access to other sources (i.e., friends, relatives, Internet cafés, and so forth.). It can be noted that 21% of the respondents are not using alternative points of access.

Seventeen percent of the respondents make use only of a telephone and only 31% was using the Internet. Nearly 47% were using both telephone and the Internet. It appears that most respondents are comfortable with using the Internet as means of accessing information.

Table 4. Alternative points of access

Type of POA	Respondents	Percentage
Home	7	9%
Internet café	22	27%
Work	3	4%
Community lab	7	9%
Other	25	30%
Not using	17	21%

Respondents between the age of 30-39 mostly own their own business. This is significant for telecentre use because Hudson (2002) argues that older people are more apt to use phones to obtain information. There's a strong positive relationship (0.542) between age and year of work.

There is a significant relationship (0.534) between business year and the times spend on computers by each respondent. A respondent doing their level of business appears to use less time on computers. This is because they have less work to do. The correlation (0.255) indicates that respondents make effective use of both Internet and telephone. Respondents value information that they obtain online and telephone. Respondents mostly rated the information to be fair and good (both Internet and telephone). The researcher correlated degree and the type of work reaching a relationship (0.11) between these two variables. The relationship is not strong and no casualty can be claimed. There is a negative relationship on the type of work being done by respondents and the time effect of their application.

In summary, respondents can use telecentres for work, entertainment, and to obtain information. telecentres can play a role for small business owners in their work. They make phone calls, play games on computers, use word processing, and spreadsheets. Telecentres can however be used more effectively by smaller businesses.

Recommendation and Conclusion

This section will summarize the issues previously discussed. It involves the recommendations and conclusion regarding the use of telecentres, based on the data obtained from respondents.

Telephone System

According to the findings, respondents make effective use of the Internet. Approximately 99% of the respondents have access to a telephone (either cell- or telephone). They use it for social, academic, and business purposes. Respondents make phone calls for different tasks. The researcher has identified the most common uses of a phone by respondents:

- Make calls to enquire (i.e., call admin or experts).
- Make calls to make bookings (i.e., call Computicket to make a ticket booking).

- Make personal calls (i.e., call a friend or family).
- Make calls for business purposes.

Although respondents have stated that the time for accessing information over the phone is not sufficient for them to enquire to do all their work. They have commented that the information that they get over the phone is mostly fair. Most of the problems experienced by respondents involve cost of making phone calls.

The Telecentre

The telecentre has grown to become a global powerful tool of accessing information. Respondents agree that this facility should help to communicate, do work, and conduct research. According to the information presented, the telephone is utilized efficiently by respondents to perform tasks. Respondents spend more time accessing information, researching and playing cell phones games. Although respondents are spending more of their time phone, the time they spend does not have an impact on their performance and their social lives. Common problems that were stated by respondents with regards to telephone were related to the following:

- **Slow:** It takes long to get information over the phone.
- **Cost:** Respondents are being charges for using the telephones.
- **Less telephones:** There are no enough machines to accommodate all the respondents.

Answers to Research Questions

How can telecentres be utilized in the small business environment?

Telecentres will enable easy communication between the small business owners. Respondents will be able to make inquiries fast and easy by using a telephone. They can call experts and make inquiries. Research can also be conducted using telephones.

Is there a need by the small business owners for such a facility?

Based on the information obtained on the completed questionnaire, respondents show a need to have a telecentre facility. It will provide them with a convenient and less convenient way of accessing information whenever they need it. When using telephones, there is no need to physically go and fetch it.

What services should this facility supply?

Telecentres have to provide different services to the students. The following are some of the suggested services that a telecentre should have:

- Telephone
- Fax
- Scanner
- Television
- Computer
- Photocopier

Recommendations

This study has proved that telecentres can be effectively used by small businesses. In order for the people to fulfil the use and availability of telecentres effectively, the following recommendations could be made:

- It must develop a hot line that will operate 24/7 with different experts available. This will enable small business owners to effectively use telephone anytime they are in need of any help.
- Affordable fax services must be offered by community telecentres rather than private telecentre shops that operate expensively.
- Small business owners should be informed that they could call the experts when they need to enquire.

Summary and Conclusion

In conclusion, small business owners need to make effective use of the Internet rather than a telephone to obtain information they need. Although computers are not enough to cater for all the students, the owners manage to run their businesses without the use of privately owned computers. Telephone services should be made available to every small business owner. Telecentres should be developed and implemented gradually.

References

Amicas telecentres. (2002). *Information, communication, and learning*. Retrieved May 30, 2004, from http://www.worldbank.org/worldlinks/telecentres/workshop/sbt-pdf/case-studies/allcasestudies_pdf.pdf

Benjamin, P. (2003). *The Gaselani telecentre in Northern Province, South Africa*. Retrieved May 20, 2004, from http://www.col.org/telecentres/chapter%2007.pdf

Commonwealth of Learning, The. (2001). *Using telecentres in supporting distance education*. Retrieved May 20, 2004, from http://www.col.org/knowledge/ks_tele-centres.htm

CommunitySA. (2001). *Universal service fund*. Retrieved May 15, 2004, from http://lists.sn.apc.org/ pipermail/communitysa.mbox/communitysa.mbox

EDEN Third Research Workshop. (2004). *Proceedings of supporting the learner and distance education*. Retrieved May 15, 2004, from http://www.uni-oldenburg.de/zef/cde/eden.pdf

Etta, F. (2000). *Telecentre overview*. Retrieved March 29, 2004, from http://web.idrc.ca/uploads/ users/105552710501._PAN_African_studies_vol_2_telecentres_capter3.doc

Etta, F. M. (2002). *The trouble with community telecentres*. Retrieved May 15, 2004.

Gómez, R., & Hunt, P. (1999a). *Report of an international meeting on telecentres evaluation*. Retrieved May 15, 2004, from http://www.bellanet.org/gkaims/documents/ docs/wrkshp.pdf?ois=no

Gómez, R., & Hunt, P. (1999b). *What types of telecentres do exist?* Retrieved May 20, 2004, from http://www.econolink.org/elerningICT/o1nam01.asp?categoryID=432

Gómez, R., & Hunt, P. (1999c). *Telecentre evaluation: A global perspective*. Retrieved May 20, 2004, from http://www.idrc.ca/pan/wrksh2.pdf

Healthyplace.com. (n.d.). Retrieved October 30, 2004, from http://www.healthyplace.com/communities/addictions/articles/apa_computer_addictions_students.htm

Hudson, H. E. (1999). *Telecentre evaluation: Issues and strategies*. Retrieved May 15, 2004, from http://www.usfaca.edu/fac_staff/hudson/papers/telecentre%20evaluation.htm

Hudson, H. E. (2000). *The Acacia programme: Developing evaluation and learning systems for African telecentres*. Retrieved May 20, 2004, from http://www.col.org/ telecentres/charper%2015.pdf

Hudson, H. E. (2002). *Telecentres evaluation. Issues and strategies*. Retrieved May 30, 2004, from http://www.col.org/telecentres/chapter%2016.pdf

IDRC—The International Development Research Centre. (2003). *Information and communication technologies for development in Africa.* Retrieved May 15, 2004.

Jensen, M. (1999). *University students*. Retrieved May 23, 2004, from http://www. pewinternet.org.pdfs/ pip_college_report.pdf

Jensen, M., & Esterhuysen, A. (2001). *The telecentre cookbook for Africa*: Recipes for self-sustainability, UNESCO.

Jensen, M., & Walker, D. (2000). *Telecentre technology*. Retrieved May 30, 2004, from http://www.col.org/ telecentres/chapter%2019.pdf

Laird, N. (2004). *Contributing to an equal and diverse Scotland*. Retrieved May 30, 2004, from http://www.beyondbarriers.org.uk/beyond_barriers/research/ ?CFID=1157188&CFTOKEN=65942640

Lubbe, S. (1997). *The assessment of the effectiveness of IT investments in South African organisations*. PhD Dissertation, University of the Witwatersrand, Johannesburg, SA

Market Vintage. (2004). Retrieved from http://www.internetperformancemarketing. com/ educate/newsletter/newsletter-0203.html

Smith, M. (2003). *Internet addiction*. Retrieved October 30, 2004, from http://www. studentaffairs.com/ ejournal/summer_2004/surfnwithapurpose.html

Student Monitor. (2004). *Computing and the Internet*. Retrieved April 20, 2005.

The Surveys Systems. (2002). *Correlation*. Retrieved May 20, 2004, from http:// www.surveysystem.com/ correlation.htm

Oestmann, S., & Dymond, A. C. (2001). *Telecentres overview*. Retrieved May 20, 2004, from http://www.col.org/telecentres/chapter%2001.pdf

Townsend, D. N. (2003). *Universal service/access policy and creation and operation of universal service*. Retrieved May 30, 2004, from http://www.itu. int/itu-D/finance/work-cost-tariffs/events/tariffs-seminars/moscow-03/03-usmodel_part_doc.pdf

Twigg, C. (2004). *Surfin' with a purpose: Examining how spending time online is related to student engagement*. Retrieved April 20, 2005, from http:www. student-affairs.com/ejournal/Summer_2004

Chapter III

Impact of Organisational Intranets on Profitability in Organisations

Udo Richard Averweg, eThekwini Municipality and University of KwaZulu-Natal, Durban, South Africa

Abstract

Organisations are being forced to invest heavily in the deployment of information systems (IS) to obtain value and benefit in the new knowledge-based environment. Organisational intranets are being used as the platform for developing and deploying critical business applications to support business operations and managerial decision-making across the Internet-worked enterprise. Executive Information Systems (EIS) grew out of the information needs of executives. Web-based technologies are causing a revisit to existing information technology (IT) implementation models, including those for EIS. Some technologies include intranet, Internet, extranet, e-commerce business-to-business (B2B), e-commerce business-to-consumer (B2C), wireless application protocol (WAP), including other mobile technologies. The author conducted a survey of 31 well-established organisations in KwaZulu-Natal, South Africa, which successfully implemented EIS. A validated survey instrument was administered to an EIS stakeholder in each organisation surveyed to rank Web-based technologies in order of their perceived impact on EIS implementation in organisations surveyed. The author reports that an organisational intranet has the highest level of impact on EIS implementation in organisations surveyed in KwaZulu-Natal, South Africa. Given this impact, justifying investment in such IS and IT should be carefully evaluated and quantified.

Introduction

Organisations are being forced to invest heavily in the deployment of information systems (IS) to obtain value and benefit and to stay competitive in the new knowledge-based environment. Managerial tasks in organisations typically require more collaborative work than day-to-day operational tasks (Abraham & Seal, 2001). Abraham and Seal (2001) report that an intranet facilitates the communication behaviour between individuals who have to accomplish a task together. Giesecke (2001) foresees that creating information will become a team process. Communication is facilitated because the intranet provides the platform to integrate communication tools (e.g., electronic mail) as well as information sharing mechanisms (e.g., databases and file servers). Information technology (IT) investment uses certain of an organisation's resources. It makes it easier for people in managerial roles to make use of IT to carry out their work. Users in organisations are demanding that the IS used by the organisation should be more efficient and effective (Wessels, 2003). The use of the intranet becomes integral to the success of the managerial functions in the organisation.

Intranets are being used as the platform for developing and deploying critical business applications to support business operations and managerial decision-making across the Internet-worked enterprise (O'Brien, 2000). Many applications are designed to interface with and access existing organisation databases and legacy systems so that employees (within the organisation) can access and run such applications using Web browsers from anywhere on the network whenever needed. O'Brien (2000) reports that some intranet-using organisations are in the process of Web-enabling operational and managerial support applications including executive information and decision support. One theme in information communication technology (ICT) management theory is the effect of IT investment on the risk of managers in the IT-using industry and this serves as a backdrop. Although IS expenditure is regarded as risky and costly, many IS investments appear to go ahead without the use of formal investment appraisal and risk management techniques (Ward, 1996). The impact of organisational intranets on executive information systems (EIS) implementation in organisations is a focus of this chapter.

Organisational Intranets

An intranet (or internal Web) is a network architecture designed to serve the internal information needs of an organisation using Web (Internet) concepts and tools (see, for example, Cortese, 1996). Turban, Rainer, and Potter (2005) indicate that an intranet is a private network that uses Internet software and TCP/IP protocols. Defined technically, intranets are the application of Internet technology (and specifically the World Wide Web service) for a prescribed community of users (Scheepers & Rose, 2001). An intranet is a network designed to serve the internal informational needs of an organisation, using Internet concepts and tools (Turban, McLean, & Wetherbe, 2004).

Organisations can use Internet networking standards and Web technology to create intranets (Laudon & Laudon, 2000). It provides similar capabilities, namely inexpensive and easy browsing, communication, and collaboration (Turban & Aronson, 1998) and are used solely for intraorganisational communication activities and information flow (Abraham et al., 2001).

Intranets can create networked applications that can run on many different kinds of computers throughout an organisation (Laudon et al., 2000). Typical intranet applications include:

- Publishing corporate documents
- Providing access to searchable directories (e.g., telephone and address lists)
- Publishing corporate, departmental and individual pages
- Providing access to groupware applications
- Distributing software
- Providing electronic mail
- Transacting with other organisational computer-based IS
- Organisation-wide information searches
- Providing a consistent user interface
- Data warehousing and decision support access

Turban et al. (1998) and Turban et al. (2004) note that intranets have the power to change decision-making processes, organisational structure, and procedures and help re-engineer organisations. Strom (1996) reports that much information on intranets is available directly on the Web. The use of intranets is increasing rapidly not only as an internal communication system, but also as a facilitator of e-commerce (Turban, McLean, & Wetherbe, 1999). Robinson (1996) suggests that intranets can be applied to enhanced knowledge sharing and group decision and business processes. Information that is most frequently included in intranets *inter alia* includes data warehouse and decision support access (Chabrow, 1998). Many organisations have benefited from use of the intranet Web-based technology and have made their organisations more efficient (Sprout, 1995). KPMG Consulting (2002) reports that organisations are focusing strongly on internal communications projects (such as intranets). It is the differences in governance and communication that enables some organisations to success and flourish where others fail.

Executive Information Systems

EIS grew out of the development of IS to be used directly by executives and used to augment the supply of information by subordinates (Srivihok, 1998). An EIS is a computer-based system that serves the information needs of top executives (Turban et al., 2004). For the purposes of this chapter, EIS is defined as "a computerized system that provides executives with easy access to internal and external information that is relevant to their critical success factors" (Watson, Houdeshel, & Rainer, 1997). EIS are an important element of the information architecture of an organisation. EIS is a computer-based technology that is designed in response to executives' specific decision-making needs (Turban et al., 2005). Turban (2001) suggests that EIS capabilities are being "embedded in BI." All major EIS and information product vendors now offer Web versions of the tools designed to function with Web servers and browsers (PricewaterhouseCoopers, 2002). Business intelligence is a broad category of application and techniques for gathering, storing, analysing, and providing access to data to help users in organisations make better decisions and strategic decisions (Oguz, 2003).

With the increasing amount of IT investment and substantial evidence of failures (Remenyi & Lubbe, 1998), many managers and researchers feel that IS justification and evaluation has become a key management issue. The old argument that it is not necessary to justify the investment in IS because they are strategically important to stay "in business" is being questioned (Wessels, 2003). EIS has become a significant area of business computing and there are increasing amounts of money invested by organisations in EIS development projects (Kaniclides & Kimble, 1995) and the subsequent operation (use) of these systems (Belcher & Watson, 1993; Millet, Mawhinney, & Kallman, 1991). For example, in October 1997 the largest water utility in South Africa, Rand Water, took a decision to build an EIS (based on Oracle products) and invested ZAR4,5 million in revamping its IT infrastructure to support that deployment (Harris, 2000). In the current business environment where senior managers and decision-makers are held more accountable to their shareholders and investors for their investment decisions, there is a need for using generally accepted techniques and methods to justify IS investment decisions. For a survey of the state of EIS implementations in organisations in South Africa, see, for example, Averweg, Erwin, and Petkov (2004).

Web-based technologies are causing a revisit to existing IT implementation models, including EIS (Averweg, Petkov, Erwin, & Moolman, 2003). Web-based tools "are very much suited" to executives key activities of communicating and informing (Pijpers, 2001). With the emergence of global IT, existing paradigms are being altered which are spawning new considerations for successful IT implementation (Averweg & Erwin, 2000).

Background and Goal of the Research

Intranet technology is essentially a pull technology and intranet use is largely voluntary (Lyytinen, Rose, & Welke, 1998). Computer or IS usage has been identified as the key indicator of the adoption of IT by organisations (Suradi, 2001). Igbaria and Tan (1997) report that system usage is an important variable in IT acceptance since it appears to be a good surrogate measure for the effective deployment of IS resources in organisations. Lu and Gustafson (1994) report that people use computers because they believe that computers will increase their problem solving performance (usefulness) and they are relatively effort free to use (ease of use). From the available literature, there is little evidence to suggest that the impact of Web-based technologies on EIS implementations has previously been investigated. This creates a platform for conducting such research. User acceptance of IT has been a primary focus in IT implementation research (Al-Gahtani, 2001). Researchers in the field rely on the theories of innovation diffusion to study implementation problems. Davis' (Davis, 1989; Davis, Bagozzi, & Warshaw, 1989) technology acceptance model (TAM) is based on the diffusion of innovation model. TAM is a well-respected model of IT adoption and use (Al-Gahtani, 2001).

As the usage of IT increases, Web-enabled information technologies can provide the means for greater access to information from disparate computer applications and other information resources (Eder, 2000). These Web-based technologies include intranet, Internet, extranet, e-commerce business-to-business (B2B), e-commerce business-to-consumer (B2C), wireless application protocol (WAP), and other mobile technologies. The focus of this chapter is on organisational intranets. There exists a high degree of similarity between the characteristics of a "good EIS" and Web-based technologies (Tang, Lee, & Yen, 1997).

The technology for EIS is evolving rapidly and future systems are likely to be different (Sprague & Watson, 1996). EIS is now clearly in a state of flux. As Turban (2001) notes, "EIS is going through a major change." There is therefore both scope and need for research in the particular area of future EIS implementations being impacted by organisational intranets as executives and business end-users need systems that provide access to diverse types of information that form part of information age economies. Emerging (Web-based) technologies can redefine the utility, desirability, and economic viability of EIS technology (Volonino, Watson, & Robinson, 1995). Damsgaard and Scheepers (1999) describe intranet technology as a multi-purpose, rich networked, and malleable in terms of its application. As with all other investments, management must make a conscious decision to invest in a particular IS. Decisions to invest (or not invest) will influence the future of the organisation. With the absence of research efforts on the impact of organisational intranets on EIS implementation in South Africa, this research begins to fill the gap with a study of selected organisations in KwaZulu-Natal, South Africa, which have implemented EIS.

Research Method and Data Gathering

The questionnaire was validated using expert opinion. It was based on previous instruments used in published research papers. Particular attention was given to Straub's (1989) guideline of a pre-test for the technical validation of the research instrument. This validation included the use of "previously validated instruments wherever possible" (Straub, 1989). Watson and Frolick (1993) note that numerical information comes from the questionnaire. The findings of the author's survey will be based on the survey instrument.

As a preamble to the interview, the classification of the various types of IS and the distinguishing characteristics of EIS were discussed with each interviewee. A working definition of EIS (as used earlier in this chapter) was also given. This preamble to the actual interview meant that the interviewee was properly focused on the EIS in the organisation. The author's survey instrument consists of three parts:

- **Section 1** deals with an organisation's demographics. Questions were extracted from the Roldán (2000) EIS questionnaire, translated from Spanish to English and adapted for the author's survey. The measurement of demographic variables of interest is consistent with prior research in sociology and organisational behaviour (Venkatesh & Morris, 2000).

- **Section 2** deals with the attributes of the organisation's EIS. Questions were extracted from the Roldán (2000) EIS questionnaire, translated from Spanish to English and adapted for the author's survey.

- **Section 3** deals with how an interviewee perceives specific Web-based technologies impacts the organisation's EIS implementation. The selected Web-based technologies are (1) intranet; (2) Internet; (3) extranet; (4) e-commerce: business-to-business (B2B); (5) e-commerce: business-to-consumer (B2C); (6) wireless application protocol (WAP) and other mobile technologies; and (7) any other Web-based technologies.

Pre-testing a survey instrument is common practice. Roldán and Leal (2003) report that their "instrument was pre-tested with consultants and business and IS professors." A similar process was undertaken and experienced by the author who solicited expert opinion for additions, modifications, and/or deletions to the survey instrument. A pilot study was conducted to ensure that the interview schedule was clear, intelligible, and unambiguous. In order to evaluate the initial questionnaire design, an executive who uses EIS and four academics participated in separate field tests. One Spanish academic with EIS research interests commented "Very interesting." Their comments led to a refinement of the questionnaire instrument. Their contributions are gratefully acknowledged. The survey instrument was submitted to three EIS software vendors (Cognos, JD Edwards (amalgamated with PeopleSoft, which is now part of Oracle) and ProClarity) in South Africa. A senior employee (e.g., managing director) from each vendor independently furnished some suggestions regarding the survey instrument. Some appropriate suggestions were adopted by the author and incorporated in the survey instrument.

There are six major metropolitan Councils in South Africa. Ethekwini Municipality Area (EMA) is the most populous municipality in South Africa (SA2002-2003, 2002). EMA's geographic area size is 2,300 km^2 with a population of 3.09 million citizens (Statistics South Africa, 2001). During 2004, eThekwini Municipality was voted the best performing municipality in South Africa (Makhanya, 2004; Mthembu, 2004). The author's survey of organisations in KwaZulu-Natal, which have implemented EIS, is confined to organisations in the EMA. It is acknowledged that some organisations may have implemented more than one EIS. In those cases and for this study, only the latest EIS implementation is used in the author's survey.

Some studies suggest that EIS should not only be accessed by executive users (see, for example, Rai & Bajwa, 1997; Volonino et al., 1995). Salmeron (2001) notes EIS as the technology for information delivery for all business end-users. Kennedy (1995) and Messina and Sanjay (1995) report that EIS have spread throughout organisations. It is evident that EIS requires continuous input from three different stakeholder groups (known as constituencies):

- EIS executives/business end-users

- EIS providers (i.e., persons responsible for developing and maintaining the EIS)

- EIS vendors or consultants

All constituencies are surveyed in the author's data sampling. The sample was selected using the unbiased "snowball" sampling technique. Cooper and Emory (1995) state that this technique has found a niche in applications where respondents are difficult to identify and are best located through referral networks. A formal extensive interview schedule was compiled and used for the semi-structured interviews. Interviews were conducted during May-June 2002 at the interviewee's organisation.

Data Analysis and Interpretation of the Results

From the 31 interviews conducted using the author's survey instrument, 31 completed questionnaires were analysed. A tally of the responses to question 1.1-1.5 (Section 1) and question 2.1, 2.3, and 2.5-2.13 (Section 2) was made. Where there was a null (or blank) response recorded, this null (or blank) response was excluded from the respective tally. Frequency tables were constructed for each tally. For the responses to question 2.2 and 2.4, the data was arranged, sorted and frequency tables constructed. Such approaches are common in EIS research (see, for example, Kaniclides & Kimble, 1997; Meneely & Pervan, 1994; Roldán & Leal, 2003; Salmeron, Luna, & Martinez, 2001). As Meneely and Pervan (1994) report, the questionnaire data was analysed using basic statistical methods including frequencies. The author adopted a similar descriptive statistical process.

Demographics of Organisations Participating in Study

From a tally of interviewees' responses to question 1.1, the organisations participating in the study belongs primarily to the manufacturing (22.6%) and financial services (19.5%) sectors. (See Table 1) The prominence of these two sectors is reported in the Spanish EIS survey by Roldán and Leal (2003). The corresponding Spanish activity sector percentages are manufacturing (37.1%) and banking/financial services (24.3%).

From a tally of interviewees' responses to question 1.2, the gross annual turnover in South African Rands of organisations surveyed is given in Table 2. One respondent was unsure of his organisation's turnover and was not able to give a response to question 1.2. This null response was not included in Table 2. From Table 2, 27 (90.0%) of the organisations surveyed were large enterprises in the EMA. One organisation surveyed had an annual "sales for the year exceeding R12 bn" (Butcher, 2002).

From a tally of interviewees' responses to question 1.3, the number of permanent employees in organisations surveyed is given in Table 3. From Table 3, 20 (64.5%) of these organisations had more than 500 employees. This percentage compares

Table 1. Activity sector list of organisations surveyed which have implemented EIS

Activity Sector	Number of Activity Sectors in survey sample and associated percentage of total sample surveyed (N=31)
Agriculture	1 (3.2%)
Catering	1 (3.2%)
Construction and Automotive	1 (3.2%)
Education	1 (3.2%)
Electrical Power Distribution	1 (3.2%)
Financial Services	6 (19.5%)
Food Processing	1 (3.2%)
Information Technology Services	2 (6.5%)
Manufacturing	7 (22.6%)
Medical Scheme Administrators	1 (3.2%)
Public Administration	1 (3.2%)
Public Transportation	1 (3.2%)
Publishing	1 (3.2%)
Retail	2 (6.5%)
Software Development	1 (3.2%)
Warehousing and Distribution	2 (6.5%)
Water Distribution	1 (3.2%)
TOTAL	31 (100.0%)

Table 2. Gross annual turnover of organisations participating in study

Gross annual turnover (in South African Rands)	Number of organisations in survey sample and associated percentage of total sample surveyed (N=30)
More than 500 Million	16 (53.3%)
Between 100 and 500 Million	8 (26.7%)
Between 20 and 100 Million	3 (10.0%)
Between 5 and 20 Million	0 (0.0%)
Between 1 and 5 Million	3 (10.0%)
Less than 1 Million	0 (0.0%)
TOTAL	30 (100.0%)

Table 3. Number of permanent employees in organisations participating in study

Number of permanent employees in organisation	Number of organisations in survey sample and associated percentage of total sample surveyed (N=31)
More than 5,001 employees	6 (19.5%)
Between 2,001 and 5,000 employees	5 (16.1%)
Between 501 and 2,000 employees	9 (29.0%)
Between 251 and 500 employees	5 (16.1%)
Between 51 and 250 employees	5 (16.1%)
Less than 51 employees	1 (3.2%)
TOTAL	31 (100.0%)

Table 4. Number of years that organisations, which participated in the study, have existed

Number of years that the organisation has existed	Number of organisations in survey sample and associated percentage of total sample surveyed (N=31)
More than 25 years	25 (80.6%)
Between 10 and 25 years	3 (9.7%)
Between 5 and 10 years	2 (6.5%)
Less than 5 years	1 (3.2%)
TOTAL	31 (100.0%)

favourably with the Spanish EIS survey percentage of 71% (Roldán et al., 2003).

From a tally of interviewees' responses to question 1.4, the number of years of existence of organisations surveyed is given in Table 4. From Table 4, 28 (90.3%) of organisations surveyed have existed for more than a decade. This suggests that these organisations are well-established in the EMA. The surveyed organisation which existed for less than five years was from the Information Technology Services sector (see Table 1).

From a tally of interviewees' responses to question 1.5 the classification of organisations surveyed is given in Table 5. Table 5 suggests that the existence of EIS in organisations is not limited to a single organisational classification. As EIS differ considerably in scope and purpose "the primary purpose of the system will change from one organization to another" (Roldán et al., 2003). In the case of the Foreign enterprise classification, both organisations were locally based (South African) but wholly owned by their respective overseas (based in Germany and Switzerland) parent organisations.

Interviewee names and their corresponding organisation names were recorded against question 1.6. These are not reported in this chapter. From the recorded responses to question 1.7, an inventory of interviewee's job titles was compiled. These are also not reported in this chapter. Some interviewees had identical job titles (director, managing director, regional manager, and systems analyst). Twelve (38.7%) interviewees held IT positions in organisations surveyed. Earl (1996) suggests that if IS implementation is left to IS professionals and users alone, the investment is rarely recouped.

From an interviewee's response to question 1.8, the author objectively classified respondents into one of three stakeholder groups: EIS executive/business end-users, EIS providers and EIS vendors or consultants. The three EIS constituencies and number of surveyed respondents and associated percentages per constituency are given in Table 6. Most research of IT acceptance and use does not distinguish senior executives as a separate group (Pijpers, 2001).

Table 5. Classification of organisations participating in study

Classification of organisation	Number of organisations in survey sample and associated percentage of total sample surveyed (N=31)
Public listed	11 (35.5%)
Public non-listed	3 (9.7%)
Government or quasi-government body	6 (19.3 %)
Foreign enterprise	2 (6.5%)
Private company	9 (29.0%)
TOTAL	31 (100.0%)

Table 6. EIS constituencies and number of interviewees surveyed per constituency

Stakeholder groups (constituencies)	Number of respondents surveyed and associated percentage of total sample surveyed (N=31)
EIS executives/business end-users	20 (64.5%)
EIS providers	7 (22.6%)
EIS vendors or consultants	4 (12.9%)
TOTAL	31 (100.0%)

From an analysis of interviewee's responses to question 1.8, 29 respondents indicated that they were EIS users in their organisations. Two respondents reported that they were EIS implementers.

This concludes the analysis and findings of the interviewee's responses to Section 1 of the author's survey instrument. Interviewees' responses to question in Section 2 of the survey instrument are now analysed and discussed.

EIS in Respondent's Organisation Participating in Study

Roldán et al. (2003) surveyed organisations whose EIS were "operative or in an implementation stage sufficiently advanced." From a tally of interviewees' responses to question 2.1, the current (i.e., during the interview period) EIS situation in the respondent's organisation is given in Table 7. From Table 7, one EIS implementation failure was reported by a respondent. This failure was ascribed to the most *recent* EIS implementation. In the Pervan and Phau (1997) EIS survey of organisations in Australia a similar experience was reported—"only one of the organisations had experienced complete failure, in which the system had fallen into disuse."

From the 27 operational EIS and in use by executives/business end-users (see Table 7) in organisations surveyed, a tally of interviewees' responses to question 2.2 is given in Table 8. Two respondents were not able to report the time taken before the EIS was in use by executives/business end-users. They stated "EIS in use before I joined the company." Their null responses are not included in Table 8.

From Table 8, the average time taken before the EIS was in use by executives and business end-users is 9.01 months. This compares favourably with the Roldán et al. (2003) average time of 8.53 months. Salmeron et al. (2001) report that the development of an EIS (in Spain) usually takes 6-12 months. These average times should be

Table 7. Current EIS situation in respondent's organisation

Current situation of EIS in respondent's organisation	Number of respondents surveyed and associated percentage of total sample surveyed (N=31)
Based on the evaluation, the EIS has been accepted and is under development and implementation	3 (9.7%)
The EIS is operational and in use by executives/business end-users	27 (87.1%)
EIS failure (where the latest EIS implementation has been successful)	1 (3.2%)
TOTAL	31 (100.0%)

considered long term when compared with previous studies (Watson, Rainer, & Koh, 1991; Watson, Rainer, & Frolick, 1992; Park, Min, Lim, & Chun, 1997), which could negatively affect the users' acceptance of the system (Young & Watson, 1995).

From a tally of interviewees' responses to question 2.3 (more than one answer could be given), the applications for which the EIS is used in organisations surveyed is given in Table 9.

Research has found that the accessibility of information is more important than its quality in predicting use (O'Reilly, 1982). Access to updated online information is a basic characteristic of EIS (Houdeshel & Watson, 1987; Martin, Brown, DeHayes, Hoffer, & Perkins, 1999). Pervan and Phua (1997) report that the ability to access current status information, such as performance reports, is the main feature most highly used by executives in obtaining the day-to-day information needed for their decision-making. From Table 9, the two highest scoring (see shaded areas) EIS applications used in respondents' organisations confirms the Australian EIS survey findings. Jones (2002) notes, "Executives need to be able to draw upon corporate

Table 8. Time taken before EIS was in use by executives/business end-users

For operational EIS, time taken before EIS was in use by executives/business end-users	Tally and associated percentage of the time taken as reported by respondents in sample surveyed (N=25)
3 days	1 (4.0%)
10-15 days	1 (4.0%)
14 days	1 (4.0%)
1 month	2 (8.0%)
2 months	1 (4.0%)
2-3 months	1 (4.0%)
3 months	2 (8.0%)
3-6 months	3 (12.0%)
5 months	1 (4.0%)
6 months	2 (8.0%)
8 months	2 (8.0%)
12 months	3 (12.0%)
15 months	1 (4.0%)
18 months	1 (4.0%)
24 months	2 (8.0%)
36 months	1 (4.0%)
TOTAL	25 (100.0%)

Table 9. Applications for which EIS is used in organisations surveyed

EIS applications used in respondent's organisation	Tally and associated percentage of the number of applications reported by respondents in total sample surveyed (N=31)
Office automation activities	5 (16.1%)
Access to current status information	22 (71.0%)
Access to projected trends of the organisation	23 (74.2%)
Querying corporate and external databases	16 (51.6%)
Performing personal analysis	16 (51.6%)
Measuring key performance indicatiors	1 (3.2%)

knowledge and make decisions based on hard facts, not assumptions." The value of an intranet for managing knowledge is largely dependent on the calibre of the content and tools it provides to its users and their ultimate application in the organisation's business operations (Hall, 2001). An IS investment can either have a negative effect, a positive effect or no effect on the objectives of an organisation and these effects can be of a long-term duration.

From the 27 operational EIS and in use by executives/business end-users (see Table 7) in organisations surveyed, the EIS user statistics of interviewees' responses to question 2.4 is given in Table 10.

The EIS user statistics for *all* interviewee's responses (31 organisations surveyed) to question 2.4 is given in Table 11. The mean number of EIS users per organisation in both samples (see shaded areas in Tables 10 and 11) is similar.

Roldán et al. (2003) report that "the average number of users in all organisations studied is 75.93 persons." This figure is significantly higher than the author's means of 54 (N=27) and 50 (N=31) in Tables 10 and 11 respectively. A possible explanation for this is that in the Spanish survey, three organisations surveyed each had more

Table 10. EIS users in organisations surveyed

EIS user statistics in organisations (N=27)	
Minimum number of EIS users reported	6
Maximum number of EIS users reported	700
Mode	20
Mean	54
Standard deviation	134

Table 11. EIS users in organisations surveyed

EIS user statistics in organisations (N=31)	
Minimum number of EIS users reported	2
Maximum number of EIS users reported	700
Mode	20
Mean	50
Standard deviation	126

than 400 users. One of these three organisations had a total of 1,800 EIS users. In the author's research, the largest number of reported EIS users in one organisation was 700. Roldán et al. (2003) suggest that it would therefore be more appropriate to take into account the mode values. They report "the number of 20 users as a measure of the central trend." This mode corresponds exactly to the author's survey results given in Tables 10 and 11.

From a tally of interviewees' responses (more than one answer could be given) to question 2.5, the hierarchical employee levels where EIS is used in organisations surveyed is given in Table 12. Liang and Hung (1997) report that in their survey of organisations in Taiwan, middle-level managers are primary EIS users (78.94%) "but lower-level managers (24.58%) are also popular." From Table 12, middle managers show significant higher EIS use levels (77.4%) than top managers (managing director/chief executive officer (45.2%) and director (58.1%)). This middle manager use level (77.4%) corresponds with the Liang et al. (1997) survey but is higher than the Roldán et al. (2003) middle manager survey result of 68,6%. While Roldán et al. (2003) report a "close similarity" between EIS use by middle managers (68.6%) and EIS use by managing directors (70.0%), this similarity is not evidenced by the author's findings in Table 12. There is a significant use difference between these two hierarchical levels. Furthermore Roldán et al. (2003) report that "21.4% of organizations declare that they have other users' below the line manager hierarchical level."

From Table 12 there are 12 (38.7%) business end-users and one (3.2%) financial consultant below the line manager hierarchical level. The total percentage (41.9%) of these EIS users is significantly higher than the Roldán et al. (2003) survey. This tends to suggest that the degree of EIS diffusion to lower organisational hierarchical levels and use by these levels in organisations surveyed in South Africa, is on par with organisations surveyed in Taiwan but is significantly higher than experienced by organisations in Spain. As Liang et al. (1997) note, a "reason for this may be the extension of EIS to everybody information systems." EIS are becoming less strictly defined to support professional decision-makers throughout the organisa-

Table 12. Hierarchical employee levels where EIS is used in organisations

Hierarchical employee level where EIS is used in organisation	Tally and associated percentage of the number of employee levels reported by respondents in total sample surveyed (N=31)
Managing director/ chief executive officer	14 (45.2%)
Director (or delegated)	18 (58.1%)
General manager	20 (64.5%)
Senior operations manager	19 (61.3%)
Middle manager	24 (77.4%)
Line manager	14 (45.2%)
Business end-user	12 (38.7%)
Financial consultants	1 (3.2%)

tion (Turban et al., 1998). Turban et al. (1998) state that "there is now increasing number of tools designed to help functional managers (finance, marketing); these tools are integrated with EIS."

From a tally of interviewees' responses to question 2.6 (more than one answer could be given), the functional areas where EIS are used in organisations is given in Table 13. The highest scoring functional areas are Finance (64.5%) and Marketing (64.5%). The lowest scoring functional area is Personnel (16.1%). Table 13 shows that the functional areas where EIS are used in organisations surveyed are quite broad. Similar broad findings are reported by Liang et al. (1997) in organisations surveyed in Taiwan. One must ensure that the cost of the technology is able to justify its usage (Agarwal, Higgins, & Tanniru, 1991).

Table 13. Functional areas where EIS is used in organisations

Functional area where EIS is used in organisation	Tally and associated percentage of the number of functional areas reported by respondents in total sample surveyed (N=31)
Finance	20 (64.5%)
Planning	10 (32.3%)
Marketing	20 (64.5%)
Sales	16 (51.6%)
Personnel	5 (16.1%)
Production/ Operations	12 (38.7%)
Entire Organisation	7 (22.6%)

From a tally of interviewees' responses to question 2.7 (more than one answer could
be given), the different types of information held by an EIS in an organisation is
given in Table 14. From Table 14, Financial information (90.3%) appears as the
most important item followed by Business/Sales (74.2%) and then Strategic Planning (35.5%). In the Roldán et al. (2003) survey, the three highest ranking types of
information held by an EIS in an organisation were commercial and sales information (89.2%), financial information (65.7%) and production information (55.7%).
While previous research studies agree in presenting these three types of information
(sales, financial, and production) as the most relevant ones (Allison, 1996; Kirlidog,
1997; Thodenius, 1995) the author's findings partially support these findings with
business/sales (74.2%) and finance (90.3%) types of information. Holding strategic
planning information in EIS in organisations in South Africa appears to have a higher
importance than holding production information. Wessels (2003) conducted a survey
about IS investment decisions in organisations in South Africa and found that 66.0%
of respondents stated that they justified their investment on strategic reasons.

Watson et al. (1996) recognise that executives require "soft" information (often
provided informally) for decision-making. Soft information is "fuzzy, unofficial,
intuitive, subjective, nebulous, implied, and vague." Watson et al. (1996) found that
soft information was used in most EIS but the author's findings (12.9%) do not support this. One possible explanation is that it is often policy not to allow unsubstanti-
ated rumours into IS without a reference to a source and tagged by the individual
entering the information (Turban et al., 1998). In the justification of investing in IS

Table 14. Functional areas where EIS is used in organisations

Types of information held by EIS in organisation	Tally and associated percentage of the number of types of information as reported by respondents in total sample surveyed (N=31)
Strategic planning	11 (35.5%)
Inventory management/suppliers	10 (32.3%)
"Soft" information	4 (12.9%)
Finance	28 (90.3%)
Business/Sales	23 (74.2%)
Trade/Industry	4 (12.9%)
Human resources	9 (29.0%)
Quality	7 (22.6%)
External news services	1 (3.2%)
Production	8 (25.8%)
Competitors	3 (9.7%)
Stock exchange prices	1 (3.2%)

and the process of making decisions (whether to invest in a new IS on not), "soft" factors also need to be incorporated (Hinton & Kaye, 1994).

From Table 14 it can be observed that the information that appears predominantly in EIS has an internal characteristic (Preedy, 1990). External information obtains low response levels: trade/industry (12.9%), external news services (3.2%), competitors (9.7%) and stock exchange prices (3.2%). Roldán et al. (2003) report similar low response levels. Salmeron et al. (2001) note that "it is surprising that external information is so seldom included in Spain." Intranets and knowledge sharing can assist to "capture, organise, store, and transmit" source material from which an individual may acquire knowledge (Gundry & Metes, 1996). An IT investment decision is a process of filtering and distilling often complex data, information, and knowledge to levels manageable to the human mind (Bannister & Remenyi, 2000).

From a tally of interviewees' responses to question 2.8 (more than one answer could be given), how information is held by EIS in an organisation is given in Table 15. From Table 15, information is generally presented by products (71.0%), operational areas (64.5%) and geographical areas (58.1%). Roldán et al. (2003) report similar findings for operational/functional areas (62.9%), products (61.4%), and geographic areas (52.9%). Roldán et al. (2003) note that "information according to processes ranks quite low, existing in only 20% of participating entities." From Table 15, there is a striking commonality with the author's finding of 19.4%. This situation was highlighted by Wetherbe (1991) as one of the traditional IS problems for top managers (i.e., these systems are considered as functional systems rather than being considered as systems crossing functions).

From a tally of interviewees' responses to question 2.9 (more than one answer could be given), the different types of sources of information that support an EIS

Table 15. How information is held by an EIS in an organisation

How information is held by EIS in organisation	Tally and associated percentage of how information is held as reported by respondents in total sample surveyed (N=31)
By products	22 (71.0%)
By projects	5 (16.1 %)
By operational areas	20 (64.5%)
By geographic areas	18 (58.1%)
By strategic business units	10 (32.3%)
By processes	6 (19.4%)
By key performance areas	14 (45.2%)
By company	11 (35.5%)
By customers	1 (3.2%)

in an organisation are given in Table 16. One of the capabilities or characteristics of EIS is the filtering, organisation, and consolidation of multiple data sources. This quantitative data stems from corporate databases (80.6%) and operational databases (64.5%). Data aggregation is to integrate data from various sources to provide critical information requested by decision-makers (Liang et al., 1997). A significant advantage of using an intranet involves its facilitation of decentralised decision-making (Van der Merwe, 2001). This occurs because everyone has access to information and there is no reliance on a limited number of employees who have access to different types of information from different departments within the organisation.

As previously discussed, Table 14 reflects that the information that appears predominantly in EIS has an internal characteristic. Table 16 reflects that a significant majority of the information came from internal sources. External sources have a low presence: external databases (25.8%) and Internet, intranet, or extranet (16.1%). This trend towards internal sources supports the results obtained in previous research studies (Basu, Poindexter, Drosen, & Addo, 2000; Kirlidog, 1997; Roldán et al., 2003; Watson et al., 1991; Watson et al., 1992). In the opinion of Salmeron et al. (2001) "the extent to which information coming from the environment is included in the EIS of Spanish big businesses should reach higher figures, due to the fact that all elements that currently form economy are interrelated". Given the presence of Web-based technologies and from Table 16 it is therefore somewhat surprising that the Internet, intranet and extranet rank as the lowest source of information which support an EIS in the organisations surveyed in the EMA. One of the contributions of the Web has been streamlining and co-coordinating the internal communication structure of organisations by using the Web as a standard (Abraham and Seal, 2001).

System justification implies first an evaluation and then the activity of justification, showing that the IS is appropriate for the particular business context (Remenyi, Money, & Twite, 1995). From a tally of interviewees' responses to question 2.10,

Table 16. Sources of information that support EIS in an organisation

Sources of information that support EIS in organisation	Tally and associated percentage of sources of information as reported by respondents in total sample surveyed (N=31)
Corporate databases	25 (80.6%)
Individuals	12 (38.7%)
Operational databases	20 (64.5%)
External databases	8 (25.8%)
Documents or reports	7 (22.6%)
Internet, intranet or extranet	5 (16.1%)

Table 17. Approaches taken for EIS development in organisations

Approach taken for EIS development in organisation	Tally and associated percentage of approach taken for EIS development as reported by respondents in total sample surveyed (N=31)
In-house development using existing software tools	6 (19.4%)
In-house development with critical EIS features developed initially and optional features added over time, using existing or commercially purchased software tools	9 (29.0%)
Fully developed by vendor	7 (22.6%)
In-house development with assistance from vendor	12 (38.7%)

the approach taken for EIS development is given in Table 17. In-house development with assistance from the vendor (38.7%) was the most common approach taken. A "piece meal" strategy where in-house EIS development with critical features was conducted initially then operational features added over time using existing or purchased software tools was most preferred (33%) by organisations surveyed in Australia (Pervan et al., 1997). From Table 17, a similar pattern (29.0%) was evidenced in organisations surveyed in South Africa.

Roldán et al. (2003) report a "low number of cases in which the systems have been developed with software produced by the organization itself (5.7%)." In the author's survey, in-house development using existing software tools is somewhat higher (19.4%). A possible explanation is that some organisations surveyed may not yet have migrated from their first (in-house developed) EIS.

Pervan et al. (1997) report that for organisations surveyed in Australia, only 17% of EIS were developed in-house with assistance from a vendor/consultant. Roldán et al. (2003) report in-house development with assistance from the vendor (47.1%) as the most common approach taken in organisations surveyed in Spain. From Table 17, it can be seen that while this approach is taken by organisations surveyed in South Africa, the occurrence is slightly less. Many organisations do not perform evaluations or cost benefit analysis on there is and those who do sometimes report mixed or confused results (Remenyi et al., 1995).

From a tally of interviewees' responses to question 2.11 (more than one answer could be given), the distribution of the market amongst vendors of EIS tools used in organisations surveyed is reflected in Table 18.

One respondent indicated that his organisation *only* used in-house developed software. This response was therefore not included in Table 18. From Table 18, Cognos is the most frequently (60.0%) reported commercially packaged EIS software tool.

Table 18. Distribution of market amongst vendors of EIS tools according to responses

Name of commercially purchased EIS software tools and/or ERP software with EIS features	Tally and associated percentage of commercially purchased EIS software tools and/or ERP software with EIS features as reported by respondents in total sample surveyed (N=30)
Business Objects	2 (6.7%)
Cognos	18 (60.0%)
Crystal Enterprise	1 (3.3%)
Holos	1 (3.3%)
Hyperion	3 (10.0%)
JDEdwards BI	4 (13.3%)
Lotus Notes	3 (10.0%)
Oracle	4 (13.3%)
Pilot	2 (6.7%)
ProClarity	1 (3.3%)
SAP/EIS	1 (3.3%)
MIMMS	1 (3.3%)
MISYS	1 (3.3%)
BI Query	1 (3.3%)

Cognos has 2.5 million users at 18,000 customers in 120 countries and its business intelligence solutions are available from more than 3,000 worldwide partners and resellers. See http://www.cognos.com

Pervan et al. (1997) report that "Pilot was the most popular choice with 26%, followed by Powerplay with 16%" in organisations surveyed in Australia. Roldán et al. (2003) found that "Commander from Comshare (39.1%), DSS Agents from MicroStrategy (21,9%), Forest & Trees from Platinum Technology (15.6%), and Focus/EIS from Information Builders (10.9%)" were the popular EIS software tools in organisations surveyed in Spain. From Table 17 and the Australian and Spanish survey findings, it appears that little use is made of ERP software with EIS features. EIS products "tend to be included in larger software systems, becoming a module integrated in quite a few ERP systems such as SAP" (Roldán et al., 2003). However, the author's findings suggest that there is a strong *usage* preference for commercially purchased EIS software tools (as opposed to ERP software with EIS features) by organisations surveyed in South Africa. Usage of ERP software with EIS features appears to be minimal in organisations surveyed in South Africa.

From a tally of interviewees' responses to question 2.12 (more than one answer could be given), the frequency of EIS use in organisations surveyed is given in Table 19.

Table 19. Frequencies of EIS use in organisations

Frequency of EIS use in organisation	Tally and associated percentage of EIS use in organisation as reported by respondents in total sample surveyed (N=31)
Very rarely or not at all	1 (3.2%)
Rarely (a few times per month)	1 (3.2%)
Occasionally (a few times per week)	1 (3.2%)
Sometimes (about once per weeks)	1 (3.2%)
Fairly regularly (several times per week)	4 (12.9%)
Regularly (once a day)	12 (38.7%)
Frequently (several times per day)	13 (41.9%)

This EIS use measure was self-reported by respondents. Although previous research suggests that self-reported frequency measures are appropriate as relative measures (Blair & Burton, 1987), they should not be regarded as precise measures of actual use frequency (Davis et al., 1989).

From Table 19, frequent (several times per day) and regular use of the EIS were reported by a total of 25 (80.6%) respondents (see shaded area in Table 19). In the survey of EIS applications in Taiwan, Liang et al. (1997) state that "over half of the respondents reported using their systems every day. Twenty-two percent used the system very often." Liang et al. (1997) report that organisations with EIS "rely heavily on their systems for support decision making." In the author's survey, some respondents reported different EIS use frequencies during the month (e.g., higher EIS use during month end). One respondent stated, "First week of month is a lot busier. Towards end of the month not more than an hour." An EIS has the effect of multiplying the frequency of use (Palvia, Kumar, Kumar, & Hendon, 1996).

The low EIS use frequencies can be ascribed to the fact that three EIS implementations in organisations are currently under development and implementation (see Table 7). Despite this, Davis (1989) notes that users are often willing to cope with some difficulty of use in a system that provides critically needed functionality. System use is the most crucial aspect of EIS operation.

From the responses to question 2.14, a smorgasbord of some interviewee's comments is now given. Twenty-nine interviewees expressed a positive personal expectation to the success of the EIS implementation in their organisations. Some interviewee comments recorded were "Positive," "Very optimistic," "We knew it would be a success from our previous history," "I though the guys would really go for it," "Had a very high expectation of success," "We had nothing. We believed it would sort out all our problems," "I knew it would be successful because we had done a lot of research," and "I knew it would work as we were reliant on the mainframe."

One interviewee's response was neutral with a reply "Can't comment. Before my time." Another interviewee "thought it would fail...had old style managers who were not into new kinds of things...things have now changed." Perlman (1986) notes that overcoming inherent human conservatism associated with any change is crucial. The right determination is seen as a key to EIS success (Salmeron, 2001).

From a synthesis of interviewees' responses to question 2.15, the first author identified that 27 interviewees reported the most recent EIS implementation in their organisation as successful, three interviewees reported partially success, and one interviewee reported failure with his organisation's most recent EIS implementation.

For the 27 successful organisations, some interviewee comments recorded were "Yes, definitely growing now," "Yes, it was successful due to the ease of implementing the Cognos product. It is very scalable. We staged the implementation," "Absolutely, yes!" "Oh, yes. Without a doubt," "To a large degree it achieved what we had originally set out to achieved," "Successfully implemented but not widely used," and "Yes, once up and running."

For the partially successful EIS implementations some interviewee comments recorded were "It has not yet been completed...serious mindset to get rid of" and "thought it would be successful but needed executive team buy-in." Support from senior management is considered to be the most critical issue affecting EIS operation (Kaniclides et al., 1997).

For the not successful (i.e., failure) EIS implementation in response to question 2.16, the interviewee stated for the latest EIS implementation his organisation had "tried to pilot a project ... but there were some political reasons for its failure." Politically motivated resistance from executives is a highly rated factor affecting the success of EIS development (Kaniclides et al., 1997). Kaniclides et al. (1997) note that politically driven tactics can originate from both executives designated as initial users of the system and those regarded as potential future users of the system. This scenario appears to be present in the organisation, which the interviewee reported that the latest EIS implementation had not been successful. Furthermore, there seemed to exist an interest in letting the EIS system fail rather than a lack of interest in system success. A similar finding was reported by Poon and Wagner (2001) in organisations surveyed in Hong Kong.

There is little information available to assist practitioners regarding the question of how to minimise the risk of EIS failure (Watson et al., 1991). Watson and Glover (1989) carried out a study of 21 EIS failures. From their findings, they identified the following factors that contribute to the EIS failure: inadequate or appropriate technology, failure of the system to meet user needs, lack of executive commitment and executive resistance to technology. In the Pervan et al. (1997) study of EIS failures in organisations surveyed in Australia, inadequate or appropriate technology was reported as being the major EIS failure factor. During the author's interview of the respondent who reported his most recent EIS implementation as not successful, the interviewee cited that "there were some political reasons for its failure." At first glance this finding appears to be inconsistent with the Watson et al. (1989) and the more recent Pervan et al. (1997) studies.

A further investigation reveals that in the Pervan et al. (1997) study, "with only 16% of organisations having EIS that are in full operation, this may be the reason for political problems being rated the least important." Pervan et al. (1997) note that "this issue may increase in significance as more organisations progress from the evaluation stage to the operational stage in the near future." During the author's survey, the respondent who reported his most recent EIS implementation as not successful *had* progressed from an EIS evaluation stage to the operational stage. Consequently, the author's findings do not appear to be inconsistent with the Pervan et al. (1997) study. Willcocks (1996) suggest that the high failure rates of new IS in organisations stems from the fact that there is a wide gap between the level of investments in IS and an organisation's ability to achieve the necessary benefits from such investments. Most organisations do not formally evaluate their investment in IS (Wessels, 2003).

From the responses to question 2.15 for successful and partially successful EIS implementations in organisations surveyed, some interviewee's comments are now given. "Software had to be user friendly...the way that we had done our reporting did not display well...our MD wants to look at something more visual," "a very clear understanding of user requirements is necessary because they don't know what they want," "the ease of extracting the data...must be very easy and flexible," "...the buy-in was already there," "that we can use our data for analysis," "management support," "the immediate access to data, drill down, KPIs to customers and products," "presents answers in a presentable way...user-friendly," "reliable, timeliness, and flexibility," "accurate, timeous, relevant to what's happening in business at moment... also ease of use," "needed to be backed by management to be successful," "needed an executive sponsor," "stable technology," and "data integrity."

Rockart and Delong (1988) observed several factors in organisations which appear to be the most important for effective EIS implementation. Some factors which Rockart et al. (1988) report as critical to a successful EIS implementation, are a committed and informed executive sponsor, an operating sponsor, appropriate IS staff, appropriate technology, management of data, clear link to business objectives, management of organisational resistance, and management of system evolution spread. Pervan et al. (1997) report that these factors will be refined by other researchers as the EIS field evolves. While there is no consensus on the "ingredients for EIS success" (Paller & Laska, 1990) there appears to be a strong degree of commonality between the identified factors and interviewee's comments. The process of evaluating IT is the application and absorption of a range of input information which includes data, evaluation techniques, personal experience, personal knowledge, corporate or departmental politics, personal decisions and intuition (Wessels, 2003). This concludes the analysis and findings of the interviewee's responses to Section 2 of the author's survey instrument. Interviewees' responses to questions in Section 3 of the survey instrument are now analysed and discussed.

Level of Impact of Web-Based Technologies on EIS Implementation

From Section 3 of the author's survey instrument, a tally, and associated percentage of the perceived degree to which specific Web-based technologies impacted a respondent's EIS implementation is given in Table 20. The shaded area in Table 20 suggests that there is little (if any) perceived impact by Web-based technologies on EIS implementation in organisations surveyed in KwaZulu-Natal.

Table 20 shows that only seven (22.5%) of organisations surveyed reported that the organisational intranet significantly impacted their EIS implementation. From a managerial perspective, intranet technology's cost, flexibility, and wide spectrum of uses does render it an attractive IT in the organisational environment (Scheepers et al., 2001). The level of impact by the Internet on EIS implementation is slightly

Table 20. Tally and associated percentage of the expected degree to which specific Web-based technologies impacted respondent's EIS implementation

Web-based technology	The degree to which Web-based technologies impacted respondent's EIS implementation (N=31)						
	Not at all	Very little	Somewhat little	Uncertain	Somewhat much	Very much	Extensively
Intranet	17 (54.8%)	2 (6.5%)	2 (6.5%)	0 (0.0%)	3 (9.7%)	4 (12.9%)	3 (9.6%)
Internet	21 (67.7%)	1 (3.2%)	1 (3.2%)	0 (0.0%)	2 (6.5%)	3 (9.7%)	3 (9.7%)
Extranet	24 (77.4%)	1 (3.2%)	2 (6.5%)	1 (3.2%)	1 (3.2%)	2 (6.5%)	0 (0.0%)
E-commerce (B2B)	28 (90.4%)	1 (3.2%)	0 (0.0%)	0 (0.0%)	0 (0.0%)	1 (3.2%)	1 (3.2%)
E-commerce (B2C)	26 (83.9%)	1 (3.2%)	1 (3.2%)	0 (0.0%)	2 (6.5%)	0 (0.0%)	1 (3.2%)
WAP and other mobile technologies	29 (93.6%)	1 (3.2%)	0 (0.0%)	0 (0.0%)	0 (0.0%)	0 (0.0%)	1 (3.2%)
Portal	26 (83.8%)	0 (0.0%)	0 (0.0%)	0 (0.0%)	2 (6.5%)	2 (6.5%)	1 (3.2%)

lower with six (19.4%) of organisations surveyed reporting that the Internet had significantly impacted their EIS implementation. While 24 (77.4%) of the organisations surveyed reported the extranet had no impact on their organisation's EIS implementation, the balance of the data sample (22.6%) reported different degrees of impact. Turban et al. (2004) note that the use of extranets is rapidly increasing due to the large savings in communication costs that can materialise. The author reported relatively low-level impact by the extranet on EIS implementations in organisations surveyed, and this may be an avenue for further investigation. The Internet, intranet, and extranets can be used in various ways in a corporate environment in order to gain competitive advantage (Turban et al., 2004). As a mission critical corporate tool, Internet technology has to support all the core business functions and it must do this more effectively and economically than is possible using other concepts and tools (Van der Merwe, 2001). The Internet provides global access and is the conceptual start of both intranets and extranets (Askelson, 1998).

The results show that the vast majority (90.4%) of respondents reported that e-commerce (B2B) had not impacted EIS implementation in organisation surveyed. A slightly lower result (83.9%) was reported for e-commerce (B2C). One possible explanation for e-commerce (B2B) and (B2C) low impact levels is that the software development tools are still evolving and changing rapidly. E-commerce is a rapidly evolving area that is continuing to penetrate into new application areas (Hawryszkiewycz, 1999). Another possible reason is it is difficult to integrate the Internet and e-commerce software with some existing applications and databases. However, Ciborra and Hanseth (1998) suggest that intranet technology may even emerge without a grand plan in the organisation.

WAP and other mobile technologies have no (93.6%) or very little (3.2%) impact on EIS implementations. Of the seven Web-based technologies given in Table 20, WAP and other mobile technologies have the *least* impact (combining "Somewhat much," "Very much," and "Extensively") on EIS implementation in organisations surveyed. Only one respondent (3.2%) reported that WAP and other technologies had extensively impacted the EIS implementation in her organisation. A possible explanation for this result is that the EIS consultant was technically proficient in WAP technologies.

From Table 20, three interviewees reported that their organisation's EIS implementations were significantly impacted ("Very much" and "Extensively") by portal technologies. This is noteworthy as the portal technology impact on EIS implementations (9.7%) is higher than the extranet (6.5%), e-commerce (B2B) (6.4%), e-commerce: (B2C) (6.4%) and WAP and other technologies (3.2%) impacts. For a discussion of the impact of portal technologies on EIS implementation in organisations, see Averweg et al. (2004).

Combining the results ("Somewhat much," "Very much," and "Extensively") for each of the seven Web-based technologies, Table 21 gives a descending ranking

Table 21. Descending rank order of impact levels of Web-based technologies on EIS implementation

Rank	Web-based technology	Tally and level of impact on EIS implementations
1	Intranet	10 (32.2%)
2	Internet	8 (25.9%)
3	Portal	5 (16.2%)
4	Extranet	3 (9.7%)
5	E-commerce (B2C)	3 (9.7%)
6	E-commerce (B2B)	2 (6.4%)
7	WAP and other mobile technologies	1 (3.2%)

order of the levels of impact on EIS implementations. From the selected Web-based technologies, intranets have the highest level of impact on EIS implementation in organisations surveyed in KwaZulu-Natal. Organisational intranets are envisioned as platforms for organisational knowledge management (Davenport & Pruzak, 1998). This information is particularly useful for IT practitioners in the planning of future EIS implementations. The key point is that an organisational intranet utilizes Internet and Web-based technologies to conduct internal communication and collaboration activities within an organisation and provides a level of integration and access.

This concludes the analysis and findings of the interviewee's responses to Section 3 of the author's survey instrument. Some concluding remarks will now be given.

Concluding Remarks

Ezingeard et al. (1998) report that in their survey, more than half of the respondents did not formally list the benefits expected of their IT and IS investment but justified the investment as an "act of faith." Intranet technology calls into question some of our traditional IT implementation wisdom and presents new challenges for seeking to implement the technology (Balasubramanian & Bashian, 1998; Scheepers, 1999). Consequently, approaching an EIS implementation with a traditional mindset or using existing implementation models may be short-sighted. Emergent processes require new modelling methods and technologies to build successful systems that support them. The advent of the organisational application of Internet-based technologies (especially intranets), now marks the ubiquitous computing paradigm that weaves together a complex array of existing ICT into one rich medium (Dahlbom, 1996).

There is a need to identify crucial differences in existing IT implementation models that enable some organisations to success with their IT investment where others have failed. Developers must be aware of emerging trends in the organisational intranet market to create systems that will be able to incorporate the latest technological developments and new methods of information delivery and presentation. Organisations need to build connections between information and organise it in ways that most individuals can navigate through choices for themselves. As the use of Web-based technologies in the distribution of internal information in organisations in KwaZulu-Natal, South Africa becomes more widespread, it is envisaged that future EIS implementations will be further impacted by organisational intranets. Given this impact, justifying investment in such IS and IT should be carefully evaluated and quantified.

References

Abraham, D. M., & Seal K. C. (2001). CLASIC: Collaborative layered system using intranet capabilities. *Logistics Information Journal, 14*(1), 99-107.

Agarwal, R., Higgins, C., & Tanniru, M. (1991). Technology diffusion in a centralized MIS environment. *Information & Management, 20*, 61-70.

Allison, I. K. (1996). Executive information systems: An evaluation of current UK practice. *International Journal of Information Management, 16*(1), 27-38.

Al-Gahtani, S. S. (2001, June 4-6). The applicability of the technology acceptance model outside North America: An empirical test in the Arab World. In *BITWorld 2001 Conference Proceedings*, American University in Cairo, Cairo, Egypt.

Askelson, K. (1998). *Extranets; all part of the third wave.* Retrieved December 15, 2004, from http://www.itfac.co.uk/chartech/issue73/page6.htm

Averweg, U., Erwin, G., & Petkov, D. (2004, October 4-6). A survey of the state of executive information systems in organisations in South Africa. In *Proceedings of the South African Institute of Computer Scientists and Information Technologists Conference (SAICSIT-2004)*, Stellenbosch, Western Cape, South Africa (pp. 216-220).

Averweg, U., Petkov, D., Erwin, G., & Moolman, H. (2003, December). Impact of portal technologies on EIS implementations in organizations in KwaZulu-Natal. *South African Journal of Information Management, 5*(4). Retrieved November 24, 2006, from http://www.sajim.co.za/default.asp?to=peer1vol5nr4

Averweg, U. R. F., & Erwin, G. J. (2000, November 1-3). Executive information systems in South Africa: A research synthesis for the future. In *Proceedings of the South African Institute of Computer Scientists and Information Technologists Conference (SAICSIT-2000),* Cape Town, South Africa.

Balasubramanian, V., & Bashian, A. (1998). Document management and Web technologies: Alice marries the mad Hatter. *Communications of the ACM, 41*(7), 107-115.

Bannister, F., & Remenyi, D. (2000). *Value perception in IT investment decisions.* Retrieved December 15, 2004, from http://is.twi.tudelft.n./ejise/vol2/issue2/paper1.html

Basu, C., Poindexter, S., Drosen, J., & Addo, T. (2000). Diffusion of executive information systems in organizations and the shift to Web technologies. *Industrial Management & Data Systems, 100*(6), 271-276.

Belcher, L. W., & Watson, H. J. (1993). Assessing the value of CONOCO's EIS. *MIS Quarterly, 17*(4), 239-253.

Blair, E., & Burton, S. (1987). Cognitive processes used by survey respondents to answer behavioral frequency questions. *Journal of Consumer Research, 14,* 280-288.

Butcher, C. (2002, May). SPAR: Striving for excellence. *Professional Management Review,* 18-20.

Chabrow, E. (1998, October). Instruments of growth. *InformationWeek, 5.* Retrieved November 24, 2006 from http://www.informationweek.com/703/03ssgro.htm;jsessionid=MLOUBEFC04BVAQSNDLPSKHSCJUNN2JVN?queryText=Instruments

Ciborra, C. U., & Hanseth, O. (1998). From tool to gestell: Agendas for managing the information infrastructure. *Information, Technology & People, 11*(4), 305-327.

Cooper, D. R., & Emory, C. W. (1995). *Business research methods.* Richard D. Irwin, Inc.

Cortese, A. (1996, February 26). Here comes the intranet. *Business Week, 3464,* 76-84.

Dahlbom, B. (1996). The new informatics. *Scandinavian Journal of Information Systems, 8*(2), 29-48.

Damsgaard, J., & Scheepers, R. (1999). Power, influence, and intranet implementation: A safari of South African organizations. *Information, Technology & People, 12*(4), 333-358.

Davenport, T. H., & Pruzak, L. (1998). *Working knowledge: How organizations manage what they know.* Boston: Harvard Business School Press.

Davis, F. D. (1989). Perceived usefulness, perceived ease of use, and user acceptance of information technology. *MIS Quarterly, 3*(3), 319-342.

Davis, F. D., Bagozzi, R. P., & Warshaw, P. R. (1989). User acceptance of computer technology: A comparison of two theoretical models. *Management Science, 35*(8), 982-1003.

Earl, M. J. (1996). Putting information technology in its place: A polemic for the nineties. *Journal of Information Technology, 7*, 100-108.

Eder, L. B. (2000). *Managing healthcare information systems with Web-enabled technologies.* Hershey, PA: Idea Group Publishing.

Ezingeard, J. N., Irani, Z., & Race, P. (1998). Assessing the value and cost implications of manufacturing information and data systems: An empirical study. *European Journal of Information Systems, 7*(4), 252-260.

Giesecke, M. (2001). The end of the author. *Deutschland, E6*(3), 54-55, June/July.

Gundry, J., & Metes, G. (1996). *Team knowledge management: A computer-mediated approach.* Retrieved December 15, 2004, from http://www.knowab.co.uk/wbeteam

Hall, H. (2001). Input-friendliness: Motivating knowledge sharing across intranets. *Journal of Information Science, 27*(3), 139-146.

Harris, L. (2000). Rand Water derives bottom-line benefits from EIS. *E-Business or Out of Business*, an Advertising Supplement compiled and published by Computing S.A., TML Business Publishing, Pinegowrie, South Africa, 28-29.

Hawryszkiewycz, I. (1999). *Workspace networks for knowledge sharing.* Retrieved December 15, 2004, from http://ausWeb.scu.edu.au/aw99/papers/hawryszkiewycz/paper/html

Hinton, C. M., & Kaye, G. R. (1994). The hidden investments in information technology: The role of organizational context and system dependency. *International Journal of Information Management, 16*(6), 413-427.

Houdeshel, G. S., & Watson, H. J. (1987). The Management Information and Decision Support (MIDS) system at Lockheed-Georgia. *MIS Quarterly, 11*(1), 127-140.

Igbaria, M., & Tan, M. (1997). The consequences of information technology acceptance on subsequent individual performance. *Information & Management, 32*(3), 113-121.

Jones, B. (2002, July 22). Automating balanced scorecards mobilises resources. *Computing S.A., 22*(27), 19.

Kaniclides, T., & Kimble, T. (1995). A framework for the development and use of executive information systems. In Lourens (Ed.), *Proceedings of GRONICS '95*, Groningen, The Netherlands (pp. 47-52).

Kaniclides, T., & Kimble, T. (1997). *Assessing the relative importance of factors affecting executive information systems success* (Rep. No. YCS283). Department of Computer Science, University of York, UK.

Kennedy, D. H. (1995). Everybody's information systems? *Management Accounting London, 73*(5), 4.

Kirlidog, M. (1997). Information technology transfer to a developing country: Executive information systems in Turkey. *OCLC Systems & Services, 13*(3), 102-123.

KPMG Consulting. (2002, May). Reality bites. *The second annual report on e-business in the UK.*

Laudon, K. C., & Laudon, J. P. (2000). *Management information systems* (6th ed.). Upper Saddle River, NJ: Prentice-Hall.

Liang, T. P., & Hung, S. Y. (1997). DSS and EIS applications in Taiwan. *Information Technology & People, 10*(4), 303-315.

Lu, H. P., & Gustafson, D. H. (1994). An empirical study of perceived usefulness and perceived ease of use on computerized support system use over time. *International Journal of Information Management, 14*(5), 317-329.

Lyytinen, K., Rose, G., & Welke, R. (1998). The brave new world of development in the Internetwork computing architecture (InterNCA): Or how distributed computing platforms will change systems development. *Information Systems Journal, 8*, 241-253.

Makhanya, P. (2004, December). eThekwini voted best metro in SA. *The Mercury*, p. 10.

Martin, E. W., Brown, C. V., DeHayes, D. W., Hoffer, J. A., & Perkins, W. C. (1999). *Managing information technology: What managers need to know.* Upper Saddle River, NJ: Prentice-Hall.

Meneely, J., & Pervan, G. P. (1994). Factors that contribute to the successful use of executive information systems. In Shanks and Arnott (eds), In *Proceedings of the 5th Australasian Conference on Information Systems* (Vol. 1, pp. 170-189), Monash University, Melbourne, Australia.

Messina, F. M., & Sanjay, S. (1995). Executive information systems: Not just for executives anymore! *Management Accounting, 77*(1), 60-63.

Millet, I., Mawhinney, C. H., & Kallman, E. A. (1991). Alternative paths to EIS. *DSS-91, International Conference on Decision Support Systems*, Manhattan Beach, CA (pp. 50-61).

Mthembu, B. (2004, December 10). eThekwini voted top dog for service. *Daily News*, p. 3.

O'Brien, J. A. (2000). *Introduction to information systems: Essentials for the Internetworked enterprise* (9th ed.). Boston: Irwin McGraw-Hill.

O'Reilly, C. A. (1982). Variations in decision makers' use of information sources: The impact of quality and accessibility of information. *Academy of Management Journal, 25*(4), 756-771, December.

Oguz, M. T. (2003, May 31). Strategic intelligence: Business intelligence in competitive strategy. *DM Review.* Retrieved October 5, 2004, from http://dmreview.com

Paller, A., & Laska, R. (1990). *The EIS book.* Homewood, IL: Dow Jones-Irwin.

Palvia, P., Kumar, A., Kumar, N., & Hendon, R. (1996). Information requirements of a global EIS: An exploratory macro assessment. *Decision Support Systems, 16*(2), 169-179.

Park, H. K., Min, J. K., Lim, J. S., & Chun, K. J. (1997). A comparative study of executive information systems between Korea and the United States. Seoul, Korea: Dept. of Telecommunications Systems Management, Sangmyung University. In J. J. Cano (Ed.), *Critical reflections on information systems: A systemic approach.* Hershey, PA: Idea Group Publishing.

Perlman, A. H. (1986). Building a successful executive information system. *Infosystems*, p. 66.

Pervan, G., & Phua, R. (1997). A survey of the state of executive information systems in large Australian organisations. *The Australian Computer Journal, 29*(2), 64-73.

Pijpers, G. G. M. (2001). Understanding senior executives' use of information technology and the Internet. In Anandarajan & Simmers (Eds.), *Managing Web usage in the workplace: A social, ethical, and legal perspective* (pp. 1-19), Hershey, PA: Idea Group Publishing.

Poon, P., & Wagner, C. (2001). Critical success factors revisited: Success and failure cases of information systems for senior executives. *Decision Support Systems, 30*(4), 393-418.

Preedy, D. (1990). The theory and practical use of executive information systems. *International Journal of Information Management, 10,* 96-104.

PricewaterhouseCoopers. (2002). *Technology forecast: 2002-2004. Volume 1: Navigating the Future of Software* (Document No. TC-01-12). Menlo Park, CA: PricewaterhouseCoopers Technology Centre.

Rai, A., & Bajwa, D. (1997). An empirical investigation into factors relating to the adoption of EIS: An analysis for collaboration and decision support. *Decision Sciences, 18*(1), 939-974.

Remenyi, D., & Lubbe, S. (1998). Some information systems issues in South Africa and suggestions as to how to deal with them. In S. Lubbe (Ed.), *IT investment in developing countries: An assessment and practical guideline.* Hershey, PA: Idea Group Publishing.

Remenyi, D., Money, A., & Twite, A. (1995). *Effective measurement and management of IT costs and benefits.* London: Butterworths.

Robinson, T. (1996, November 18). Intranet 100: The revolution is here. *InformationWeek,* 106-108. Retrieved November 24, 2006 from http://www.informationweek.com/606/06rev.htm;jsessionid=MLOUBEFC04BVAQSNDLPSKHSCJUNN2JVN?queryText=Intranet

Rockart, J. F., & DeLong, D. W. (1988). *Executive support systems the emergence of top management computer use.* Homewood, IL: Dow Jones-Irwin.

Roldán J. L. (2000). *Sistemas de información ejecutivos (EIS): Génesis, implantación y repercusiones organizativas.* Unpublished thesis, Universidad de Sevilla, Spain.

Roldán, J. L., & Leal, A. (2003). Executive information systems in Spain: A study of current practices and comparative analysis. In Forgionne, Gupta, & Mora (Eds.), *Decision making support systems: Achievements and challenges for the new decade* (pp. 287-304), Hershey, PA: Idea Group Publishing.

SA2002-2003. (2002). *South Africa at a glance.* Craighall, South Africa: Editors Inc.

Salmeron, J. L. (2001). EIS evolution in large Spanish businesses. *Information & Management, 1968,* 1-10.

Salmeron, J. L., Luna, P., & Martinez, F. J. (2001). Executive information systems in major companies: Spanish case study. *Computer Standards & Interfaces, 23,* 195-207.

Scheepers, R. (1999, August 21-22). Key role players in the initiation and implementation of intranet technology. In *Proceedings of IFIP TC8 WG 8.2, New Information Technologies in Organizational Processes: Field Studies and Theoretical Reflections on the Future Work,* St Louis, MO.

Scheepers, R., & Rose, J. (2001). Organizational intranets: cultivating information technology for the people by the people. In Dasgupta (Ed.), *Managing Internet and intranet technologies in organizations: Challenges and opportunities* (pp. 1-20), Hershey, PA: Idea Group Publishing.

Sprague, R. H., Jr., & Watson, H. J. (1996). *Decision support for management.* Upper Saddle River, NJ: Prentice-Hall.

Sprout, A. (1995, November 27). The Internet inside your company. *Fortune,* 161-168. Retrieved November 24, 2006 from http://money.cnn.com/magazines/fortune/fortune_archive/1995/11/27/208032/index.htm

Srivihok, A. (1998). *Effective management of executive information systems implementations: A framework and a model of successful EIS implementation.* PhD dissertation. Central University, Rockhampton, Australia.

Statistics South Africa. (2001). *Census 2001 digital census atlas.* Retrieved December 15, 2004, from http://gis-data.durban.gov.za/census/index.html

Straub, D. W. (1989). Validating instruments in MIS research. *MIS Quarterly*, *13*(2), 147-166.

Strom, D. (1996). *Finding the right intranet technologies to buy.* Retrieved December 15, 2004, from http://www.strom.com/pubwork/intranet.html

Suradi, Z. (2001, June 4-6). Testing technology acceptance model (TAM) in Malaysian environment. In *BITWorld 2001 Conference Proceedings*, American University in Cairo, Cairo, Egypt.

Tang, H., Lee, S., & Yen, D. (1997). An investigation on developing Web-based EIS. *Journal of CIS*, *38*(2), 49-54.

Thodenius, B. (1995, April 20-22). The use of executive information systems in Sweden. In *CEMS Academic Conference—Recent Developments in Economics and Business Administration*, Wirtschaftsuniversität, Wien, Austria.

Turban, E. (2001, October 7). California State University, Long Beach, and City University of Hong Kong, USA. *Personal communication.*

Turban, E., & Aronson, J. (1998). *Decision support systems and intelligent systems.* Upper Saddle River, NJ: Prentice-Hall.

Turban, E., McLean, E., & Wetherbe, J. (1999). Information technology for management. New York: John Wiley & Sons.

Turban, E., McLean E., & Wetherbe, J. (2004). *Information technology for management. transforming organizations in the digital* (4th ed.), Hoboken, NJ: John Wiley & Sons, Inc.

Turban, E., Rainer, R. K. Jr., & Potter, R. E. (2005). *Introduction to information technology.* Hoboken, NJ: John Wiley & Sons, Inc.

Van der Merwe, A. (2001, September). Managing intranets to improve knowledge sharing. *South African Journal of Information Management*, *3*(2). Retrieved November 24, from http://www.sajim.co.za/default.asp?to=student4vol3nr2

Venkatesh, V., & Morris, M. G. (2000). Why don't men ever stop to ask for directions? Gender, social influence, and their role in technology acceptance and usage behavior. *MIS Quarterly*, *24*(1), 115-139.

Volonino, L., Watson, H. J., & Robinson, S. (1995). Using EIS to respond to dynamic business conditions. *Decision Support Systems*, *14*(2), 105-116.

Ward, J. (1996). *Information systems: delivery business value?* Paper presented at the Business Information Technology Conference, Manchester, UK.

Watson, H. J., & Frolick, M. N. (1993). Determining information requirements for an executive information system. *MIS Quarterly*, *17*(3), 255-269.

Watson, H. J., & Glover, O. H. (1989, December 4). Common and avoidable causes of EIS failure. *Computerworld*, 90-91.

Watson, H. J., Houdeshel, G., & Rainer, R. K. Jr. (1997). *Building executive information systems and other decision support applications*. New York: John Wiley & Sons.

Watson, H. J., O'Hara, M. T., Harp, C. G., & Kelly, G. G. (1996). Including soft information in EISs. *Information Systems Management, 13*(3), 66-77.

Watson, H. J., Rainer, R. K., & Koh, C. E. (1991). Executive information systems: A framework for development and a survey of current practices. *MIS Quarterly, 15*(1), 13-30.

Watson, H. J., Rainer, R. K., & Frolick, M. N. (1992). Executive information systems: An ongoing study of current practices. *International Information Systems, 1*(2), 37-56.

Wessels, P. (2003, June). Justifying the investment in information systems. *South African Journal of Information Management, 5*(2). Retrieved November 24, 2006 from http://www.sajim.co.za/default.asp?to=peer4vol5nr2

Wetherbe, J. C. (1991). Executive information requirements: Getting it right. *MIS Quarterly, 15*, 50-65.

Willcocks, L. (1996). *Investing in information systems*. Oxford, UK: Chapman and Hall.

Young, D., & Watson, H. J. (1995). Determinates of EIS acceptance. *Information & Management, 29*(3), 153-164.

Chapter IV

Information Dynamics in Developing Countries

Hakikur Rahman, SDNP Bangladesh (UNDP), Bangladesh

Abstract

Revolutionary advancement in information and communication technology (ICT) with strengthening of economic and social aspects is transforming the global communities. A new kind of dynamism—the information dynamics—is emerging where communities are not restricted within boundaries and becoming competent with information, knowledge, networking, and versatility on a global basis. A new society is emerging with pervasive information capabilities, creativity other than the conventional learning system, substantially different from an industrial society; more competitive, better able to address individual needs, and steady to the ever-changing environment. The information revolution creates both the challenge and the means for the developing world to adjust to the newly developed strategic issues and action plans of the New World by accommodating the needful infrastructure of telecommunications and information systems. The information revolution has also opened up opportunities to tackle the problems of poverty, inequality, illiteracy, and environmental degradation.

Introduction

Information is the lifeblood of every economy. In more traditional economies, information may be less codified, more often conveyed in personal interaction, but it is vital nonetheless. The ways people get information, and the incentives they have to gather and provide it, are affected by the way society is organized: legal rules and social conventions, institutions and governments, all determine how much information people have and the quality (that is, the accuracy and completeness) of that information (World Bank, 1998).

Information technology is changing throughout the world. Information and communication technologies (ICTs) are generating a new industrial revolution already as significant and far-reaching as those of the past century. This revolution is based on information dynamics, and within itself the human knowledge content.

Recent years have seen rapid progress in science and technology related to the generation, processing, transmission, accumulation, storage, and utilization of information—a field known collectively as information science and technology (Council for Science & Technology, 1999). Advancement in ICT offers unprecedented promise for social and economic development on a global perspective. As the primary means of communication and performance in the networked society, ICT has become a fundamental instrument for both the developed and developing countries.

ICT can contribute to fostering empowerment and participation and making government processes more efficient and transparent by encouraging communication and information sharing among people and organizations, and within government. ICT connects individuals and local communities with information and resources beyond their geographic boundaries, encouraging information dissemination, information exchange, and communication (DOI, 2001).

Wolfensohn (1998) stated in his forwarding for the World Bank WRD1998 report, that the information revolution makes understanding knowledge and development more urgent than ever before. New communications technologies and plummeting computing costs are shrinking distance and eroding borders and time. The remotest village has the possibility of tapping a global store of knowledge beyond the dreams of anyone living a century ago, and more quickly and cheaply than anyone imagined possible only a few decades ago.

Information infrastructure comprised of the cross-country telecommunications network, the user-friendly computing tools, and easy-access information warehouses. Information backbone has the characteristics of easier transportation, manipulation, storage, and dissemination by creating the "knowledge tank" an essential element for the management of the new economy. And because the new economic development is about knowledge networking, the information revolution holds inestimable promise for downtrodden population in the developing countries.

Background

Information can be seen as any communication or representation of knowledge, such as facts, data, or opinions in any medium or form, including textual, numerical, graphic, cartographic, narrative, or audiovisual forms. It is the knowledge acquired through study or experience or instruction. Information is data and facts that have been organized and communicated in a coherent and meaningful manner (Google definition search). Dynamics is that part of the field of mechanics that studies objects in motion, and here it is taken as a representation of movement of entities (human, society, or community). By developing countries, it meant a country that is poor by world standards in terms of real GDP per capita. They are the countries with low- and medium-income in which most of the population have a lower standard of living with access to fewer goods and services.

Then information dynamics can be treated as an integrated knowledge movement of the society or community. Depending on the penetration of various applications on information and communication technologies, information dynamics in low-income countries have potential impact on the community development processes.

Information technology revolution should not be treated as innovation and just advancement, but as "general purpose technology" (Bresnahan & Trajtenberg, 1995) to adopt and improve the livelihood of the general people. This general-purpose technology has surpassed the rapidity and mobilization in many perspectives, and substantially improved the quality of life in the marginal community by simply multiplying the state of applications in everyday usage.

The striving forces behind the so-called information revolution are the sharp decline in the prices of information processing, the convergence in communication and computing technologies, and the rapid growth in network computing. Communication networks and interactive multimedia applications are providing the foundation for the transformation of existing social and economic relations into an "information society" (OECD, 1997). It is, indeed, widely believed that modern information technology will change the world, but how can such a change be measured and its impacts assessed (Pohjola, 1998)? A question that needs to be addressed properly for successful implementation of the processes before launching it.

Information technology presents the attractive possibility of bypassing older technologies ("leapfrogging"). For example, countries with old-fashioned mechanical telephone systems can skip the analog electronic era and go straight to advanced digital technologies, and that certainly is happening. Leapfrogging is also made possible in a more radical developmental sense (IMF, 2001).

An information system provides a societal capability based on the use of information that encompasses its full context of people, institutions, policies, processes, incentives, data, information technology, and infrastructure. A strategic information system provides a fundamental capability of such importance that it can enhance the scope and efficiency of an entire sector and economy (Talero & Gandette, 1996).

Radical advancement in ICT information technology reinforced economic and social changes by transforming community and society. From this advancement emerges a new kind of economy, the information economy, where information is the critical essence. Traditional ways of doing business has been drastically modified and sometimes, the old ways have been replaced by new means and methods. Technological progress now enables us to process, store, retrieve, and communicate information in whatever form it may take, unconstrained by distance, time, and volume. This revolution adds huge new capacities to human intelligence and constitutes a resource, which changes the way we work together and the way we live together (Bangemann et al., 1994).

Developing countries and especially the least developed countries (LDCs), have yet to attain measurable socio-economic benefits out of ICT. Development of this sector has often been hindered by a combination of outdated infrastructure, relatively high telecommunication costs, inappropriate technology policies, absence of skilled professionals, and the intricate culture of information interchange. With these views and practices, many of these nations could not able to be the forerunner in the global market and compete with their more fortunate neighbors (Rahman, 2004).

In developing countries, access to information infrastructure always remains inadequate, and progress on telecommunications policy reforms are lagging behind. Yet there is an opportunity for leapfrogging the new technology can provide better, cheaper links to the grass root level stakeholders, while competing global operators can provide low-cost long distance communications. Adopting new technologies, developing countries can deploy telecommunications for lower costs per capita than the industrial world and rapidify poverty alleviation processes.

To create appropriate information dynamics in developing countries, the following issues need to be resolved with greater context; issues of accessibility, intellectual property protection, fair competition, content regulation, and cultural preservation. However, due to many unintended factors, the access to the global information infrastructure by developing countries remains inadequate and dependent on major telecommunications policy reforms yet to be implemented.

Key Factors to Uphold the Information Dynamics: Issues and Problems

Information technology has become a potent force in transforming social, economic, and political life globally. There is little chance for countries or regions to develop without their incorporation into the information age. More and more, development strategies see the need for developing countries to embrace information technology both as a way to avoid further economic and social mobilization as well as to offer opportunities for both growth and diversification of their economies (Hafkin & Taggart, 2001).

Communication is no longer focusing on a single issue, but on a range of livelihoods issues and using several channels. Communication theory has not quite come to grips yet with the complexities of participatory communication. What is certain is that implies a change in roles for the main stakeholders, some of whom may be more willing to change than in roles for the main stakeholders, some of whom may be more willing to change than others (Lowe, 2001).

Poor men and women living in urban informal settlements do need knowledge and information to cope with risks and improve their livelihoods, but the urban poor obtain information hard to access (Schilderman, 2002a). Science and technology development is the fundamental driving force in pushing forward the entire process of social evolution while the creation of more advanced tools is the kernel engine of the development (Zhong, 2003).

Therefore, to harness information and communication technology for its mission of poverty alleviation and sustainable economic development, the following objectives to be set at the national level:

- Easy access to communication and information services through accelerated deployment of national information infrastructure and integration into international communication and information backbone.

- Systemic improvements in the functioning and competitiveness of key sectors of the national economy through strategic policies and implementation plans.

- New ways to use ICT to assist in solving the most prevailing problems of human and economic development—education, health, poverty alleviation, rural development, and reinforced environmental awareness.

- Increased motivation at the national level for economic development through inclusion of information contexts in each level of administration hierarchy.

Evolving Parameters:
Solutions and Recommendations

Information technology can offer significant opportunities in developing countries for virtually all societies, including marginalized communities in rural areas. In considering diversified entrepreneurial ventures associated with information technology, the following parameters need indepth study to ensure equitable participation of all societies in the information age.

- **Concept of society needs to be re-thinked:** Societal control based on closely-held information is no longer possible when information is ubiquitous and inexpensive. Uncontrolled and easy flows of information increase create opportunities for social manipulation.

- **Environmental awareness to be raised:** Due to faster information dissemination and knowledge development, the preservation of the environment has become a prime concern of a well-informed public society. Economic growth cannot be pursued at the expense of the environment, lest such growth become unsustainable and threaten the environment of the entire globe, though environment has significantly different connotations in developed and developing countries.

- **Definition of developing countries needs to be adjusted:** With the rapid advancement of the developed world, and unbalanced participation of the developing world in the global economy, developing world is in the competitiveness of their goods and services. They are threatened with a new form of information poverty that could further extend the "digital divide" and widen the gap in economic status and competitive issues. Necessary fine-tuning is essential, though extremely complex, for total diffusion of information technology, which may result in social fragmentation.

- **Information revolution:** In real sense, to keep up with the developed world, the term "information revolution" needs to be retorted. This will assist to create new paradigm to encounter problems of poverty, inequality, and environmental degradation with the potential to achieve unprecedented gains in social and human development.

- **Developing world need rapid transformation:** Information and communication technology in developing countries need transformation to overcome the dynamic challenges and create unprecedented possibilities for sustainable economic development.

- **Strategies for information dynamics to be recapitulated:** Strategic information systems for developing countries should primarily include sector-wise information systems for education, health, governance, and communication at the first phase. E-commerce, knowledge networks, e-business, environmental awareness, disaster prevention and management, and national statistical data-bank may be treated as the next phase strategic systems.

- **Sectoral information networks need to be developed:** Social networks based on computer-based communications are needed to improvise to connect institutions working in diversified sectors, like, agriculture, education, health, banking, industry, and others. Interconnected networks offer multi-dimensional opportunities in technical cooperation, research, coordination, information, and resource sharing.

- **Social and technical aspects are needed to be simplified:** Design, development, and deployment of information systems and telecommunications capabilities are socially and technically complicated, even in the face of technological advancement and sometime not completely understandable to developing communities. Countries need to depend on the substantial resources, often from abroad, to accomplish this task. They need to establish means and management schemes to facilitate adoption and effective utilization of new systems through adaptive methodologies.

- **State patronization:** Government action is a pre-requisite, but epoch making adjustments are required at the state level in the developing countries to participate in the newly emerged global economy. Governments should establish broad partnerships with the private and corporate sectors, local communities, small and medium enterprises, non-governmental agencies, international and development partners.

  Government intervention to harness information for development is necessary on several fronts: as policy makers, as major users of information technology, and as compensating influences against market failures. Also, governments must supervise and coordinate education—the key to human and economic development (Talero & Gandette, 1996).

- **Telecommunications reformation is a must:** Reformation in the telecommunications sector are a primary requisite to increase the efficiency and availability of services. Policies and regulations are needed to create the conditions for faster private sector entry, for national integration into global information infrastructure, and for efficient use of the existent infrastructure.

- **ICT policies need to be revisited:** National information strategies and action plans need to be deployed by identifying the parameters leading to based an information-based economy. The policy, institutional, legal, and regulatory changes need to be utilized to create an information-friendly environment.

Performance, competitiveness, and governance of all sectors of the economy can be improved through de-regulated information policies and systems.

- **Priorities needed to be identified:** Information systems with important and catalytic capacity to national economic activity should be considered strategic and put forward as part of national information infrastructure. Sector-wise information systems for education, health, financial management, communication, and transportation fall in this category. Similarly, some other generic value-added information facilities, like e-commerce, environmental awareness, disaster prevention, and poverty alleviation can be added to the priority categories. Each country should define its own set of guideline as part of the national information strategy.

Nation-wide networks can also accommodate:

- Network of the financial institutions, and the information industries
- Cross-country studies on ICTs and e-readiness
- Accumulation and dissemination of best practices
- Establishment of a national databank

Figure 1. Information dynamics in social uplift

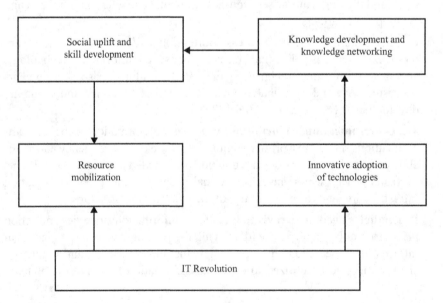

Figure 2. Information dynamics creates demand at the local level

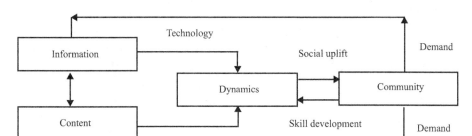

Figure 3. Global knowledge pyramid

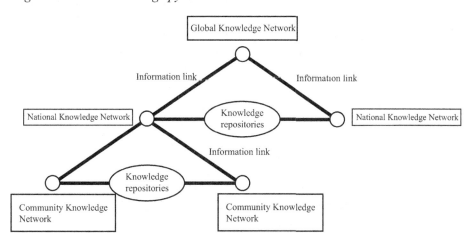

Similarly, strategies need to be taken to mobilize financial sector for development:

- Of national information infrastructure projects
- In project financing guarantees
- With technical cooperation

To implement these strategies in actions, nations need to form information dynamics as depicted in Figure 1. From this figure, it is evident that IT revolution is the core of social uplift through proper resource mobilization. Similarly, Figure 2 illustrates how information and content creates dynamics in the society for its uplift and skill development, creating demand at the local level. The entire information process can create a global knowledge network in a three tires context, as shown in Figure 3. Fed with balanced content in repositories and connected through information links community knowledge networks can form a knowledge pyramid.

Derived from these perspectives, the concept of creating an information dynamics at the national level is shown in Figure 4. Proper policy initiation, partnership, and recognition of key players would lead to the development and implementation of information dynamics by bridging the digital divide inside a country. This information dynamics can grow top-down-top fashion according to the information hierarchy as depicted in Figure 5. By pushing forward a balanced information policy to be implemented in modular form at strategic locations, and utilizing the existing infrastructure, in addition to the newly built one can create demands at the local level. Thorough understanding of local level demand and accommodation of content will enhance incremental expansion of the dynamics at the national level. Eventually, these national networks can be interlinked to form a global information backbone.

Figure 4. Concept of information dynamics at the national level

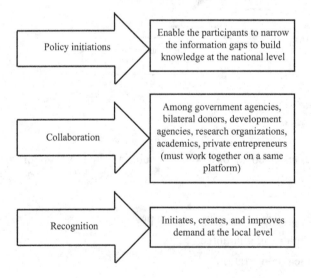

Figure 5. Information hierarchy backbone

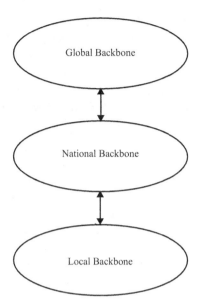

Global Challenges and Future Dimensions

The challenge of communication technologies is not only to transmit pure information but, above all, to enable a real communication between people and communities. The transmission of information is certainly important, but it is far from sufficient. Real, effective, interpersonal communication is, first of all, based upon the exchange of different kinds of messages, postures, gestures, and intonations that physical co-presence can transmit. It is also important to focus on the fact that communication follows different rhythms of interaction (Casalegno & McWilliam, 2004). To implement a successful ICT application for the development of a society, the ideologies of ICTs in social change, empirical research studies on ICTs and organizational change, changes in everyday life, or larger scale societal changes must be understood. Furthermore, relationships between conceptions of ICTs (tools, media, environments, socio-technical networks), theories of social change, workable evidence, and research methods need to be examined in depth (Kling, 2001). The future of information dynamics in developing countries needs to understand principles of information infrastructure, technologies, architecture, and scaleable use of the information (MIT Report, 1995-96).

The development of new media and the progressive spreading of the emerging and rapidly growing phenomenon of remote collaboration pave the way for interesting research in several fields, from teaching to communication, from design to architecture, from ergonomy to studying interfaces. Remote collaborative environments represent a very good opportunity to design communication spaces that allow for social interaction between people and between distant communities, supporting different forms of communication, work, and creativity in various domains. Furthermore, technological progress makes interactive media progressively more efficient, easier to use and destined to a wider public (Casalegno et al., 2004), through participatory communication.

Participatory communication not only helps to empower communities, it also does allow them to influence development. Impact assessment should therefore also consider whether two-way communication has been established, and whether local knowledge and demands have been taken into account, for instance, in policies and programmes targeted at the urban poor (Schilderman, 2002b). Therefore, understanding of principles of information technologies, pursuing these technologies to create acceptable information architecture, and using these infrastructures on highly scaleable state (MIT Report, 1995-96) at marginal to organizational to national to global level are important.

Nowadays, concept of sustainable development has arises in the emerging societies. It is the process of achieving a standard of living and a quality of life with a degree of dignity and a measure of control over their lives, including respect for the environment and the natural resources. This process demands investment, in infrastructure, in human capital, and in productive capacity. In this context, achieving the Millennium Development Goals remains another challenge in reducing poverty and improving livelihoods that world leaders have agreed on at the Millennium Summit in 2000 (http://www.undp.org/mdg/).

Conclusion

The tremendous opportunities offered by the emerging information technology often come in packages with remarkably high payoff potential and at the same time impart high risk. However, these sort of projects should not divert resources from efforts to address the basic needs of common communities and should be driven to be well-established, low-risk, and easily adaptable.

Poor countries and poor people differ from rich ones not only because they have less capital but because they have less knowledge. Knowledge is often costly to create, and that is why much of it is created in industrial countries. But developing countries can acquire knowledge overseas as well as create their own at home (World Bank, 1998).

The urban poor are often deprived by a lack of knowledge and information. The public sector often discriminates against the poor when they seek access to information, or is simply inefficient. To overcome these problems, development agencies should seek to improve their communication with the poor, reduce exclusion, support communities in building their knowledge and information assets, improve the attitudes and performance of information suppliers and invest in sustainable ICTs that are of use to the poor (ITDG, 2002).

As a starter, community information centers are a good fit. This multisectoral concept can help common citizens, non-governmental organizations, and businesses in poor rural and urban areas with economical, easy, and ready access to needed information. The centers could be a powerful engine of rural development and a preferred instrument in the fight against poverty. They could be the hub, at the community level, through which a large number of information services can be dispensed--telephone and fax, local bulletins, document searches on demand, video libraries for entertainment, and knowledge development, health and nutrition training, government utility services, market prices, self-paced learning, and more. The centers would be multisectoral facilities and eventually self-sustaining through fees and contracts (VITA, 1995).

At the social context, a new society is emerging with pervasive information capabilities, thus making it substantially different from an industrial society. It is more competitive, able to address individual needs, and environment friendly, dictating a major agenda of structural adjustment. The adjustment, therefore, is needed within the information arena to tackle uncontrolled information flows, global competition, trade unbalance, and investment opportunities.

References

Bangemann, M., et. al. (1994, May 26). *Europe and the global information society.* Unpublished recommendations to the European Council.

Bresnahan, T. F., & Trajtenberg, M. (1995). General purpose technologies: Engines of growth? *Journal of Econometrics, 65*(1), 83-108.

Casalegno, F., & McWilliam, I. M. (2004). Communication dynamics in technological mediated learning environments. *ITDL Journal, 1*(11), 15-34.

Council for Science & Technology. (1999). *Measures for the strategic promotion of information science and technology pioneering the future.* Retrieved February 7, 2005, from http://www.mext.go.jp/english/kagaku/science06.htm

DOI. (2001, July). *Creating a development dynamic*. Final report of the Digital Opportunity Initiative.

Hafkin, N., & Taggart, N. (2001, June). *Gender, information technology, and developing countries: An analytic study*. Academy for Educational Development (AED).

IMF. (2001, October). The information technology revolution. In *World Economic Outlook* (p. 135).

ITDG. (2002). *Strengthening the knowledge and information systems of the urban poor*. A project report of ITDG, 2002. Retrieved December 25, 2004, from http://www.itdg.org/?id=kis_urban_poor

Kling, R. (2001). *Information technologies and social change*. Retrieved February 7, 2005, from http://www.indiana.edu/Kling

Lowe, L. (2001). *Modeling demand in order to meet it: Can the information and knowledge management systems of the urban poor be understood and strengthened?* A paper to the DSA Conference, Manchester, 2001.

MIT Reports. (1995-96). *MIT reports to the president 1995-96*. Retrieved February 7, 2005, from http://web.mit.edu/annualreports/pres96/10.16.html

OECD. (1997). *Towards a global information society*. Paris: OECD.

Pohjola, M. (1998). *An introduction to the research issues* (UNU/WIDER Working Paper No. 153).

Rahman, H. (2004, July 6-9). *Utilizing ICT for sustainable development in developing countries*. Presented at the 18th European Conference on Modern South Asian Studies Network (SASNET), Lund, Sweden.

Schilderman, T. (2002a). *How do the urban poor obtain information and develop knowledge?* Retrieved December 25, 2004, from http://www.eldis.org/static/DOC10072.htm

Schilderman, T. (2002b). *Strengthening the knowledge and information systems of the urban poor*. A project report of ITDG, 2002.

Talero, E., & Gandette, P. (1996, March). *Harnessing information for development*. A proposal for a world bank group strategy. The World Bank.

VITA. (1995, January). Volunteers in Technical Assistance (VITA), Arlington VA, USA. *Community information centers*. Unpublished topic paper prepared for the VITA project.

Wolfensohn, J. D. (1998). *World development report 1998*. World Bank.

World Bank. (1998). Knowledge for development. *World Development Report 1998, World Bank*, pp. iii, 72.

Zhong, Y. X. (2003, October 14-16). *Information age and information engineering*. Presented at the Digital Divide World Congress, World Federation of Engineering Organization, Tunis.

Chapter V

The Impact of IT Investment in South African E-Commerce SME Organizations

Sam Lubbe, University of KwaZulu-Natal, South Africa

Abstract

This chapter considers the possibility of a link between organisational performance and information technology (IT) investment intensity in SME organisations practising e-commerce for the period 2001/2002. The answers to the research questions note that in top performing organisations; (1) IT costs as proportions of operating costs were higher; (2) IT costs as a proportion of turnover was lower, than in weak performing organisations; and (3) that a positive correlation exists between the computerisation index (CI) and the operating costs ratio. The investigation also reveals that chief executive officers (CEO)'s expect additional output while planning e-commerce operations and keeping IT budgets constant. Evidence is presented that company performance is linked to the level of IT investment intensity in the sample of organisations investigated, even though more output was expected from the IT department.

Introduction

Achieving business value from information technology (IT) and e-commerce investment at the same time is probably one of the more common organisational concerns of (CEOs) today (Lubbe & Pather, 2002). IT and e-commerce are the growing areas of investment in most organisations; in fact many organisations will not be able to function without IT or digital commerce. The role of IT has also been redefined by some organisations to include attempts to embark on e-commerce operations. The role of IT in organisations is not merely a tool for processing communication, but a strategic weapon that can thus affect an organisation's competitive position (Lubbe et al., 2002; Weill & Olson, 1989).

Some of the variables that will be discussed include IT, e-commerce, investment, and achieving value from IT investment. The contribution of this article is significant, as it will contribute to the understanding of managers that the impact of e-commerce may change the way organisations handle their total IT investment. The article will, however, review only South African organisations and aims to improve on the topic's understanding off IT and digital investment by managers and academics.

Review of Past Research

Mason, McKenney, and Copeland (1997) argue that information sstems (IS)[1] as a discipline has not yet developed a tradition of historical research. This historical analysis by them broadens the understanding of the processes and designs during which IT is introduced into organisations and the forces the shape IT investment uses. They argue that a dominant design for this shape could be manifested in several ways; a new organisational infrastructure, new functionality, new products, new services, new production functions or new cost structures. The problem with historical analysis is to discover why some organisations lead their respective industries in the use, design and application of IT, and why other organisations, having spent millions of dollars achieved modest success rates.

Hu and Plant (2001) argue that the promise of increased advantage was the driving force behind large-scale investment in IT since the 1970s. Current debate continues amongst managers and academics with reference to the measurable benefits of IT investment. Return on investment (ROI) and other performance measures in academic literature, indicates conflicting empirical findings. They also submit that it would be convincing to infer causality if IT investment in the preceding years is significantly correlated to the performance of the organisation in the subsequent year. Hu et al. (2001) used the Granger causality model with three samples of

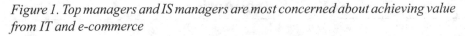

Figure 1. Top managers and IS managers are most concerned about achieving value from IT and e-commerce

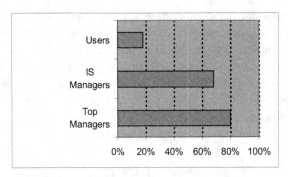

organisations and discovered that there was no increase in the level of financial performance. Rather, it is the other way round—increased financial performance lead to increased IT investment.

Li and Johnstone (2002) argue that a manager can use the framework within which the appropriateness of using real options theory in strategic IT investment by systematically justifies the use of it. They classify IT costs and provide some insight about the relationship between technology standardisation and IT investment decisions. Research by Lubbe et al. (2002) also reflects that managers of organisations are concerned whether their organisation is achieving IT and e-commerce value from their organisation's IT investment (Figure 1).

Bui, Sankaran, and Sebastian (2003) argue that technology and societal changes are moving the global market rapidly towards a new economic order rooted in e-commerce. They investigate some factors including macro economy, ability to invest, access to skilled workforce, cost of living, and pricing. The authors also state that many organisations face a chronic shortage of resources (including funding). Management should be aware that e-business is part of the complex and general economic structure and the success of organisations depend on that structure as well as the optimum allocation of resources.

Dykman (2003) notes that information systems (IS) represent a significant investment for many organisations. Managers need to know that the decision made to spend money on IS should be analysed like any other major purchase. She argues that general management often gives in to the expert power of the technologists, both internal and external to the organisation to invest in IS. The ROI on an IS acquisition may not be quite as simple or straightforward as other capital expenditure. She, however, states that it is still possible to do the financial analysis for the investment.

Dykman (2003) argues that it would be of great benefit if there were a general recipe that could assist to ensure success. Ideally all the strategies (e-commerce, IT, and organisation), including the framing of all investments, could be aligned around business requirements, rather than on technology requirements. She states that it needs a workhouse of a system to facilitate the operations of the organisation as it works to realise its strategic vision. She further argues that managers should be measured against the accuracy of their tangible financial projections for IS investment. Every investment should be justified with concrete revenue (benefit) and expense commitments. Dykman (2003) notes that managers should aim to do a better job assessing the benefits associated in a proposed IS investment in tangible and financial terms. Executives demand this when evaluating the approval, or denial, of any other capital expenditure. IS investment decisions are business decisions and therefore not technology decisions.

Moodley (2003) argues that e-commerce technologies are becoming increasingly important to South African apparel producers as they are integrated into global value chains. Moodley (2003) suggests that the empirical evidence emanating appears that e-commerce is still in its infancy but there is potential for growth. The problem is to ensure that there is sufficient financial support to sustain success. Moodley (2003) argues that South African organisations should increase their investment in e-commerce.

Quayle (2003) notes that the awareness and level of implementation of e-business in European small and medium enterprises (SME) differ in some aspects from larger organisations. He argues that the issues of highest importance are leadership, time to market, marketing and financial management, and a narrow vision of business survival. He further states that small firm's perceptions of quality, price, production reliability, service reliability, and capability to provide support are normal buyer's demands. Nowhere is the aspect of value from IT investments reflected. The idea is that the cost to execute transactions be reduced. He states that developing e-business expertise is essential to sustain the competitive advantage. SMEs must be aware that some aspects such as financial management could impact on their future plans.

It is also argued by Santhanam and Hartono (2003) that the resource-based view can be used to investigate the impact of IT investment on organisational performance. A strong IT capability can support improved organisational performance. Furthermore, their results indicate that organisations with superior IT capability, exhibit current and sustained organisational performance. They note however, that previous performance must be taken into account while doing these calculations.

Kearns (2004) states that while IT investment has the potential of providing competitive advantage, actual returns on such investment vary widely and a majority of CEO's rank past IT investment disappointing. There are many methods for investment evaluation, but traditional methods do not adequately account for the intangible benefits that characterises strategic investments. They also lack other features of portfolio selection. He describes a model based on the analytic hierarchy process that could possibly overcome the deficiencies associated with traditional approaches to economic evaluation of IT investment. This approach reflects both on tangible and intangible methods and links IT investment to business strategies.

The Research Questions and Research Methodology

Research Questions

The Relationship Between Profitability and IT Investment

Lubbe et al. (2002) noted that a relationship exists between profitability and IT expenditures in South African e-commerce organisations. Quayle (2003) notes that no relationship exists between organisational performance and the relative portion of resources allocated to IT. He argues that the measure of performance will not capture all factors that contribute to the organisation. Using case studies, Weill et al. (1989) reveal the importance of converting IT investment into productive inputs with different levels of effectiveness, depending on the organisation. There is also empirical evidence that the use of IT results in lower cost (Santhanam et al., 2003). The first research question can thus be formulated as:

Is there a negative correlation between IT investment with profitability in e-commerce intense organisations?

The Relationship Between Profitability and Computerisation Index 2

Weill et al. (1989) argue that two key factors are emerging determining the return on investments (ROI) on IT is difficult; and investment in IT alone is not sufficient. Dykman (2003) suggests that IT investment reduces the cost of revenue generation. Santhanam et al. (2003) suggest that evidence indicates that organisational performance is linked to the level of IT investment intensity. This research question specifically compares the overall performance of the organisation with the CI index (another measure of computerisation) and not the IT expense (ITEX) ratio as used previously.

The second research question can thus be stated as (based on the study of Santhanam et al. 2003):

Is there a positive correlation between IT investment intensity and organisational performance?

The Relationship Between Profitability and IT/E-Commerce Strategic Management Integration with Organisational Strategic Management

The third research question is formulated as:

Is there a positive correlation between IT investment and strategic management of IT and e-commerce operations?

Research Methodology

The author had decided to use qualitative research because it is designed to help him understand the people and the social and cultural contexts within which the organisation operates. To establish the best design it was decided to collect the data needed to answer the research questions discussed above using a structured questionnaire. The population consisted of all IT intensive organisations that have just started an e-commerce operation during the period 2001/2002. From this list, a number of companies were selected who indicated their willingness to cooperate with the investigation. They were mailed a copy of the questionnaire with a request to include financial statements for the period covered (2001/2002).

The completed questionnaires were analysed to extract the data. The CI was calculated from data collected using the questionnaires. Financial ratios were calculated using data from the statements and the questionnaires. Data showing the relationships between the CI and measure of financial performance were plotted on graphs using Microsoft Excel.

Limitations of the Study

It is acknowledged that there are other factors that could affect the research but the author has decided to limit the study to the papers that were available to him. It was assumed that the organisational financial and other figures, as rendered, were accurate and complete where they could be verified with audit/working papers. Additionally it was assumed that the respondents completing the questionnaire did so accurately. However, a possible source of error lies in the respondents' interpretation of the terminology used in the questionnaire, although it was pre-tested.

Furthermore, some data given by the respondents could not be verified fully, owing to its sensitivity. Also, it was not possible to check the method of accounting and it is acknowledged that this could have influenced some financial ratios. However, given these limitations, it was still possible to use the models to answer the research questions since these sources of error did not differ from those evident in other studies (e.g., Lubbe et al., 2002; Weill et al., 1989). It was also possible to interpret the results based on the data obtained as no statistical technique could show them to be unreliable.

The Results

Information Systems in South Africa in Context

South Africa is a medium sized country, 471,000 square miles at the southern tip of the African continent with a population of some 45 million people. Relative to the rest of Africa, South Africa is substantially industrialised. South Africa is a wealthy country from an industrial and agricultural point of view and computers have been actively in use in South African business, education, and industry since the early 1960s when both IBM and ICL opened offices in Johannesburg. Today South Africa employs computers in every aspect of industry, business and government as well as having a relatively high percentage of home computers among the middle class. All the major vendors are present and there is considerable interest in hi-tech.

The business and industrial sectors in South Africa are as sophisticated as anywhere in the world in the use of information systems. South Africa leads the world in deep level mining and supports this activity extensively with computer systems. The country also has a substantial financial services sector that has won international recognition for its excellence in information technology. For example, the First National Bank (FNB) of South Africa was named one of the world's top 100 computer users by ComputerWorld Magazine in May 1995 and in July 1996, the same bank also won the prestigious Smithsonian Institute prize for the innovative application of biometrics in their information technology.

Discussion of the Results

In order to test the validity of aspects of the questionnaire respondents may have had difficulty understanding when answering, a pilot study was conducted using some of the companies in the sample. This was done to ensure that it was possible to collect all data required for the ratios. Ambiguities were removed in order to reflect a concise research instrument.

Figure 2. Turnover vs. operating expense

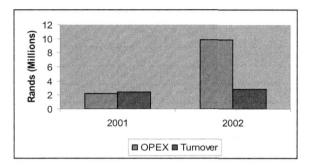

Research Question 1:

The Relationship Between Profitability and IT Investment

The data needed for this section was gathered from financial returns provided by the organisations. Figure 2 illustrates a profile of both, the turnover and operating expenses for the organisations in the sample (2001/2002). Turnover exceeds the operating expenses in 2001 as can be seen from Figure 2. However, in 2002, the effects of a low growth rate in South Africa manifests in the turnover slumping to a low. One organisation spent additional resources to expand their operations affecting the overall picture.

Operating Expense Ratio (OPEX)[3] and information technology expense ratio (ITEX)[4] were the two ratios used in this instance. These were calculated and presented in Table 1.

These ratios were calculated and averaged over the period under investigation to negate the effects of seasonal and abnormal influences as indicated. Finally, the organisations were sorted in ascending order using the OPEX ratio as a primary key in and grouped in quartiles (Table 2). This was done partly to disguise the data and to neutralise the effect of seasonal and other influences.

As stated before, Table 2 is the result of sorting the organisations (OPEX as the primary key) in ascending order and grouped together in quartiles; the first three companies were used for quartile I, the second three for quartile II, etc. Although all the previously mentioned operations were used to negate the effects of seasonal and economic fluctuations, the results of a loss by one organisation could be seen in the second quartile. There is a negative correlation of 0.5425 between the Operating expense ratio and the IT ratio. This provides evidence that there is a link between the two ratios and supports statements by authors such as Weill et al. (1989) and Lubbe et al. (2002).

Table 1. Operating expense ratios (OPEX) and IT expense ratios (ITEX)

Co	2001		2002	
	OPEX	ITEX	OPEX	ITEX
1	0.152	0.119	0.157	0.128
2	0.128	0.037	0.148	0.053
3	0.162	0.117	0.180	0.145
4	0.257	0.160	0.427	0.180
5	0.172	0.483	0.252	0.820
6	0.422	0.139	0.374	0.232
7	0.783	0.118	0.718	0.099
8	0.916	0.002	0.933	0.003
9	0.991	0.002	0.963	0.001
10	0.987	0.003	0.980	0.003
11	1.009	0.062	0.860	0.082
12	0.093	0.001	0.963	0.000

Table 2. Quartile groupings for organisations (2001/2002)

Quartile	OPEX	ITEX
I	0.155	0.100
II	0.317	0.336
III	0.734	0.037
IV	0.965	0.076

Research Question 2:

The Relationship Between Profitability and Computerisation Index

Table 3 compares the operating expense ratio, IT expense ratio, and CI[5]. The CI indicates and supports the second research question noting that there is a link between computerisation and organisational performance. The better an organisation performs, the higher the CI. From a statistical point of view, the Spearman ranking indicates a high negative correlation of 0.8842 between the CI and the OPEX, while only a positive correlation of 0.4126 was measured between the OPEX and ITEX ratios. CI is therefore a better measure for the intensity of computerisation in an organisation. Lubbe et al. (1992) indicated that the CI applies to other industries as well and this further supports this finding.

Table 3. Relationship between CI and operating and IT ratios

C	CI	OPEX	ITEX
1	73	0.155	0.124
2	47	0.138	0.045
3	13	0.171	0.131
4	10	0.342	0.170
5	7	0.212	0.652
6	6	0.398	0.186
7	5	0.751	0.109
8	5	0.0925	0.003
9	5	0.977	0.002
10	5	0.983	0.003
11	8	0.934	0.072
12	6	0.528	0.000

Figure 3. CI vs. OPEX ratio

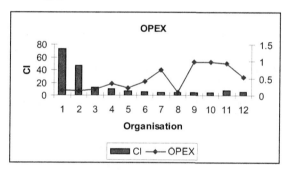

Further statistical analysis indicates an F-Ratio of 3.89 and squared mean deviation of 0.384485 between the CI, OPEX, and ITEX ratios. The correlation matrix used to estimate the coefficients produced a correlation-coefficient of -0.8778 between the CI and OPEX ratio and a correlation-coefficient of -0.675 between the CI and ITEX ratio. The correlation was in both instances negative and high. There was also a weak correlation between the CI (the constant, level of computerisation) and the ITEX and OPEX ratios (the variables). It thus helps to answer the second question by delivering proof that there is a relationship between profitability and computerisation. Figure 3 illustrates the link between CI and OPEX clearly.

Research Question 3:

The Relationship Between Profitability and IT/E-Commerce Strategic Management Integration with Organisational Strategic Management

A positive correlation of 0.54 was calculated, which led the researcher to accept the fact that there is a relationship between profitability and IT/e-commerce strategic management integration at the 95% level. A problem that all the respondents mentioned is that they still get the same amount of funding but that top management expects more from them. In real terms, this means that top management expects e-Commerce to stem naturally from the IT department. All the responding organisations placed e-Commerce as part of the IT department.

Discussion and Conclusion

The relative high correlation that is evident from Figure 3 may be attributed to the strategy employed with IT investment decisions and is supported by Dykman (2003). The strategic importance of IT investment should be emphasized and the importance of IT investment decisions needs to be considered by business managers. The reason being stated is that it may affect their e-commerce and other commercial operations. Organisations also need to ensure that e-commerce is not part of the IT department but a department on its own with an own strategy.

It is important to note that the more integrated IT and e-commerce investment decisions become the better chance for full alignment with the overall organisational strategy. This will help businesses in the long run. Although the study does not conclusively deliver proof of a positive or negative correlation in one instance, it shows that in the sample used, a strong tendency exists that:

- Organisational performance is correlated with IT investment intensity.
- IT investments will be correlated to IT and e-commerce intensive organisations with their profitability.

It should be noted that to find organisations just embarking on e-commerce is extremely difficult and explains the reason for the small sample size.

References

Bui, T. X., Sankaran, S., & Sebastian, I. M. (2003). A framework for measuring national e-readiness. *International Journal of Electronic Business, 1*(1), 3-22.

Dykman, C. A. (2003). Financial evaluation of information systems investments. In C. K. Davis (Ed.), *Technologies & methodologies for evaluating IT in business* (pp. 175-189). Hershey, PA: IRM Press.

Hu, Q., & Plant, R. (2001). An empirical study of the casual relationship between IT investment and firm performance. *Information Resources Management Journal, 14*(3), 15-25.

Kearns, G. S. (2004, January-March). A multi-objective, multi-criteria approach for evaluating IT investments: Results from two case studies. *Information Resources Management Journal, 17*(1), 37-62.

Li, X., & Johnstone, J. D. (2002). Evaluate IT investment opportunities using real options theory. *Information Resources Management Journal, 15*(3), 32-47.

Lubbe, S., Hoard, A., & Parker, G. (1992). The profit impact of IT. *Journal of IT, 1*(10), 44-51.

Lubbe, S., & Pather, S. (2002, July 15-16). A study into theoretical success factors for successful Internet commercial enterprises. Presented at ECITE 2002, held at Université Dauphine, Paris.

Mason, R. O., McKenney, J. L., & Copeland, D. G. (1997, September). Developing a historical tradition in MIS research. *MISQ, 21*(3), 257-277.

Moodley, S. (2003). The potential of Internet-based business to business electronic commerce for a technology follower: The case of the South African apparel sector. *Journal of Internet and Enterprise Management, 1*(1), 75-95.

Quayle, M. (2003). E-business in a turbulent world: Usage in European small and medium enterprise. *International Journal of Electronic Business, 1*, 41-52.

Santhanam, R., & Hartono, E. (2003). Issues in linking information technology capability to firm performance. *MISQ, 27*(1), 125-153.

Weill, P., & Olson, M. H. (1989). Managing investment in information technology: Mini case examples and implications. *MISQ, 13*(1), 3-17

Endnotes

[1]   Information technology (IT) and information systems (IS) will be used alternatively and for the purpose of this article will be interpreted as meaning the same whilst discussing the investment of IT.

[2]   Computerisation index was discussed in detail in a previous paper of Lubbe, Hoard, and Parker (1995): The profit impact of IT investment. *Journal of Information Technology (JIT)*, *1*(10), 44-51.

[3]   OPEX = non-interest operating expenses to income.

[4]   ITEX = IT expenses to non-interest operating expenses.

[5]   CI means the extent and sophistication of computerization. Ten variables (for example years using computers, management activity level, etc.) were selected to collectively represent the computerization process.

Chapter VI

The Use of IT in Small Business:
Efficiency and Effectiveness in South Africa

Sam Lubbe, University of KwaZulu-Natal, South Africa

Abstract

This chapter addresses the effective use of information technology (IT) in small businesses. Worldwide it is regarded as a problem as was illustrated in the literature review. Small business owners need to calculate and plan proper use of IT in their businesses by aligning their strategic IT planning to the business plan. A computing grid is proposed with a proper structure and guideline to help the owners.

Introduction

Information technology's (IT) use in small business had been limited to occasional glimpses of "brilliance." Most of the small business owners have rarely had training to use IT effectively and did not worry about proper use of the Internet. This article therefore investigates the present state of IT in a representative sample in Kwa-Zulu Natal, South Africa.

It firstly defines what a small business is and looks at different approaches to formalise IT in the small businesses interviewed. The instrument that is used (questionnaire) is discussed as well. The results are represented and implications as well as guidelines for small business owners are explained and linked to the theory.

Literature Review

Introduction and General Definitions

IT is impacting the roles and work of individuals and IT enabled change is also revolutionising business processes. It should also be noted that the real engine in association with IT, for economies in Africa, is small businesses. How a small business learns about its environment, how it selects and interprets information through its information system, and how it forms its information structure to get its information processing goals supported by appropriate resources is all fundamental aspects of how small businesses can process information efficiently and effectively. They should keep in mind that sparks can fly between technology and small business. Chakravorti (2003) notes that the processes by which technology have an impact on smaller business is slow even though the intrinsic benefit is enormous.

DeLone (1988) notes that the majority of business organisations are classified as small and medium (SMME) enterprises. These small businesses differ from large enterprises in terms of strategy, structure, decision-making, and resource availability. He further argues that the allusion of small business research will have an impact on bigger businesses. In an earlier paper (1981), he states that few articles have studied the differences between smaller and bigger businesses (also noted by Duxbury, Decady, & Tse, 2002; Hunter, Diochon, Pugsley, & Wright, 2001; Tagliavini, Ravarini, & Buonanno, 2001). Doukidis, Smithson and Lybereas (1992) argue that IT has made an impact on large organisations but it is not as clear on smaller organisations and that little research had been done on it. Walczuch, den Braveen, and Lundgren (2000) note that small firms are not adopting the technology (e.g., Internet, etc.) with the same speed as the larger firms do. Bunker and MacGregor

(2002) argue that it is also important to discover how IT is accepted and used with SMMEs.

Petkov, Fry, Petkova, and D'Onofrio (2003) note that small businesses need technology in order to succeed. Some of these technologies could be used to solve the problems of smaller businesses and accumulate knowledge for improvement of their services. Hunter (2002) argues that IT researchers have not differentiated businesses upon size. He notes that previous research has shown there is a difference in the management of small vs. large businesses in general, and specifically how IT is employed. Researchers, however, need to explore how small business may impact their use of IT. For this specific reason, the study had been designed to study the impact of IT on smaller businesses in KwaZulu-Natal, South Africa.

Definitions of Small Business

Small business definitions range from those that encompass as few as 10 employees to up to 500 or 1000 employees (Burgess, 2003). Other definitions include turnover, assets, or variations across industry sectors. Managers, however, cannot expect that IT will be used in a similar fashion across businesses that have these ranges in size. Duxbury et al. (2002) argue that smaller business will have simple and highly centralised structures, lack trained staff resources, experience financial constraints, and take a short-range perspective imposed by a competitive environment. They further state that staff should not be more than 99 people. The possibility also exists that a small firm could behave like a big firm from an IS perspective. It is because of this range of definitions that it was decided to tie down the definition and use a standard definition for the region of KwaZulu-Natal: The owner should be involved in the control of the operation, there should not be more than 99 staff members and turnover should be less than R10 million per annum.

Architecture

DeLone (1981) states that smaller firms had been using computers for a shorter period of time than their larger brothers. He argues therefore that some smaller organisations have to make use of external services to ensure effectiveness. Smaller businesses also have smaller revenue and this can cause owners to restrict the IT they invest into. He also notes that smaller firms spend more on IT (especially hardware) in proportion to their total revenue. On the other hand, these smaller businesses take quicker decisions to invest in IT than larger businesses. He states that firms' size is directly related to the size of their IT and inversely related to the percentage of EDP costs that are used to acquire computer equipment.

Winston (1998) notes that entrepreneurs need to have a positive attitude towards IT and the quality of its architecture. She states that positive attitudes by managers can ensure a higher quality IT architecture. Obviously, IT architecture with a low quality can impact badly on small businesses. The nature of the smaller business on the other hand would determine what type of IT architecture it would need (Rodriguez, 2003).

Purao and Campbell (1998) state that many smaller businesses get state of the art type architectures although they do not need all the computing power. Most of the issues about implementation of IS in small business also deals with the type of IT to be installed. Chakravorti (2003) argues that the players in this instance should all be connected with each other using a grid network and they should not act alone. Grid networking, however, can be an enemy of innovation and impact on the players but it should help them to work together. Barriers to prevent grid networking should be removed and connectedness would become a weapon in small businesses armoury to help diffuse the innovation and get to equilibrium faster.

Capabilities of IT

DeLone (1988) argues that the capabilities of IT should help smaller firms to react faster to market changes and their flexibility to acquire and assimilate new IT will be enhanced by this. Bharadwaj, Sambamurthy, and Zmud (1999), however, state that very little understanding as to what constitutes a firm's IT capability and how it could be measured exist. Drawing from theoretical perspectives, they conceptualize an enterprise-wide IT capability as a second order factor model. In doing this, they used structural equation modelling techniques and verified IT capability construct. They argue that recent research have paid attention to the role of IT capabilities in enabling superior IT based innovation and business performance. These studies also identified broad capability classes such as IT infrastructure, human IT skills, and organisational resources that could apply to smaller businesses. Hunter, Diochon, Pugsley, and Wright (2001) note that dependency of IT is increased by the increased use of IT in smaller businesses. Small business owners should also ensure that IT is used as efficient as possible.

Although IT usage has been identified as a significant construct in small businesses, gaps remain in the understanding of how IT is used by different organisations and organisational members (Lee, Chandrasekaran, & Thomas, 2003). Their findings were that formalised firms facing competitive pressures have higher levels of IT usage among both management and non-management staff.

IT capabilities could also reduce the cost of business transactions and increased operational efficiency of businesses. Lee et al. note that IT capability simply refers to the use of IT by staff to improve their work processes. Their study has thrown

Figure 1. Relationship among organisational scanning, interpretation, and decision-making (Source: Zheng et al., 2003)

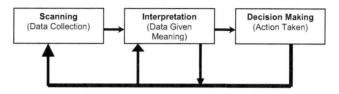

light on business processes in smaller businesses (that is formalisation, a variable in determining IT usage) (also supported by Tagliavini et al., 2001). Organisations that want to increase IT capabilities should aim to set up work procedures, teams, and committees. Tagliavini et al. (2001) further argue that small companies seldom make use of internal IT staff. IS support is also a meaningful percentage of functional areas and should be regarded as satisfactory by the small business owner if they want to be competitive.

Zheng and Zmud (2003) note that organisational scanning and organisational information processing are two critical organisational information-processing activities. Their importance is intensified with globalisation, intense competition between small businesses and dynamic environments.

They argue that governance structures for scanning and interpretation are determined by the need for environmental uncertainty reduction and problematic organisational equivocality resolution respectively. They note that interpretation is important; the more so for small businesses. Degrees of participation and hierarchy of authority is also important for small businesses and can provide a sound basis for future exploration of governance in complex organisational contexts such as small businesses. This will enhance capabilities of small business.

Critical Success Factors

Small business need to implement principles of CSF theory (Petkov et al., 2003). They also need to support learning in a distributed environment based on a distributed IT infrastructure and needs to be compatible with all technologies, enabling organisational learning at the same time. Bunker et al. (2002) argue that business types have an influence on the adoption of IT and some contextual differences, resultant skill, and process orientations make a difference. This could impact on CSFs and small businesses should keep this in mind.

Difference Between Large and Small Businesses

IT investment will make an impact on the competitiveness of small and medium organisations. SMEs are therefore starting to spend a higher percentage of their turnover on IT. The sentiment is that smaller businesses should be a growth market for the IT sector in order to create this growth market. IT should be used by smaller businesses for instance to retain present customers and win new clients. Hunter et al. (2001) state that it is also useful to consider how small businesses differ from the larger sector to discover how this market could be sustained. Duxbury et al. (2002) argue that small businesses are not just little big businesses and that all small businesses are not the same—small is not always small.

The environment for management information systems might be different for small businesses and may well be missing the needs and problems of millions of small business users (DeLone, 1981). This older paper is being cited because it is an example of how this segment of business has been neglected for quite a while in the IS research field. The strategic orientation of managers of large businesses differs from managers of small businesses (Hunter, 2002). Bunker et al. (2002) note that many Western researchers based their opinion of what should happen in SMEs on what has happened in larger businesses. They argue that cross-cultural suitability should apply to small businesses as well. Their statement is based on the incorrect assumptions that research can be used to cross-pollinate other areas.

Small business managers tend to respond to opportunities with a minimum commitment of resources in a multi-staged approach. Resource poverty must be used as an explanation of the difference between managers of large and small businesses. Resource poverty refers to the lack of both financial, technical and human resources. Managers of small businesses must therefore continually conduct their affairs with limited resources. This situation tends to increase the manager's focus on a minimum and multi-staged commitment process.

The momentum for the adoption of IT by small businesses comes from a number of sources. Small business may react to actions taken by their competition. Also, because of the prevalent use of IT, the cost to implement these systems has fallen within the reach of small business and is not exclusive to larger businesses. IT has also become more reliable and powerful and small businesses have started to recognise IT as a way to compete with larger companies. Walczuch et al. (2000) argue that a number of benefits that smaller firms are getting from using technology can be described as border crossing because these smaller businesses are always looking for potential business opportunities.

Lack of Resources

Peterson (2003) notes that the very small business suffers from lack of resources and of a sufficient customer base. Petkov et al. (2003) suggest that a lack of resources could affect the development of a CSF theory. Purao et al. (1998) argue that a deterrent for smaller business appears to be start up computerisation costs, unfamiliarity with the Internet and lack of guidance about how to start the process. The primary concern for these small business owners seems to be security hazards. All of these, according to Purao et al. could be due to a lack of resources.

Chakravorti (2003) notes that everyone was excited by the convergence of the changes happening all around and by investing resources expect this to make a profound and immediate difference. Smaller businesses had made huge up-front commitments to reap early rewards and are then disappointed by the fact that things have not changed much.

Problems Encountered

DeLone (1981) notes that the age of the business is directly related to the experience they show while using computer services. Since many smaller businesses are not that long in business, they may lack this experience on what type of computer service they need. The bigger organisations with established computer services may experience other computing problems than those with younger services. It will therefore be difficult to evaluate the payoff of their "most important" applications. Hunter et al. (2001) state that problems occurred if criteria are not linked to the overall aims of the smaller businesses. The problem is that smaller businesses cannot keep track of technological changes taking place and cannot identify the unique challenges that lie ahead.

It is also a problem with conceptualisation because measures do not take into account the vast array of IT applications with different functionalities that exist in organisations today (Lee et al., 2003). Doukidis et al. (1992) argue that the problem have increased since the early 1980s. They note that advice received in terms of IT investment conceptualisation is still not good enough and that there is little staff involvement in IS development in smaller businesses. Some of the problems that smaller businesses experience in terms of IT are insufficient training, power failures, vendor incompetence, software and hardware. There are also some problems that are encountered with suggested solutions. Some reservations include:

- Lack of computer experience
- Software and hardware selection

- Lack of productivity—people finish their work sooner but does not do more work
- Potential implementation problems
- Financial impact
- Adequate service

The biggest mistake these smaller businesses make in implementing IT is that they do not know where they cannot do everything themselves. They also do not know how to get their customers to interact with them because they do not have the knowledge or experience to do so. Other mistakes they make include trying to do too much too fast and to be afraid of making mistakes because they might lose their business.

Size of Business, IT, and Performance

Few solid results have been found linking IT, organisational structures, and performance. This is because there is a problem of defining and measuring IT, performance, and the fit between technology and structure (Raymond, Paré, & Bergeron, 1993). In smaller organizations, it was discovered that there is a link between IT and structure. Mismatches, however, could exist and could be pointed out early. Small business can compete internationally if they utilize technology in full. IT can allow them to go from high to low-entry cost and will allow them the benefit of competitive advantage. The use of IT also ensures that smaller businesses appear distinctive and allow them access to venture capital.

Research Questions

The aim of the research is:

1. To study and evaluate the approach by SA small business owners specifically in the region of KwaZulu-Natal to IT investment and benefit identification
2. To develop a preliminary theory of good practice in the field
3. To test this theory by reference to other enterprises and practitioners
4. To develop the theory into managerial guidelines

The previous literature review and the critique thereof lead directly to the fundamental objective of this study, which is to investigate the application in practice, the impact, and the effectiveness of evaluation of IT investment in small businesses in South Africa (KwaZulu-Natal). Thus, the following research questions were identified: (1) How do South African small business owners identify IT investment and IT benefits? (2) What is involved in implementing sound IT investments in small businesses? (3) Would small business owners agree that this is good practice? and (4) Is it possible to develop the theory into managerial guidelines?

Critical Assessment of Literature

This section refers to attempts by researchers (e.g., DeLone, 1981; Doukidis et al., 2003; Hunter et al., 2001) to investigate the use of IT by small businesses. All these authors note that no concrete evidence of the total impact of IT has been made in small businesses. However, these studies emphasize the impact of IT on small businesses in mind while investing scarce resources in IT. Authors like Duxbury et al. (2002) also explain the importance of business size when making an IT investment.

Over the last couple of years, authors (e.g., Hunter et al., 2001) have examined the possibility of quantifying IT expenditure in small business. Bunker et al. (2002) suggest that most surveys of small businesses underestimate the total investment in IT. Some authors (Lee et al., 2003; Raymond et al., 1993) note that the link between IT and performance varies. The problem is the measurement of the business value of IT and information in small business. They all agree, however, that the value of information for small business should be closely linked to the decision supported by the information available. DeLone (1988) claim that all the components of IT should be considered if the right pricing method for the charge back of IT is to be selected for small business.

Some authors (e.g., Doukidis et al., 1992) established a link between IT investment and an increasing profitability margin for smaller businesses. They note that an increase in the profitability margin could be found in similar organisations in the same industry. All the studies researched agree that investing in IT for small businesses could make a contribution towards the benefits, which the organisation receives.

As can be seen from the previous, not much of the work has been carried out in the field of measuring the impact of IT investment on the profitability and risk of small organisations. Because of the fact that researchers have investigated different perspectives and these credited experts have expressed different views, the authors believe that a need exists for conducting a study in SA that will make a useful contribution for managers in their attempts to obtain results from the application of information systems in small businesses.

Research Methodology

The main objective of the study is to determine whether small business owners use guidelines when purchasing (investing) IT and how they apply and use IT in their business activities and whether using IT has obtained effective results.

Limitations

This study is only an overview of the aspects that should, according to the literature review, be included in the evaluation and selection process of suitable IT for smaller businesses.

Delineation of the Study

The researcher had decided to exclude legal procedures and focused on IT investments from a technical viewpoint. The research scope does not include the processes (e.g., contract negotiation) followed after the decision has been made, as the researcher feels that these steps might not have relevance to the selection of the best IT.

Development of Questionnaire

The researcher compiled a questionnaire consisting of two sections (demographics and details of the small business and "grand tour" IT questions). The first section was divided into several sub-sections and covers the demographic details of the respondent and some aspects of the small business. The grand tour consists of a focus of the IT in use.

The questionnaire was completed (on behalf of the researcher) by a reliable data collector who interviewed small business managers or somebody they identified who allowed her to speak to the identified employees. The objective of the first section was to ensure they used IT as discussed in the theory. Section B was used to collect data about the IT in use. The objective of section B was to determine what procedure they use to invest into IT, whether they where satisfied with the present IT and does it deliver on demand.

All questions where derived from the literature survey as described earlier in this paper. Open ended questions were used in the questions. The reason for this is to evaluate areas where answers from the respondents indicate in depth approaches to the use of IT.

Data Discussion

The data was collated (EXCEL, 2000) and the statistics were calculated with the use of Excel. Figure 2 details the demographics of the respondents.

As can be seen, more than 60% of the small business owners delegated the task to complete the interview to an employee. It is of no coincidence that there are 50% more men than women in this exercise (60% men vs. 40% women). However, it might be argued that managers allow men more freedom in the running of their business and this could be the reason why more men participated in this data collection exercise. Table 1 explains the market the respondents serve.

The market served by these small businesses range from local to international (1 only). The total adds up to more than 100% because the respondents ticked more that one option. It agrees with the literature that these small businesses can (by using computers) change, to a certain extent, the customers it serves. Many of the respon-

Figure 2. The type of position the respondent holds

Table 1. Market served

Market served	Number	%
Local	60	61
Provincial	23	23
National	23	23
International	1	1

dents supply only local communities and this agrees with the statement by Hunter et al. (2001) that smaller businesses are unique and community based. Most of these smaller businesses employ less than 10 employees (96%) and only one employs more than 30 employees (stated in the literature review). Three of the businesses employs between 11-20 employees. This supports the statement that most smaller businesses in KwaZulu-Natal employ less than 30 people (99%) (see definitions in the literature review). About 80% of the smaller businesses are connected to the Internet and it eventually will help them with starting a computing grid.

More than half of the small business owners are younger than 30 years old (56%) while 6% of the owners are over 40 years. This auger well for the small business sector in South Africa and can assure continuity in the sector. The one problem is that most of them lack experience. DeLone (1988) argues that experience is directly related to the application of the computer services. This could be interpreted that if they are not experienced enough that they will not apply IT as frequently in their business operations. Nearly 75% of the people working in small businesses have less than 10 years experience and another 20% have 11-20 years business experience. There is a high correlation between the years of overall experience and the years of work-related experience. Most of the small business owners have a Grade 12 or college qualification (66%). Thirty-one percent has a degree and the rest have a postgraduate qualification. This shows that you do not have to have a doctorate to be successful. Most of the people that completed the questionnaire help with normal business activities and the rest is either in an administrative position or management.

Details About the Small Businesses

Nearly 90% of the small businesses interviewed have retail (they were selling general goods (83%) and some services (17%)) as their main business activity while the rest of the respondents deliver services (e.g., medical, plumbing, etc.). Most of their revenue is stable (91%) while only 8% has regarded their income as expanding. One of the small businesses stated that they are insolvent and would probably close their doors. This could impact on the use of IT and how they investment into IT. Only one business exists longer than 10 years.

Means of Communication

Very little internal communication using digital communication takes place in the sample. Only 45% of the communication is done using e-mail. The rest of the communication takes place in the form of messages per paper (83%), using the telephone (100%), and personal messages (96%). It is clear that a new culture has to be cre-

Figure 3. Internal communication

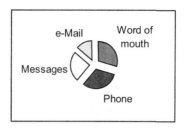

ated to ensure that total acceptance of IT takes place. External communication is by all means no different from internal communication. Ninety five percent of the respondents use oral communication as means to convey a message. Nearly all of them use the telephone to speak to people and snail mail usage is 80% while digital communication with outside people is only 30%. This needs attention and should be solved by some active research in this area in SA. This result is in agreement with the findings by Duxbury et al. (2002) who noted that smaller business do not trust digital media and has received little training in this aspect.

Advertising displays a similar trend where TV is used by only 3% to advertise their service and goods; word of mouth is used by 24%; and business cards by 3%. Newspapers are used by for advertising by 73% of the smaller businesses and the yellow pages by only 8%. Only one small business uses the Internet to market their goods. This is in agreement with Zheng et al. (2003) that small businesses do not rely too much on the Internet or electronic communication as means of advertising their business. Most of the times they use a fax or letter to order to items.

More than 60% noted that they have their own Web page, while only one small business does not know what it means. Most of the respondents know about the Internet but do not know how it will impact their business performance. About 50% of the small business owners had a clue what should be classified as IT. It is therefore clear that half of these small businesses do not have a suggestion what IS/IT entails and how it should be used. This is in accordance with Chakravorti (2003) who noted that the more things change the more (and less) they stay the same. DeLone (1981) argues that firm size and the use of computers have an impact on IT, and the previous figures support the statement he made.

The use of IT is spread over a spectrum and this agrees with the study by Bharadwaj et al. (1999) who argued that there is no defined use for IT in small businesses. The top use of IT/IS in small businesses in South Africa is the use for increased productivity and to handle their money on the Internet (e.g., payment of accounts, investment, etc.). This needs to be further investigated. This finding is also in agreement with Purao et al. who noted that there are some critical concerns and one is

Figure 4. The use in small businesses (IT)

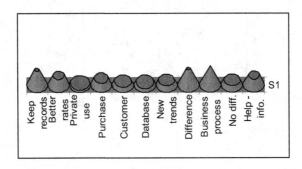

that there is no definitive application that stands out in smaller businesses. About 17% of the smaller businesses noted that IT/IS makes a difference but could not explain where the difference is that they noticed. Some of the uses of the computers amount to no more than number crunching and all resources that the computer offer them is not utilised at all. These include private use, some e-marketing, organising the business, maintaining databases on stock and customers, and researching and looking at new trends on the Internet. As it is evident that there is no consistent use of IT available although it seems that small business owners need to be trained on how to apply their IT.

The top uses of IT in the small business sample include the following:

- Software applications in business process (74%)
- Word-processing for typing letters (all of the small businesses use their IT for word-processing)
- Point of sales (86%)

It is clear that the smaller businesses that have computers use it for three types of exercises. There is little use in terms of WWW applications and they make employ it mainly for tasks that were done manually previously (e.g., cash register changed to point of sale application). Only 4% of the small businesses use their IT for searching on the Internet. The statement by Raymond et al. (1993) is supported because they note that organisational business processes' structure is not changed even though their processes are computerised.

The investment process into IT is initiated by the owners (92%) and the managers of the small business. The investment process is based mainly on a "flashes-of-commercial-insight" (gut feeling) principle. No benefits are really considered by the investors because they do not have the experience or the knowledge how to do it, nor the time. Most of the times the small businesses are being "misled" while investing money into IT by the salesman who works on a commission base to earning a living. The IT investment done by the small business were mainly for private use (9%), business use (25%) and the main purpose why the IT was purchased was because their competitors have one and they got one but do not know how to use it. This shows there is a link between the use in the business of the IT and the actual reason for the purchase. This explains why most of them do not know what to use the IT for.

Most of the respondents stated that they have a strategic plan but this plan is not tied to their IT. They also do not tie the purchase of the IT to the strategic plan of the business. Most of them (88%) argue that their IT is delivering results but they could not explain what the results are and how this is being measured. This explains the reason why only 60% is satisfied with their investment in IS. Also, to further support this, nearly all the respondents stated that they are not too sure where it is failing them. This is supported by Raymond et al. (1993) who argued that people do not have the capacity to plan properly for the use of IT. They do not understand what the implications for performance in their business are. Nearly 60% of the small businesses agree that software developments can make the biggest impact but they stated that they do not know how to measure this impact. There is therefore a need to help the small business owner to understand and use IT properly. This agrees with the statement by Winston (1998) that attitude impacts on IT quality.

The biggest limitation to full implementation of IT into these small businesses comes down to the fact that 80% do not know how to use IT correctly. Other limitations include items such as:

- The correct use of software (7%)
- Too few clients (4%)
- Does not deliver service promised (3%)
- Not a good investment (3%)

More than 90% stated that they do not trust the information completely on the Internet (in agreement with a statement made by Lee et al., 2003). More than 80% noted that it did not help with any decision-making and is in agreement with the statement above that they do not trust information from the Internet. They all need help to apply IT correctly in the following fields:

- Marketing
- Financial
- Manufacturing

- HRM
- SCM

The research questions could thus be answered as follows:

- The data discussion demonstrated that small business owners do not have an idea of what is classified as IT investment. This is agreement with the theory discussion as well. They can therefore not identify the benefits that they should get.
- Because of the problem, they have of identifying and classifying it is difficult to nominate sound IT investments. Most of the organisations invest into IT as a token but not necessarily as part of their business procedures. This is also in agreement with the literature.

The guidelines as presented next were issued to some focus groups and they all agree that this could be good practice but that the education of small business owners needs to be kept up to date to ensure proper application.

It was possible to develop some guidelines using the data discussion. The guidelines are presented below.

Managerial Guidelines and Conclusion

As well as developing theory as to how IT investments are developed and evaluated in small businesses, the research also has an objective—to create a series of management guidelines, which will assist small businesses in applying formal procedures when making any IT investments.

These guidelines have been developed from the theory as well as from the results of all the different evidence gathering activities undertaken by the author during the research. The 10 principles so developed reflect elements of the theory developed into practical management guidelines for IT investment.

In order for IT investment to be formulated, implemented, and evaluated in an effective format, the small business owner should:

- **Clarify targets:** IT investments occur as the result of targets identified by small business owners. It means the organisation must look for one or more drivers that could be emphasised. IT investment is thus not just easy internal targets for IT investments. There is evidence from nearly all the case studies to support the principle and it is in line with the studies of DeLone (1988), Hunter et al. (2001), and Duxburry et al. (2002).

- Get to know the drivers for IT investment well and what is likely to change in the short to medium term. It involves monitoring the basic economics of the industry, the industry's technology, the competition, and developments in the IT industry. It would probably require the setting up of a scanning group and incorporating these reports into the IT investment planning process. The outward process is supported by the work of Lee et al. (2003).

- Develop IT investment targets that are clear and understandable to all parties in the small business. Sub-ordinates that develop the action plans and test the IT should know what they need to do and what managers expect from them.

Outcome (benefit) objectives should be spelled out clearly because they would affect the action plans that would ensure the success of the IT investment. It applies to both tangible and intangible outcome (benefits). All these should be in a format to ensure that everything is running smoothly and that nobody will be able to state that they did not know what to do at any stage. Documentation should thus be available at all times.

Keep the small business's IT investment objectives and IT strategy in the consciousness of the staff as much as possible. Match all IT investment proposals to IT investment strategy and action plans. Make sure that all persons measuring and noting outcome (benefits) have a known and reliable performance index or measure with which to evaluate each outcome (benefit) type, both tangible and intangible. Raymond et al. (1993) support the principle in their study.

Determine the attitude of the owner. Is he or she sensitive to IT investment processes and its potential? It implies that owners are fully aware of the IT strategy and targets. Does the rest of the small business have the skills to make the IT investment process work? Furthermore, the work by Hunter (2002) and Doukidis et al. (1992) support the principle.

The small business must ensure that staff involvement receives the required attention. It may be achieved by ensuring that everybody is fully briefed. Specific thought must be given to training schedules. Training should be part of the IT investment costs.

Develop adequate support facilities, which can handle a wide range of problems. The basis should be a partnership between all stakeholders in such a way that a two-way communication channel (a grid network exists) between groups of stakeholders who must ensure that the IT investment process is successfully completed. Petersen (2003) conducted work on the topic.

Look for IT investment targets across a wide range of issues, especially in areas that relate directly to the IT strategy and small business strategy. IT outcome (benefits) should be high on the lists of targets searched for. Regular evaluation needs to be conducted to ensure outcome (benefit) realisation. The work by Bharadwaj et al. (1999) also supports the principle.

Adequately staff the IT investment process and implementation with suitably trained and experienced personnel. Such staff must have both the skills of general workers as well as be fluent in IT. Hunter et al. (1999) support the principle.

It is clear that such a practical guideline requires considerable time and resources. Also owners need to be committed to ensure that all concerned promptly comply with these guidelines and that people do not get side-tracked by issues. In applying the guidelines suggested, many smaller businesses would have to face change of a cultural change exercise.

References

Bharadwaj, A. S., Sambamurthy, V., & Zmud, R. W. (1999, December 12-15). *IT capabilities: Theoretical perspectives and empirical operationalization.* Presented at ICIS 1999, Charlotte, NC.

Bunker, D. J., & MacGregor, R. C. (2002, August 9-11). *The context of information technology and electronic commerce adoption in small/medium enterprises: A global perspective.* Presented at the 8th AMCIS, 2002, Dallas, TX.

Burgess, S. (2003). *A definition of small business.* IRMA Special Research Cluster information. Retrieved September 2, 2005, from http://www.businessandlaw. vu.edu.au/sbirit/

Chakravorti, B. (2003). *The more things change, the more (and less) they stay the same.* Ubiquity. Retrieved September 10, 2003, from http://www.acm.org/ubiquity/interviews/ v4i28_chakravorti.html

DeLone, W. H. (1981, December). Firm size and characteristics of computer use. *MISQ, 5*(4), 65-77.

DeLone, W. H. (1990, December 16-19). *Lessons learned from information technology research on small organizations.* Paper presented at the Eleventh International Conference on Information Systems, Copenhagen, Denmark.

Doukidis, G. I., Smithson, S., & Lybereas, T. (1992, December 13-16). *Approaches to computerization in small businesses in Greece.* Presented at ICIS 1992, at the Hyatt Regency in Dallas, TX.

Duxbury, L., Decady, Y., & Tse, A. (2002). Adoption and use of computer technology in Canadian small business: A comparative study. In S. Burgess (Ed.),

Managing IT in small business: challenges and solutions (pp. 19-47). Hershey, PA: Idea Group Publishing.

Hunter, M. G., Diochon, M., Pugsley, D., & Wright, B. (2001, May 20-23). Small business adoption of IT: Unique challenges. In *Proceedings of the IRMA 2001 Conference*, Toronto, Canada.

Hunter, M. G. (2002). *The use of information systems by small business: An international perspective*. IRMA Special Research Cluster. Retrieved September 2, 2005, from http://www.businessandlaw.vu.edu.au/sbirit/

Lee, C. S., Chandrasekaran, R., & Thomas, D. (2003, August 4-6). *Examining IT usage across different hierarchical levels in organizations: A study of organizational, environmental, and IT factors*. Presented at the 9th AMCIS, 2003, Tampa, FL.

Peterson, R. L. (2003, August 4-6). *The small IT business, the university, and community partners: A model for synergy*. Presented at the 9th AMCIS, Tampa, FL.

Petkov, D., Fry, G. S., Petkova, O., & D'Onofrio, M. (2003, August 4-6). *Assisting small information technology companies identify critical success factors in Web development projects*. Presented at the 9th AMCIS, Tampa, FL.

Purao, S., & Campbell, B. (1998, August). *Critical concerns for small business electronic commerce: Some reflections based on interviews of small business owners*. Presented at AMCIS 1998, Baltimore.

Raymond, L., Paré, G., & Bergeron, F. (1993). Information technology and organizational structure revisited: Implications for performance. In *Proceedings of the ICIS*, Orlando, FL (pp. 5-8).

Rodriguez, W. (2003, August 4-6). *Managing small-business/university IT partnerships*. Presented at the 9th AMCIS, Tampa, FL.

Tagliavini, M., Ravarini, A., & Buonanno, G. (2001, May 20-23). Information systems management within SMEs: An Italian survey. In *Proceedings of the IRMA 2001 Conference*, Toronto, Canada.

Winston, E. (1998, August). *How attitude impacts IT implementation quality: An exploratory investigation of the small business entrepreneur*. Presented at AMCIS 1998, Baltimore.

Walczuch, R., den Braveen, G., & Lundgren, H. (2000, August 10-13). *Internet adoption barriers for small firms in The Netherlands*. Presented at AMCIS 2000, 2000, Long Beach, CA.

Zheng, W., & Zmud, R. W. (2003, August). *Structuring environmental scanning and organizational information interpretation: An organization-level contingency model*. Presented at the 9th AMCIS, Tampa, FL.

Chapter VII

The Creation of a Commercial Software Development Company in a Developing Country for Outsourcing Purposes

Sam Lubbe, University of KwaZulu-Natal, South Africa

Abstract

SDC has financial services knowledge with cross-industry technical skill capabilities. Their emphasis is on advanced development techniques and tools. The model they used is proving to be successful for all parties and the growth process had provided them with invaluable experience and expertise in the HR transformation. The lesson they have is that they need to ensure that they have a strong presence in the market.

Introduction

Some case studies are qualitative while some are not. Custom also has it that not everything is a case, but firstly having established the criteria for case studies, it was therefore decided to subsequently follow the case study method. This was also done because the authors felt that the creation of a software development company (SDC) justified a case study. This was further motivated because there has been a growing interest in the use of qualitative techniques in the administrative sciences and the case study could do justification to research.

This case study will therefore report on the creation of a software development company (SDC) in South Africa using a detailed description of interrelationships between perceptions of what is happening in developing countries and what is happening in developed countries. The case describes the scenario and contributions stemming from the methodological point of view. The case study also illustrates points such as the value of following a structured method of establishing a methodology for starting such an SDC. The need is discussed for context specific measures of the characteristics for an SDC and the reporting of process measures while establishing an evaluation of the SDC that is being created. Also the need to explore the necessary relationships between the clients and the systems that are created and the perceptions of the clients are discussed. This is because the unidirectional assessment of the SDC can impact on the users and user characteristics and on computer software implementation. Despite the normative nature of the SDC the most important conclusion is the desirability for a variety of approaches to studying SDCs. No one approach to SDC research can provide the richness that information systems research needs for further advancement of the skills in a developing country.

Information Systems in South Africa in Context

South Africa is a medium sized country, 471,000 square miles at the southern tip of the African continent with a population of some 43 million people. Relative to the rest of Africa, South Africa is substantially industrialised. The Republic of South Africa is a wealthy country from an industrial and agricultural point of view and computers have been actively in use in South African business and industry since the early 1960s when both IBM and ICL opened offices in Johannesburg. Today South Africa employs computers in every aspect of industry, business, and government, as well as having a relatively high percentage of home computers among the middle class. All the major vendors are present and there is considerable interest in hi-tech.

The business and industrial sectors in South Africa are as sophisticated as anywhere in the world in the use of information systems. South Africa leads the world in deep level mining and supports this activity extensively with computer systems. The country also has a substantial financial services sector that has won international recognition for its excellence in information technology. For example, the First National Bank (FNB) of South Africa was named one of the world's top 100 computer users by *ComputerWorld Magazine* in May 1995 and in July 1996; the same bank also won the prestigious Smithsonian Institute prize for the innovative application of biometrics in their information technology.

Background

Information systems play an important role in the survival of a country and its organisations. Coupled with the lower costs, increased processing capabilities of hardware, and cost conscientiousness of many CIOs and CEOs, it becomes a vital source of deriving efficient and cost effective solutions for organisational problems. A good manager using a well-organised information system enhances any organisation's ability to compete favourably and it minimizes the assumptions and presumptions in decision making that could lead to bad performance and eventually the downfall of the organisation.

In many organisations, information technology (IT) (especially software) also shapes the process of product development. Organisations that are able to adapt new software technology into their development process have often seen increased productivity and improvement overall in product quality. This is why so much emphasis is being placed in South Africa on the correct procedure for software development. This has provided the motivation for many organisations to strive to become a software development company (SDC).

The cost of software development systems, like information systems, stems directly from the cost of resources required to provide and support the functions of systems. The decision to outsource development to SDCs can be a serious strategic change. Therefore, before managers can support software engineering, these SDCs must have a realistic understanding of the viability and of the costs and benefits of the tools. Cost benefit analysis usually can mean continuous reaching of goals (Lubbe, 1997). Benefits must usually exceed costs to justify the expense and this is another reason why organisations will look at SDCs as an alternative to developing software in-house.

The economics of software engineering has often focused on software cost estimation. Essentially this is a consideration of the costs related to single development projects. First world sophistication, which is in demand, requires worldwide growth of the use of information technology. However, a worldwide shortage of information technology skills exists. The high level of South African skills (business and technical) consequently causes an alarming rate of loss of top skills and thus a shortage of quality human resources in the IT sector.

Motivation for Starting a Commercial Software Development Operation

The external business pressure causes conversions and downsizing of industry sectors. This in turn causes a trend towards more efficient, focused business SDCs. The increasing competition in the global market place and new entrance is another motivation for starting a new commercial software development operation. The demand for faster and more cost-effective software systems delivery causes better local content as well as flawless production services, which can also be another motivating factor.

Some of the internal IT pressures such as skill shortages, the need for incentives to retain IT staff, perceived lack of professionalism, better productivity, delivery speed, quality, and clear career paths could be a very good motivating factor for starting an SDC.

Further motivation for starting an SDC in developing countries could be to stop the outflow of South African talent by creating job opportunities for new graduates. The worldwide dispersion of these talents could be prevented, ensuring a nucleus of software developers.

For all software developers, recruitment opportunities would be created, thus enabling a contracting option and keeping their talent for the newly proposed SDCs. The SDC should ensure retraining of these people—ensuring interest, loyalty, and the driving force to succeed in the company. Creating the previously mentioned nucleus of software experts makes it easier for customers to rely on excellent solutions and maintenance of the completed products. The solution could be a result of a mixture of the right professionals leading to applicable end products.

Creating a Commercial Software Development Company

Background to Starting a New SDC

The vision of the SDC company is to become the leading SA systems integrator for speed of delivery, quality, and value, using the most advanced tools and techniques, and to be the most appealing IT employer in SA.

One should keep in mind that to start a large-scale software development company, some projects, such as high-volume commercial transactions processing systems, require advanced analysis, design, and development techniques. This will also entail doing an evaluation of the SDC's software development process in respect of the capability maturity model (CMM). Currently a minimum of CMM Level 3 has been targeted. This will ensure that a standard system development process is integrated throughout all development activities of the SDC. As a result, of this a degree of certainty in the quality of the software products will be guaranteed. Furthermore, this will also allow the SDC to benchmark its development process against international standards.

The present SDC company has signed and completed more than 1700 maintenance requests in their first year of operation. On the other hand, they have finished 99 projects in the first year and the following figures were provided in respect of the attainment of their goals:

- Of 78 projects with planned end dates:
  o   18% were delivered ahead of time.
  o   44% were delivered on time.
  o   27% were delivered within one month of the planned dates giving them a completed figure of 89%.

An issue of concern is that they did not speak about the 11% that were needed to complete a 100% record. Of the 60 projects with initial costs estimates:

- 52% were delivered under estimate.
- 28% were delivered on estimate.
- Only 20% were delivered slightly over.

The 20% delivered slightly over, needs to be defined but they declined the offer to clarify this.

The company was created in the late 1990s by combing an established existing organisation and some key staff from the present organisation in the ratio of 3:2. The organisation presently has nearly 200 staff members and is based in one of the harbour cities of South Africa. Their future aim is to expand into international markets. They have some academic connections with one SA university since 1990 and had recruited some of the IS graduates from this university. They regard this as a long and mutual friendship.

The managing structure of the company starts as a normal hierarchical organisation with a managing director at the top and directors for various departments. The operations director controls the following sectors: strategy and architecture, software

Figure 1. Organogram for SDC

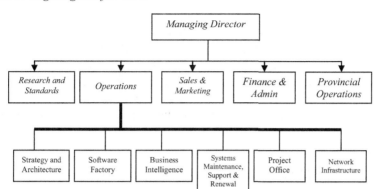

factory, business intelligence, systems maintenance, support and renewal, project office, and network infrastructure (see Figure 1).

The company identified the software manufacturing industry in South Africa as a situation of concern. They identified the current outputs of the IT industry as of a low standard and regard this as a future challenge for the success of the SDC. Their strategy is basically to prevent high staff turnover and to keep abreast of dramatic changes in the software manufacturing business.

Services and Operations of the SDC Company

The company's services include items such as strategy and architecture, software factory, business intelligence, systems maintenance, and support renewal.

On the strategic architecture side of the SDC, IT enabled business transformation consulting for this newly established organisation consists of project definition, planning, and management. Analysis is an important aspect of any SDC and for this specific SDC that had been set up.

The design of processes, applications, and technology are important factors for managers of SDC and the organisation. Business migration and development coordination is an aspect that should be kept in mind by the managers when they want to develop a new system or application and development of technology.

All of this ensures business change and proper development coordination. The SDC can evaluate packages on behalf of any organisation and look at gap analysis in order to ensure that all variations are within all acceptable norms.

Project management is an important facet of systems development. The SDC would, however, struggle to do some systems integration if they are not an integral part of the company. The SDCs staff however, needs some training in order to ensure a successful implementation.

On the other hand, business systems development is the main thrust for the company that had been selected as part of the case study component. They specialise in enterprise systems groups and the distributed systems for any organisation. Their approach is an engineered, model-driven approach with tight project definition, management, and control. They feel that this approach would enable them to satisfy requirements from organisations that approach them. They implement changes and new systems with a minimum disruption to any organisation.

The problem they face is that as an organization, they have only six years component-based developing experience. However, overall the combined experience of the staff might be several years. They specialise in applications such as GEN (Sterling), Microsoft, DB2, SQL server, and Oracle.

The business intelligence section of SDC entails the formulation of a data warehouse strategy for the organisation by designing, developing, and helping to implement the data warehouse. They regard their duties as including the following: data analysis and DB design, data sanitisation and transformation, data warehouse development, and metabase management. The important aspect of this part of their duty includes data distribution, data mining, information reporting, and decision support. Here they use software such as SA.S, BO, DB2, and the SQL server.

The systems maintenance, support, and renewal sectors include some of the following duties:

- Service level agreement
- Production maintenance, running, and control
- Help service desk
- Request logging and work tracking
- Change control and management
- Production management, support, and standby
- Optimisation of platform
- Legacy renewal via internet enablement and component wrapping
- They use software such as COBOL, IDB2, IDMS, ADS/Online, MS, and Delphi.
- The strong point of the SDC is whole personal finance solutions. The system entails personal insurance (life and risk), employee benefits, and medical aid thus ensuring a well-developed financial package that ensures that the human resources section of any organisation is well run. In this regard, they use an EB2000/Dataway.

- Their customer base expansion strategy includes the EB centre (retirement funds, life insurance, properties, healthcare, and investments) while they work across industry into telecommunications, transport, utilities and manufacturing.
- Their approach to systems development

They use a twin track type of development. This entails the following:

- The first step is the usual application requirements gathering, analysis, and design. During requirements gathering and analysis, the underlying philosophy is centred around in-depth identification of business needs. It is recognised that these phases of development are as crucial in terms of final product quality, as is the choice of development technology and actual construction. Therefore, the deployment of good analysts with sufficient experience in the client's business area is given a priority.
- Thereafter, development is split in two different tracks along a component based development timeline.
- The first track entails component design and operation specification and the specific development of components. They release the component and the two tracks meet each other.
- During the first track's process they also release the component interface release to the second track developers.
- The second track entails the application interface prototyping, building the application and application integration testing. There is communication between these two tracks all of the time in order to ensure that tile timeline is honoured.
- The last combined step is the application release builds whereby the application is installed and tested in the organisation.

The important step for SDC is the tactical delivery approach that the organisation follows. They follow the European approach whereby code and older software is re-used. If this approach is not applicable, they would investigate. If it is not better to buy, they build the application. If this is not applicable, then build for re-use would be their suggestion to their clients. Their target market is existing systems in the open market but their conceptual approach might differ. They keep a stock of component objects they can re-use. During the development process, they adopt an approach such that the end product is the application that can be generalized and used for other companies as well.

Taxonomy of Components

Their taxonomy could be divided into two sections. The first section is the technical section and deals with the following aspects:

- The security aspect has eight entities in the component and more than 30 public operations. The ADPV is a purchased component as well as the audit part of it. They do registration of all the parts they develop and install.

- The main taxonomy of components can be found in the business side of the organisation. They have 40 FIC applications and 19 public operations.

- The important aspect of their business is the client environment (69 entities and 11 public operations), investment applications (12 entities and 2 public operations), contribution applications (14 entities and 3 public operations), annuity costing basis (11 entities and public operations), EB event (1 entity and 3 public operations), client agreement role (68 entities and 14 public operations), fees (12 entities and 2 operations), Notation (5 entities, 2 public operations), annuity calculations (2 entities), global operations (no entities or public operations), agreement applications (40 entities, 11 public operations), portfolio applications (34 component entities and 5 public operations), and some investment switching applications which they have finished but nothing is sold yet.

- Components in the developing pipeline entails issues such as EB late pay limits, EM membership fixed property, EB bonus rates, EB commutation limits, and global tax rates and limits.

- The results of the joint venture are that they had a successful HR transformation ensuring that they do not lose too many of their employees (8% vs. 25% previously). Their productivity is 100% better and therefore they can deliver systems faster. There is an international demand for their products.

Broad Requirements for Sustaining SDC Development

In order to succeed, an aggressive government plan is needed. Industry and regional initiative need to be coordinated and correlated. The important aspect is free movement of information and skills. This means the elimination of inflow barriers for high-tech skills. To reach this goal, the government needs to do aggressive international marketing. Furthermore, the government needs to offer incentives for sustaining the growth of SDCs. Some ideas could be tax holidays for new start-ups, facilitation of international links, and knowledge exchange programmes, and so forth.

Sustaining the Generation of SDCs

Companies need to copy examples of the growth of a national software capability that will ensure survival. This would require a prototype roadmap for the growth of a software centre. A lesson can be learned from the government of India: The Indian government has drawn up some software companies contracts with multi-nationals to send Indian programmers to work in the USA or Europe at the client's site or under direct suspension of clients' technical managers.

Indian companies set up development centres in India where development and maintenance was done under Indian managers. Typical projects were systems maintenance, software test development, and execution as well as software components. Furthermore, some value adding is required while companies are building their research and development capabilities. This would require:

*   Highly developed project management capabilities
*   Quality by decision
*   Extensive employee training
*   The highly evolved practise of process engineering and relationship management

The South African software industry and the SDCs need extensive domain knowledge in banking, insurance, and financial services. They also need to create new technical capabilities and products to sell overseas.

For all of this, SDCs in developing countries need a highly educated work force, low cost of labour, highly developed information and telecommunication infrastructure and business modules consisting of:

*   Pilot project
*   Larger scale development
*   Dedicated development centres
*   Own development units

The success factors of countries such as India and Ireland need to be copied. South Africa and other developing countries would like to educate a young, highly educated workforce with strong technical and business skills. These workers need to be highly effective and efficient.

SDCs need full government support for the industry, with both financial and non-financial industries for both indigenous and overseas companies. This would make these countries an ideal gateway to the international markets.

To summarise some patterns:

- A well-educated work force is mandatory.
- Do not start building independent products.
- Take advantage of regional markets.

Conclusion

They have strong financial services knowledge with strong cross-industry technical skill capability and an emphasis on advanced development techniques and tools. The model they are using is proving to be successful for all parties and the growth process had provided them with invaluable experience and expertise in the HR transformation. They think they are well positioned for significant growth.

Reference

Lubbe, S. (1997). *The assessment of the effectiveness of IT investments in South African organisations*. PhD dissertation. University of the Witwatersrand, Johannesburg, SA.

Chapter VIII

Organizational Performance and IT Investment Intensity of South African Companies

Johan Nel, Brisbane Solution Centre, Australia

Abstract

This chapter considers if a link exists between company performance and information technology (IT) investment intensity in selected South African companies. The study, which covered the period 1989–1991, was based on the hypotheses viz: that in top performing companies (1) IT costs as proportions of operating costs were higher; (2) IT costs as a proportion of turnover was lower, than in weak performing companies; and (3) that a positive correlation exists between the computerization index and operating cost efficiency ratio. Evidence is presented that company performance was linked to the level of IT investment intensity in a sample of organizations in the RSA. Findings of later case study research supporting this are also presented.

Introduction

Getting business value from information technology (IT) investments is probably one of the most common business concerns of the chief executives in organisations today. IT is one of the growing areas of investments for most organizations; many organizations would not be able to function without IT. The role of IT has changed from being a tool for processing transactions to a "strategic weapon" that can affect a company's competitive position (Benjamin, 1984; Cash & Konynski, 1985; Weill & Oson, 1989). More recently however, there have been reports of real business and human benefits delivered by IT falling short of expectations (Beck, 2000; Du Plooy, 1993; Earl, 1994; Lee & Barua, 1999; Mahmood, 1994; Thorp & Leadership, 1998).

From its research findings, Butler Cox Foundation (1990) observed that managers of organizations are concerned about whether their organization is getting value from IT investments. Weill et al. (1989) noted that the product portfolio and profit impact of marketing strategy (PIMS) established average IT expenditure in 1983 as 2% of revenues. The Diebold Group survey in 1984 revealed that centralized management information systems expenditures on average accounted for 1.4% of revenues. Shoval and Lugasi (1988) postulated that the selection of alternative computer systems must consider the relative importance of the benefit and cost factors. Kwong and Mohamed (1985), in a case study of petroleum-producing companies in Malaysia, adduced that the computerization index (CI) measures the extent and sophistication of computerization.

In an empirical study among insurance companies in the USA, Harris and Katz (1988) established a relationship between an organization's profitability and their IT capital intensity. They concluded that the most profitable firms, or top performers, are more likely to spend a significantly higher proportion of their non-interest operating expense on IT. They observed further that the least profitable firms are more likely to spend a significantly smaller proportion of their non-interest operating expense on IT. Sippel (1989) stated that life insurance, like most of the financial services sector, is an "information intensive" industry. Lubbe et al. (1992) conjectured that the ratios used by Harris and Katz, and the CI model of Kwong et al. (1985) are applicable in the South African long term insurance industry.

Ward (1987) observed that a trend towards decreasing IT costs and increasing IT capabilities will make the use of IT both economically and technically feasible in the next decade. Bender (1986) examined the relationship between the ratio of information processing expense to operating expense and the ratio of operating expense to premium income in life insurance companies. The correlation between the two ratios was negative, indicating that higher values of the ratio of information processing expense to operating expense were associated with better performance.

Allen (1987), in a literature study on methods to make information systems (IS) pay its way, postulated that companies gain a competitive advantage if IT is run as a profit centre. Surveys done (Choudhury, 1986; Drury, 1980) in both charge-back and non-charge-back environments showed that MIS managers are in favour of using charge-back to control the use of scarce information resources.

Nel (1991) in an empirical study conjectured that the amount of IT expenditure is larger in some industry sectors than others. In addition, that rates of increase in expenditure are also significant. Industry sectors for which information is a key asset, (often referred to as "information intensive" or "strategically dependent on IT" industries), rely heavily on IT to support their organizations and their expenditure is relatively high. In the South African financial sector, IT budgets can easily account for 40% of operating expenditure.

Strassmann (1991) found little or no correlation between the proportion of corporate revenue spent on IT, return on assets or shareholder's investments.

The Hypotheses and Research Methodology

The Hypotheses

Relationship Between Profitability and IT Investment

Harris and Katz (1988, 1991) studied the relationship between profitability and information technology expenditures in American insurance companies. Turner (1985) noted no relationship between an organization's performance and the relative portion of resources allocated to IS. He observed that the measure of performance will not capture all factors that contribute to high performance. Using case studies, Weill et al. (1989) noted the importance of converting IT investment into productive inputs with different levels of effectiveness, depending on the organization. There is empirical evidence that the use of IT can result in lower labour costs (Harris & Katz, 1997).

Thus, the first hypothesis, based on the hypotheses of Harris et al. (1991), can be formulated as:

- **H1:** IT investments will be negatively correlated, in IT intense companies, with their operating expense ratio.

Relationship Between Profitability and Computerization Index

Weill et al. (1989) identified two key factors, which are: (1) that determining the return on investments in IT is difficult and (2) that investment in IT alone is not sufficient. Kwong et al. (1985), in a case study of the profit impact of computerization, suggested that IT investment reduces the cost of revenue generation. Harris et al. (1991) observed that evidence indicates that firm performance was linked to the level of information technology investment intensity.

The second hypothesis can thus be conjectured, based on the hypothesis of Kwong et al. (1985):

- **H2:** Organizational performance is positively correlated with information technology investment intensity.

Relationship Between Profitability and IT Strategic Management Integration with Corporate Strategic Management

The third hypothesis was formulated as:

- **H3:** IT investments will be positively correlated, in IT intense companies, with their strategic management of IT.

Research Methodology

In order to gather the data needed to calculate all statistical and other indicators, a structured questionnaire was used. The population consisted of listed companies on the JSE and other companies in South Africa. All the identified companies were sent a questionnaire with a request to include financial statements for the period covered.

The completed questionnaires were analyzed to extract the data. The CI was calculated from data collected by the questionnaire. The financial ratios were calculated using data from the statements and the questionnaire. Data showing the relationships between the CI and the measures of financial performance were plotted on graphs using Quattro Pro Version 4.0. Additionally to the graphs, it was decided to perform statistical analysis. Stat graphics was used for regression analysis and the Spearman Rank Correlation Test.

Pilot Study

In order to test for aspects of the questionnaire, which respondents may have had difficulty in understanding, a pilot study was completed using some companies in the sample. This was to ensure that it was possible to collect all data required for the ratios. Ambiguities were removed in order to reflect a concise research instrument.

Data Collection Instrument Reliability

It was assumed that the company's figures were accurate and complete. In addition, it was assumed that the respondent completing the questionnaire did so accurately. Some data given by the respondent in the questionnaire could not be verified. The study also did not check the method of accounting and it is therefore acknowledged that it could influence results obtained.

Results

Hypothesis 1

The data needed for this section was gathered from financial returns provided by the companies. Figure 3 illustrates a profile of both the turnover and operating expense for the companies in the sample from 1990 to 1991. As it can be observed from the figure, turnover normally exceeds the operating expenses. However, in 1991, the effects of the economy could be seen as turnover slumped to a low. One of the companies did spend more money on expansion of their operations and this does affect the picture as painted.

Table 1 shows the calculated operating expense (OPEX) ratio and information technology expense (ITEX) ratio, the ratios were averaged over the period under investigation to negate the effects of seasonal and abnormal influences as seen in Figure 1. Finally, the companies were sorted in ascending order of the OPEX ratio and grouped in quartiles as shown in Table 2. This was done partly to disguise the data and to neutralize the effect of seasonal and other influences.

In Table 2, the first three companies being used as quartile I, the second three as quartile II, and so forth. Figure 2 shows the average OPEX ratio vs. the average ITEX ratio.

Table 1. Operating expense ratios and IT expense ratios

C	1990		1991	
	OPEX	ITEX	OPEX	ITEX
1	0.152	0.119	0.157	0.128
2	0.128	0.037	0.148	0.053
3	0.162	0.117	0.180	0.145
4	0.257	0.160	0.427	0.180
5	0.172	0.483	0.252	0.820
6	0.422	0.139	0.374	0.323
7	0.783	0.118	0.718	0.099
8	0.916	0.002	0.933	0.003
9	0.991	0.002	0.963	0.001
10	0.987	0.003	0.980	0.003
11	1.009	0.062	0.860	0.082
12	0.093	0.001	0.963	0.000

Figure 1. Operating expense ratio vs. IT expense ratio (1990-1991)

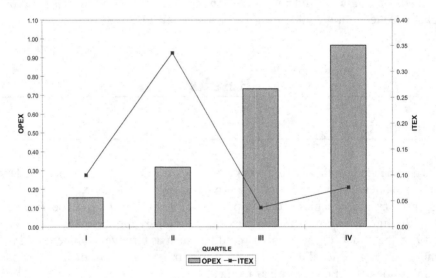

Although all the previously mentioned operations were used to negate the effects of seasonal and economical fluctuations, the result of a loss could still be seen in the second quartile. The overall effect, however, supports the first hypothesis. Using Statgraphics, there seems to be a negative correlation of 52.45% between the operating expense ratio and the information technology ratio. This further supports the first hypothesis.

Table 2. Quartile groupings for companies (1990-1991)

QUARTILE	OPEX	ITEX
I	0.155	0.100
II	0.317	0.336
III	0.734	0.037
IV	0.965	0.076

Figure 2. Turnover vs. operating expense (1990-1991)

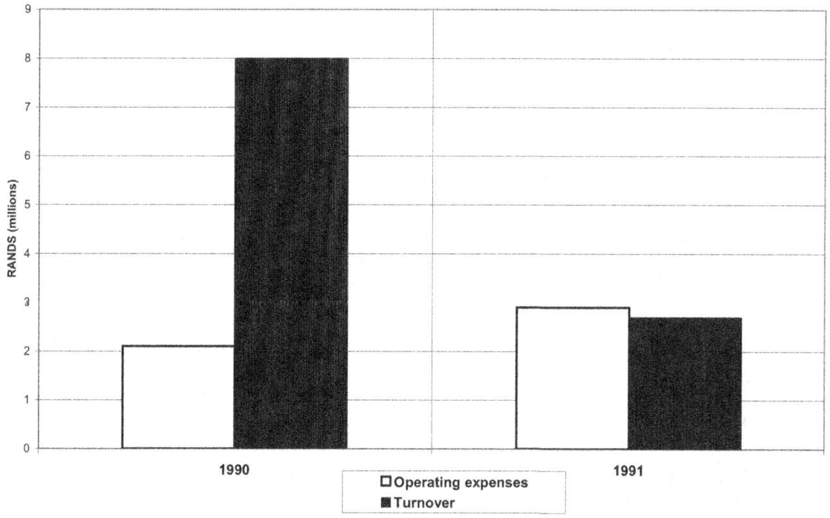

Hypothesis 2

Table 3 compares the OPEX ratio, ITEX ratio, and the CI. The figures in this table support the second hypothesis that the better a company performs, the higher the computerization index. Statistically, the Spearman correlation indicates a high negative correlation of 88.42% between the CI and the OPEX while a positive correlation of 41.26 was discovered between the OPEX and ITEX ratios. This indicates that the CI is a good measure of the intensity of computerization in any company. It also supports the assertion made in a previous study by Lubbe et al. (1992) that the CI applies to other industries and thus.

Further, statistical analysis indicates an F-ratio of 3.89 and a squared mean deviation of 0.34485 between the CI and the OPEX and ITEX ratios. The correlation matrix used to estimate the coefficients produced a correlation coefficient

Table 3. Relationship between CI and operating and IT ratios

C	CI	OPEX	ITEX
C1	73	0.152	0.119
C2	47	0.128	0.037
C3	13	0.162	0.117
C4	10	0.257	0.160
C5	7	0.172	0.483
C6	6	0.422	0.139
C7	5	0.783	0.118
C8	5	0.916	0.002
C9	5	0.991	0.002
C10	5	0.987	0.003
C11	8	1.009	0.062
C12	6	0.093	0.001

Figure 3. CI vs. operating expense ratio

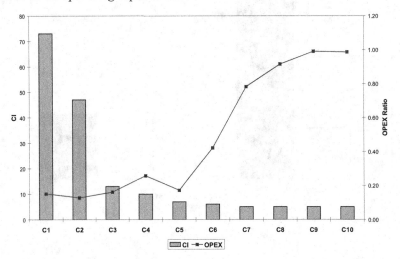

of -.8778 between the CI and OPEX ratio and a correlation coefficient of -.675 between the CI and the ITEX ratio. A positive correlation coefficient of 0.4894 was calculated between the OPEX and ITEX ratios. These results produced a high degree of correlation between the CI (the constant) and the ratios of ITEX and OPEX (the variables). Thus, it further supports the second hypothesis and leads to the acceptance of this hypothesis. Figure 3 supports these findings.

Hypothesis 3

A positive correlation of .54 was discovered which led to the acceptance of Hypothesis 3. This was at the 95% level.

Following a pilot case study, case analysis of five South African Banks done by Nel (2004) using the following sources of information, as well as a case study protocol with personal interviews:

- Annual reports
- Monthly reports
- All classified minutes of all management committees (the author was an assistant to the inter-company secretary to all the South African banks studied)
- Strategy documents (author facilitated the strategic management process in ABSA BANK)
- Personal interviews with most general managers, at least twice a year
- Brief interviews with the managing directors
- User satisfaction surveys (author conducted these)
- Competitor analysis reports
- Independent expert's reports

It can be concluded that the top two financial performing banks had a high degree of alignment and integration between the business- and IT strategic management of the organisation.

Conclusion

The relative high correlation that is evident from Figure 5 may be attributed to the strategy employed with IT investment decisions and is supported by the studies of Nel (1991) and Nel (2004). The strategic importance of IT investment's needs to be emphasized and the importance of IT investment decision's needs to be considered by business managers, as it may affect their company's profitability in the long run.

Although the study does not conclusively prove a positive correlation for all organizations in the Republic of South Africa, it shows that in the sample a strong tendency exists that:

- Organizational performance is positively correlated with information technology investment intensity.
- IT investments (strategic management of IT) will be positively correlated, in IT intense companies, with their profitability.

References

Ahituv, N., & Igbaria. M. (1988). A model to facilitate costing, prices, and budgeting of computer services. *Information and Management, 14*.

Ahituv, N., Neumann, S., & Zviran, M. (1989, December). Factors affecting the policy for distributing computer resources. *MIS Quarterly*.

Allen, B. (1987, January-February). Make information services pay its way. *Harvard Business Review*.

Bender, D. H. (1986). Financial impact of information processing. *Journal of Management Information Systems*.

Butler Cox Foundation. (1990). *Value from IT investments*. Working Paper Series.

Davis, F. D. (1989, September). Perceived usefulness, perceived ease of use, and user acceptance of information technology. *MIS Quarterly*.

Harris, S. E., & Katz, J. L. (1988, July). Profitability and information technology capital intensity in the insurance industry. *IEEE*.

Harris, S. E., & Katz, J. L. (1991). Organization performance and information technology investment intensity in the insurance industry. *Organization Science*.

Hufnagel, E. M., & Birnberg, J. G. (1989, December). Perceived chargeback system fairness in decentralised organisations: An examination of the issues. *MIS Quarterly*.

Kwong, H. C., & Mohamed, M. Z. (1985). Profit impact of computerisation. *Hong Kong Computer Journal*.

McFarlan, F., Pyburn, P., & McKenney, J. (1983). The information archipelago—plotting the course. *Harvard Business Review*.

Mullany, M.J., Miller, R., & Dos Santos Gomes, A. (1991). An enquiry into property-goal type definitions of the term 'information system. Unpublished.

Nel, J. F. (1991). Die effektiwiteit-en produktiwiteit van 'n Stelselontwikkelings-funksie. Unpublished.

Shoval, P., & Lugasi, Y. (1988). Computer systems selection: The graphical cost benefit approach. *Information and Management*.

Strassmann, P. (1991). *The business value of computers*. New York: The Free Press.

Ward, J. M. (1987). Integrating information systems into business strategies. *Long Range Planning, 20*(3).

Chapter IX

Information Technology Investment Evaluation and Measurement Methodology:

A Case Study and Action Research of the Dimensions and Measures of IT-Business-Value in Financial Institutions

Johan Nel, Brisbane Solution Centre, Australia

Abstract

The chapter reviews the present methodology and comes to the conclusion that there is a solution for the predicament of the managers. The author is convinced that the ITIEM methodology is the solution.

Introduction

The study was motivated by the researcher's concern that a fundamental area of business, ITIEM, has been found to be extremely problematic for most organisations. The lack of an integrated methodical approach to the problem as well as the isolated non-integrated research done to date on the effective measurement of IT-business-value enhanced the need for this study.

The Research Objective

The objective of this study was to identify from empirical evidence, using both case study, as well as action research techniques, a pragmatic ITIEM methodology that would enable organisations to identify their IT investments with the greatest IT-business-value; that will enable the greatest business benefits, while at the same time rigorously assessing all risks, being business risks, IT risks or people (human) risks.

Thus the research question:

What information technology investment evaluation and measurement methodology can organisations use to effectively evaluate and measure IT investments according to their IT-business-value?

In order to take advantage of the researcher's experience with the financial sector, the study focused on large, publicly held financial institutions. In addition, the financial sector is perhaps the most information intensive sector and has proportionally high investments in IT with proportionally high potential benefits.

The research question has not been made specific to financial institutions, as it was not anticipated that the study results nor ITIEM methodology will be specific to financial institutions. Nonetheless, the study has been conducted entirely within financial institutions, and for this reason, we have much less confidence extending the findings beyond this context.

The Investigative Questions

The next level of specific investigative questions that needed to be answered in order to address the research question was:

- What are the major dimensions of IT-business-value?
- How is IT-business-value measured?
- What are the main risks to IT-business-value?
- What are the relative strengths and weaknesses of known ITIEM methodologies in a practical setting?

The Study Design

In order to gain better understanding of the practical issues surrounding effective ITIEM, it was decided to conduct a series of case studies of organisational attempts to successfully implement and apply ITIEM methodologies. This was followed by action research to implement a proposed ITIEM methodology. The researcher played a pro-active role in the latter case. In both the case studies and the action research study, the unit of analysis is the ITIEM methodology.

The study design included:

1. A literature survey to identify the dimensions of IT-business-value, to identify the measures of IT-business-value, and to identify a candidate starting ITIEM methodology that is most comprehensive, addressing the most relevant measures of IT-business-value. This information was to be used to produce a draft case study protocol.

2. A single, exploratory pilot case study of a South African bank yielding amongst other things, a revised case study protocol.

3. A cross-case analysis of a multiple case study of five South African banks (including the pilot) yielding a draft ITIEM model.

4. A cross-case analysis of three Australian banks, further enhancing the draft ITIEM model, and a cross-country analysis of the South African and Australian banks. The multiple case studies within South Africa and within Australia represent literal replications, while the cross-country comparison represents

theoretical replication (Yin, 1994). It is predicted that there will be differences between the Australian and South African experience that are due to known differences in country contexts:

- Inflation
- Political stability

1.   The ITIEM methodology identified in (1) was then revised to reflect the draft ITIEM model and a hybrid ITIEM methodology was proposed.
2.   The hybrid ITIEM methodology was implemented and revised with action research resulting in the final ITIEM methodology and final ITIEM model.

What are the Major Dimensions of IT Business Value?

Cronk and Fitzgerald (1997, p. 410) suggest that the value resulting from investing in IT can be seen as IT-business-value. They provide a precise definition of IT-business-value:

The sustainable value added to the business by IT, either collectively or by individual systems, considered from an organisation perspective, relative to the resource expenditure required.

They also propose a model representing the relationships between the main dimensions of IT-business-value as depicted in Figure 1.

The literature review aided in the confirmation of the dimension of IT-business-value and following the literature review, the dimensions of IT-business-value suggested by Cronk and Fitzgerald (1997) were adapted to the following:

- Business strategy alignment
- "Soft" value
- Financial value
- Contextual value

Figure 1. Groupings or dimensions of IT business value (Based on Cronk & Fitzgerald, 1997, p. 412)

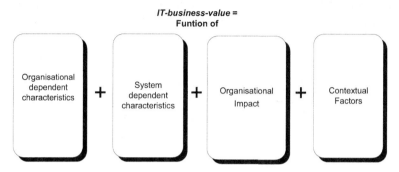

How is IT-Business-Value Measured, and What are the Main Risks to IT Business Value?

The Literature Review

The literature review aided in the identification of a comprehensive set of measures of IT-business-value, as well as the main risks to IT-business-value. By reviewing literature relevant to ITIEM, it also aided in the identification of an ITIEM method (information economics) that addresses most of the identified measures of IT-business-value.

A positive measure of IT-business-value refers to a positive value contribution to the business; where as a negative measure of IT-business-value refers to a possible negative impact to the business, a risk to the business. Table 1 summarises the measures of IT-business-value by IT-business-value dimension, as addressed by Parker, Benson, and Trainor (1988).

The Case Studies

The IT-business-value dimensions and IT-business-value measures identified in the literature review were used to put forward a draft case study protocol, which was refined and finalised during the pilot case study and was then used for an exploratory, descriptive case study involving five banks in South Africa.

Table 1. Measures of IT-business-value according to Parker et al. (1988)

IT-business-value Dimension	Measures of IT-business-value Dimension		Positive/Negative	
Business strategy alignment	❑	Degree of integration	❑	Positive
	❑	Competitive advantage	❑	Positive
	❑	Project and organisational risk	❑	*Negative*
	❑	Strategic architecture	❑	Positive
	❑	Definitional uncertainty	❑	*Negative*
	❑	Systems infrastructure	❑	Positive
	❑	Technical uncertainty	❑	*Negative*
	❑	Competitive response	❑	*Negative*
"Soft" value	❑	None		
Financial value	❑	The quantified financial return of the IT investment	❑	Positive
Contextual value	❑	MIS	❑	Positive

The South African case studies resulted in the addition of three more measures of IT-business value, namely:

- Organisational power and politics

Organisations are composed of internal constituencies that seek control over the decision process in order to enhance their position. Organisational power and politics refers to the manipulation of power in organisations using one or more power base available to the individuals. Power refers to the potential of an individual to control the behaviour of others. Hersey and Blanchard (1980) identified five kinds of power use by people:

- **Legitimate power:** Refers to the position of the person in the organisation
- **Expert power:** Power because of knowledge, information, or expertise

- **Reward power:** Power to give or withhold rewards (praise, salary increases, promotions

- **Coercive power:** Ability to ensure compliance by using physical, emotional, or psychological threats

- **Referent power:** Power due to loyalty to identify with a leader or evoked by the charisma of the leader

Better Sourcing of Inputs

Better sourcing of inputs refers to the organisations ability to obtain required inputs more effectively and efficiently with the use of the IT investment. In the case of banks, this refers to the ability to attract deposits.

Better Product Design

Product design refers to a way to add product distinctiveness through design. In the case studies, the banks referred to computer-aided design (Web pages design, etc).

These measures of IT-business-value were added due to large banks as SAB1,[1] SAB3, and SAB4 having included these measures when evaluating IT investments. These banks were also of the opinion that these measures should be compulsory when a bank evaluates IT investments.

Although information economics (IE) addresses a single measure of "project and organisational risk," the management of the banks were of the opinion that this single aggregated IT-business-value measure does not fully address their need to assess the human factors involved when investing in IT. Mitigating strategies were developed to lower the organisational power and political risk to an acceptable level when there was consensus that organisational power and politics may hamper the successful implementation of the IT investment.

The latter two measures of IT-business-value were added by the banks mainly due to their importance in the new financial services digital economy.

The Australian case studies contributed one additional measure of IT-business-value, namely:

- **Organisational culture:** An organisation's culture refers to the core values that are shared by a majority of the organisation's members (Robbins, 1987). A strong culture is characterised by the organisation's core values being intensely held, clearly ordered and widely spread. The stronger an organisation's culture, the less management need to concern themselves with developing formal rules and regulations to guide staff behaviour.

The Action Research

The action research contributed two additional measure of IT-business-value, namely:

- **Organisational communication:** Effective organisational communication was seen to be a prerequisite to realise the foreseen IT-business-value of an IT investment. All employees, managers, executives, and board of directors must understand the IT-business-value of the IT investment as well as the required behaviour to achieve the proposed IT-business-value of the investment.

- **Staff and management skill sets:** The management team of AUS3 also wanted to include the business staff and management skills in the contextual value dimension. They were of the opinion that strategic skills, training levels and skill advantage needs to be assessed because all of these are needed to realise IT-business-value.

This measure of IT-business-value was added due to two Australian banks, which included these measures when evaluating IT investments. As an example, AUS2 consisted of several financial services with different sub cultures. These services were all lumped together and future IT investments were faced with a possible weak corporate culture, at the time.

The South African case studies concluded with a draft ITIEM model. The Australian case study was used to further validate the draft ITIEM model. This model was then used as input to a hybrid ITIEM methodology.

What are the Relative Weaknesses of Known ITIEM Methodologies in a Practical Setting?

The case studies and literature review revealed the following:

- ROI methods are less successful where IT-business-value cannot be precisely estimated in cash-flow terms and there is considerable uncertainty about the value of the estimates, or the intangible benefits are given a zero value because they cannot easily be expressed in cash flow terms (Kaplan & Norton, 1996).

- Decision analysis can be used in pre-implementation evaluation (as employed by Ozernoy, Smith, & Sicherman, 1992), to choose between geographic information systems), but it cannot perform post-implementation assessment. As a vehicle for interpretative debate, it is very reliant on the analyst and participants for inclusion of social and organisational issues.

- The most well known ITIEM methodologies are not comprehensive enough.

- IE is too complex with regards to value linking and value acceleration.

- More focus is needed on the human factors in ITIEM.

Research Results

This chapter proposes a new ITIEM model that addresses the dimensions constituting IT-business-value, as well as how to measure IT-business-value. The ITIEM model of the dimensions and measures of IT-business-value was used to propose a more comprehensive, pragmatic ITIEM methodology than is available today and suggests how:

- IT investments can enable measurable IT-business-value.

- To determine which IT investments will yield the most IT-business-value for the organisation

- To ensure that IT investments and business initiatives complement each other

Table 1 lists all measures of IT-business-value identified from the literature and case studies. The measures are cross-referenced with their source ((literature and/or case study(ies)). In the sixth column, the measures are cross-referenced with IE. All measures are included in the ITIEM model.

The last five columns of the table shows which measures of IT-business-value are included in the:

- Draft ITIEM model
- Hybrid ITIEM methodology
- Action research
- The final ITIEM methodology
- Final ITIEM model

Table 2. Summary of study

Dimension	Measure	L1	L2	L3	L4	L5	L6	L7	L8	L9	L10	L11	L12	L13	L14	SAB1	SAB2	SAB3	SAB4	SAB5	AUS1	AUS2	AUS3	1E	Draft Model	Hybrid Methodology	Action Research	Final Methodology	Final Model
Business strategy alignment	Degree of integration	x					x				x		x	x	x	x		x	x	x	x	x		x	x	x	x	x	x
	Fulfilment of CSFs												x			x		x		x	x	x		x	x	x	x	x	x
	Competitive advantage								x	x	x			x	x	x		x	x	x	x		x	x	x	x	x	x	x
	Project & Organisational risk						x		x		x					x		x	x				x	x	x	x	x	x	x
	Strategic architecture						x		x		x			x		x		x	x	x	x		x	x	x	x	x	x	x
	Definitional uncertainty						x		x		x					x		x		x			x	x	x	x	x	x	x
	Systems infrastructure						x	x	x	x	x			x		x		x	x	x	x		x	x	x	x	x	x	x
	Technical uncertainty							x						x		x	x	x	x	x			x	x	x	x	x	x	x
	Competitive response							x						x		x		x	x	x	x		x		x	x	x	x	x	x
	Better sourcing of inputs															x		x	x	x							x	x	x
	Better product design															x		x	x	x							x	x	x
	Project size risk							x							x						x						x	x	x
"Soft" value	User satisfaction	x	x	x		x	x		x		x	x		x	x	x	x	x	x	x	x	x	x	x	x	x	x	x	x
	Organisational learning & growth	x	x	x			x		x	x	x	x		x	x	x	x	x	x	x	x				x	x	x	x	x
	Employee satisfaction	x	x	x			x		x		x	x		x	x	x	x	x	x	x	x				x	x	x	x	x
Financial value	Quantifiable financial measures - ROI, ROA, NPV	x	x	x		x	x		x	x	x	x		x	x	x	x	x	x	x	x	x	x	x	x	x	x	x	x
Contextual value	Organisational power & politics	x	x	x		x	x		x	x	x	x		x	x	x	x	x		x	x	x		x	x	x	x	x	x
	MIS	x	x	x		x	x		x		x	x		x	x	x	x				x	x		x	x	x	x	x	x
	Organisational culture																					x						x	x
	Organisational communication																										x	x	x
	Staff and management skill sets																										x	x	x

Other Main Findings of the Study

The following are findings from the case studies and action research in addition to addressing the investigative and research questions.

The Case Studies

The case studies contributed the following key findings:

- Although IE addresses a single measure of "Project and organisational risk," the management of the banks were of the opinion that this single aggregated IT-business-value measure does not fully address their need to assess the human factors involved when investing in IT. When there was consensus that organisational power and politics may hamper the successful implementation of the IT investment, mitigating strategies were developed to lower the organisational power and politics risk to an acceptable level
- During the case study, several important external factors influencing IT-business-value were identified:
  - Political stability of the country
  - The state of economy
  - Community considerations
  - Government

Although they were presented in the draft ITIEM model, the study did not attempt to address these influencing factors. These are factors beyond the control of the organisation and though of interest, beyond the scope of the study. However, this is a very important subject for further research.

The Action Research

The following are key findings from the action research:

- A strategic management process in an organisation is prerequisite to successful implementation of an ITIEM methodology in the organisation.
- Top management support for the implementation is also a prerequisite to successfully implement an ITIEM methodology in the organisation.

- The proposed ITIEM methodology by itself does not establish the IT investment priorities, but rather is an integral part of the business case presented to the IT steering to approve or reject the proposed IT investment.

- The Delphi technique used in the action research proved important for attaining consensus on the weights of the IT-business-value measures.

- An agreed ITIEM management process, taking into account the current decision-making process, is needed in the organisation to successfully implement ITIEM.

- All parties concerned with ITIEM need a clear understanding of the ITIEM methodology.

- Clear roles and responsibilities needs to be assigned to all concerned with ITIEM in the organisation.

- The weights agreed on for the measures of IT-business-value may change when the local and/ or international economic climate changes.

- The action research confirmed that a complex set of measures will not work in practice.

- Although the researcher at first was initially of the opinion that the more thorough the evaluation criteria are, the better the initial investment evaluation would be, this now seems to be only partially true. The fact that all dimensions of IT-business-value were covered seems to be more important than the completeness of the individual IT-business-value measures. The discussion and consensus reached about the IT investment, facilitated by the ITIEM scorecard and business case details, is in the most cases more important than the actual IT-business-value "score."

- The area of "human factors" was perceived to be highly valuable when evaluating and managing IT investments. It was confirmed that without focusing on the human aspect, the IT investment would not be appropriately used.

Assessment and Validation of IE

Although this study did not set out to test or validate the goodness of the dimensions, measures or methodology of IE, having selected IE in the literature review, it became central to the hybrid methodology we ultimately tested through action research.

From the literature survey, IE seems to be the most comprehensive method in its treatment of benefits and risks. From Table 17 it is evident that Parker et al.'s (1988) IE most comprehensively covers the identified IT-business-value measures identified in the literature, ten out of an identified fifteen measures of IT-business-value.

Although IE addresses a single measure of "Project and organisational risk," the management of the case study banks was of the opinion that this single aggregated IT-business-value measure does not fully address their need to assess the human factors involved when investing in IT.

In all instances, the case study banks used quantifiable IT-business-value measures, which ranged from simple pay-back-period to more sophisticated measures like NPV to take into account the time value of money.

In three instances, SAB1, SAB2, and SAB3, management confirmed that they had knowledge of Information Economics, but did not use the value acceleration or value linking concepts of Parker et al. (1988). The main concerns expressed by senior management were:

- It is complex to determine and costly to perform.
- It is sometimes impossible to "link back" the true benefit to just the IT investment itself; many other factors also influence the accelerated outcome of "value."
- Most of the banks had an IT investment benefit analysis process established through which the projected financial return of the IT investment could be established and evaluated in aggregate with all the other measures of IT-business-value already employed by the banks. These processes were well understood and applied by the banks.

The ITIEM Model

The draft ITIEM model was further refined through the South African case study. The proposed ITIEM model was then further validated in three Australian Bank case studies and finalised during the action research. Figure 2 represents the final revised ITIEM model.

The ITIEM Methodology

Drawing on the literature surveyed, the knowledge gained from the case studies, the ITIEM model was applied to propose a more comprehensive, practical ITIEM methodology. The final ITIEM methodology integrated all the dimensions of IT-

Figure 2. The final ITIEM model

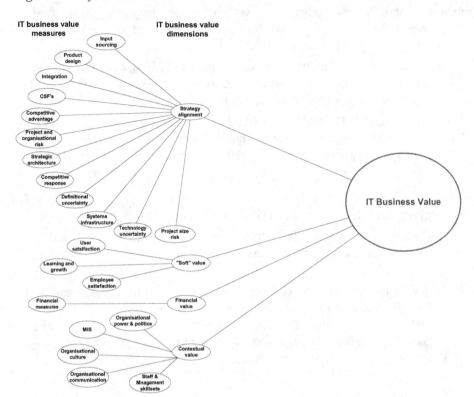

business-value and the measures of IT-business value from the ITIEM model. This methodology was successfully implemented and tested in AUS3 after four rounds of reflection, change, and re-implementation. The additional identified measures of IT-business-value were integrated to complete the ITIEM methodology. The structure of the methodology is depicted in Table 2.

The MD is still satisfied today that business is taking the lead in all IT investments and that "value for money" is being attained. The head of IT can focus on his contribution, namely to deliver quality IT assets to the business. The weights needed adjustment only once, after which all parties concerned were satisfied. It took four cycles before all parties concerned were satisfied and comfortable with the methodology. Today all IT investments above $100,000 need to be prioritised using the methodology.

Table 2. Structure of the methodology

IT-business-value dimension	Evaluation and measures of IT-business-value dimension
Business strategy alignment	• Degree of integration • Fulfilment of CSFs • Competitive advantage • Strategic and organisational risk • Strategic architecture • Definitional uncertainty • Systems infrastructure • Technical uncertainty • Competitive response • Better sourcing of inputs • Better product design
"Soft" value	• User satisfaction • Organisational learning and growth • Employee satisfaction
Financial value	• Quantifiable financial measure: NPV
Contextual value	• Organisational power and politics • MIS • Organisational Culture • Organisational communication • Staff and management skill sets

Limitations of the Study

The research was confined to large financial institutions and action research carried out in only one financial institution. Thus, we cannot generalise the findings to other lines of business. At most, we can conclude that the proposed methodology appears to be successful in financial institutions in Australia.

The proposed ITIEM model was minimally tested. The possible importance of the relationships between the dimensions of IT-business-value was not addressed in this study and should be seen as a limitation.

The management decision-making structure needed to implement the ITIEM methodology successfully was not fully discussed in this thesis. Though not a focus of the study, it was addressed during the action research.

As mentioned, the author is aware of the important mediating role of "appropriate use" and other variables, but as previously stated, it could be seen as a limitation that this study only focused on (1) how to evaluate IT investment proposals on the basis of IT-business-value as defined by Cronk and Fitzgerald (1997), and (2) measurement of the IT-business-value resulting from the use of IT.

Implications of the Research

The study suggests that all financial institutions need to evaluate and measure IT investments to ensure appropriate use and positive IT-business-value. The proposed methodology can be adapted for a particular financial institution assist financial institutions to practically align their IT investments with business strategy, and measure the success of their IT investments.

The proposed ITIEM methodology can only be used for discretionary IT investments. It does not address IT investment categories like statutory requirements, ongoing maintenance, or any other non-discretionary categories.

Study results suggest several implications for further ITIEM research:

- The dimensions of IT-business-value and the measures of IT-business value should be further empirically researched to establish their relative importance to an effective ITIEM.
- The measures of IT-business-value identified by this study, exceeding the IE measures, need to be analysed in further research as to establish their completeness and relative importance. Al-Tameem and Wheeler (2000) also sug-

gest that further research considering human and organisational aspects will be an important departure from the conventional ITIEM approaches. This is also supported by Jones and Hughes (2000) who argue that it is now time to challenge traditional ITIEM methodologies based on hard data. Because they have failed, a soft data approach may be more appropriate.

- Although the methodology was successfully implemented in a financial institution, it needs to be extended to other lines of business.

- Jones et al. (2000) also suggest that ITIEM encompasses a complex process. This process is worthy of articulation and analysis in further research.

- Khalifam, Irani, and Baldwin (2000) argue that there is evidence to support the view that ITIEM is affected by budgetary limitations and that the way organisations justify their IT investments affects the strategy adopted. More in-depth studies are required to address this.

References

Al-Tameem, A. A., & Wheeler, F. P. (2000). *A process view of information system benefits management and evaluation.* Presented at the Americas Conference on Information Systems, Long Beach, CA.

Bacon, C. J. (1992). The use of decision criteria in selecting information systems/ information technology investments. *MIS Quarterly, 16*(3), 335-353.

Bergeron, F., & Raymond, L. (1995). *The contribution of IT to the bottom line: A contingency perspective of strategic dimensions.* Presented at the International Conference on Information Systems, Amsterdam, The Netherlands.

Brynjolfsson, E., & Hitt, L. (1993). *Is information systems spending productive? New evidence and new results.* Presented at the 14th International Conference on Information Systems, Orlando, FL.

Buss, M. (1983). How to rank computer projects. *Harvard Business Review, 61*(1), 119-125.

Butler-Cox (1990). *Getting value from IT* (pp. 1-55). London: Butler Cox Research Foundation.

Chan, Y. E., & Huff, S. L. (1994). *Investigating information systems strategic alignment.* Presented at the 14th International Conference on Information Systems, Orlando, FL.

Clemons, E. K. (1991). Evaluation of strategic investments in information technology. *Communications of the ACM, 34*(1), 22-36.

Cronk, M. C., & Fitzgerald, E. P. (1997). *A conceptual framework for furthering understanding of IT-business-value and its dimensions.* Presented at the Pacific Asia Conference on Information Systems, Brisbane, Australia, Information Systems Management Research Concentration, Queensland University of Technology.

Du Plooy, N. F. (1993). *The social aspects of information systems.* SACLA, Johannesburg, South Africa: University of Pretoria.

Earl, M. J. (1989). *Management strategies for information technology.* Prentice Hall.

Earl, M. J. (1994). The new and old of business process redesign. *Strategic Information Systems, 1*(3), 21-32.

Farbey, B., Land, F., & Targett, D. (1993). *How to assess your IT investments.* Oxford, UK: Butterworth-Heinemann.

Farbey, B., Land, F., & Targett, D. (1999). *IS evaluation: A process for bringing together benefits, costs and risks, rethinking management information systems.* In W. Currie & B. Galliers (Eds.), *Rethinking management information systems* (pp. 204-228). New York: Oxford University Press.

Gable, G. G. (1994). Integrating case study and survey research methods: An example for information systems. *Journal of Information Systems, 3*(2), 112-126.

Galliers, B. (1992). Information technology—management's boon or bane? *Journal of Strategic Information Systems, 4*(34), 1-4.

Gibson, C., & Jackson, B. (1987). *The information imperative: Managing the impact of information technology on business and people.* Lexington, KY: Heath and Company.

Gitomer, J. (1988). Simulation and modelling: Systems development tools. In R. E. Umbaugh (Ed.), *Handbook of MIS management* (2nd ed.). Boston: Auerbach Publishers.

Grabowski, M., & Lee, S. (1993). *Linking information systems applications portfolio and organisational strategy.* Hershey, PA: Idea Group Publishing.

Hersey, P., & Blanchard, K. H. (1993). *Management of organizational behavior* (6th ed.). Englewood Cliffs, NJ: Prentice-Hall.

Hirschheim, R. A. (1992). *Information system epistemology: A historical perspective. Information systems research, issues, methods, and practical guidelines.* Oxford, UK: Blackwell Scientific Publications.

Hochstrasser, B., & Griffiths, C. (1991). *Controlling IT investments, strategy and management.* Tokyo, Japan: Thomson Publishing.

IBM. (1982). *Business systems planning.* New York.

Jones, S., & Hughes, J. (2000). *Understanding IS evaluation as a complex social process.* Presented at the Americas Conference on Information Systems, Long Beach, CA.

Kaplan, R., & Norton, D. (1996, January-February). Using the balanced scorecard as a strategic management system. *Harvard Business Review,* 75-85.

Keen, P. G. W. (1993). *Decision support systems: Putting theory into practice* (3rd ed., pp. 57-73). Upper Saddle River, NJ: Prentice-Hall, Inc.

Khalifa, G., Irani, Z., & Baldwin, L. P. (2000). *IT evaluation methods: Drivers and consequences.* Presented at the Americas Conference on Information Systems, Long Beach, CA.

Land, F. (1992). *The information systems domain. Information systems research, issues, methods, and practical guidelines.* Oxford, UK: Blackwell Scientific Publications.

Lee, A. (1989). A scientific methodology for MIS case studies. *MIS Quarterly, 24*(6).

Lee, B., & Barua, A. (1999). An integrated assessment of productivity and efficiency impacts of information technology investment: Old data, new analysis, and evidence. *Journal of Productivity Analysis, 27*(2), 21-43.

Lincoln, T. (1986). Do computer systems really pay-off? *Information and Management, 11*(1), 52-60.

Loh, L., & Venkatraman, N. (1993). Corporate governance and strategic resource allocation. *Accounting, Management, & Information Technology, 3*(4).

Lubbe, S., & Nel, J. F. (1993). *Organisational performance and IT investment intensity in RSA companies.* Presented at the National Conference for Masters and PhD Students in Computer Science, Johannesburg RSA, Department of Computer Science, UNISA.

Lucas, H. C. (1993). *The business value of information technology: A historical perspective and thoughts for the future.* Hershey, PA: Idea Group Publishing.

Mahmood, M. (1994). Evaluating organisational efficiency resulting from information technology investments. *Journal of Information Systems, 4*(1), 83-115.

Mahmood, M., & Mann, G. J. (1993). Impact of information technology investment: An empirical assessment. *Accounting, Management, & Information Technology, 1*(4), 23-32.

Markus, M. L., & Soh, C. (1993). *Banking on information technology. Converting it spending into firm performance. Strategic information technology management.* Hershey, PA: Idea Group Publishing.

Matlin, G. (1979). What is the value of investment in information systems? *MIS Quarterly, 3*(3), 105-109.

McFarlan, F. W., & McKenney, J. L. (1983). *Corporate information systems management*. Homewood, IL, Richard D Irwin.

McGraw-Hill Open Learning Centre. (n.d.). Retrieved from http://highered.mcgraw-hill.com sites/0072823755/student_view0/glossary.html

Miller, J. (1989). *Information systems effectiveness: The fit between business needs and system capabilities.* Presented at the International Conference on Information Systems, Boston.

Mooney, J. G., Gurbaxani, V., Tallon P. P., & Kraemer, K. L. (1995). *A process oriented framework for assessing the business value of information technology.* Presented at the 16ᵗʰ International Conference on Information Systems, Amsterdam, The Netherlands.

Morris, I. (1992). *Strategic information systems planning.* London: White Head Morris.

Nel, J. F. (1995). A theoretical perspective on information and information technology. In *Proceedings of the 10ᵗʰ National Conference for Masters and PhD Students in Computer Science*, UNISA, Pretoria, South Africa.

Nel, J. F. (1997). IT investment management: A case study and survey on the effects of IT usage on organisational strategic performance in financial institutions. In *PACIS '97*, Brisbane, Queensland Australia, ISMRC/QUT.

Neumann, S., & Sprauge, R. L. (1994). *Competitive advantage, strategic resources, and information technology: An empirical study.* Presented at the International Conference on Information Systems, Vancouver, British Columbia, Canada.

OASIG. (1996). *The performance of information technology and the role of human and organisational factors.* London: Economic and Social Research Council of UK.

Orlikowski, W. J. (1992). The duality of technology: Rethinking the concept of technology in organisations. *Organisation Science, 3*(3).

Ozernoy, V., Smith, D., & Sicherman, A. (1992). Evaluating computerised geographic information systems using decision analysis. *Organisation Sciences, 3*(3).

Parker, M., Benson, R. J., & Trainor, H. E. (1988). *Information economics: Linking business performance to information technology.* Englewood Cliffs, NJ: Prentice-Hall.

Porter, M. E. (1996, November-December). What is strategy? *Harvard Business Review*, 61-78.

Prince, C. J. (1997). IT's elusive ROI. *Chief Executive, 122*, 12-13.

Remenyi, D., & Sherwood-Smith, M. (1996). *Active benefits realisation using a formative evaluation approach.* Johannesburg, South Africa: University of the Witwatersrand.

Remenyi, D., Money, A., & Twite, A. (1995). *The effective measurement and management of IT costs and benefits*. Oxford: Butterworth-Heinemann.

Robbins, S. P. (2002). *Organisational behaviour* (10th ed.). Englewood Cliffs, NJ: Prentice-Hall.

Sambamurthy, V., & Zmud, R. (1995). *Organisational competencies for managing investments in visionary applications of IT*. Presented at the 16th International Conference on Information Systems, Amsterdam, Netherlands.

Semich, J. W. (1994). Here's how to quantify IT investment benefits. *Datamation*, 45-48.

Soh, C., & Markus, L. M. (1995). *How IT creates business value: A process theory synthesis*. Presented at the 16th International Conference of Information Systems, Amsterdam. Netherlands.

Strassmann, P. (1990). *The business value of computers*. New York: The Free Press.

Strassmann, P. A. (1997). Will big spending on computers guarantee profitability? *Datamation*, *43*(2), 75-85.

Symons, V., & Walsham, G. (1988). The evaluation of information systems: a critique. *Journal of Applied Systems Analysis*, *15*, 119-132.

Thorp, J., & D. s. C. f. S. Leadership. (1998). *The information paradox: Realising the business benefits of information technology*. Toronto, Canada: McGraw-Hill Ryerson Limited.

Tinsley, T., & Power, A. C. (1990). Why IS should matter to CEO's. *Datamation*, 85-88.

Venkatraman, N. (1994). IT-enabled business transformation. *Sloan Management Review*, 73-87.

Veryard, R. (1991). *The economics of information systems and software*. London: Butterworth-Heinemann.

Walsh, P. (1999). *Building the balanced scorecard: A core process perspective* (pp. 1-27). Sydney, Australia: Graduate School of Business University of Sydney.

Ward, J., Griffiths, P., & Whitmore, P. (1990). *Strategic planning for information systems*. John Wiley & Sons.

Ward, J., Taylor, P., & Bruce, C. (1996). Evaluation and realisation of IS/IT benefits: An empirical study of current practices. *European Journal of Information Systems,* (4), 214-225.

Weill, P., & Olsen, M. H. (1989). Managing investments in information technology: Mini case examples and implications. *MIS Quarterly*, *13*(1), 3-15.

Willcocks, L. (1992). IT evaluation: Managing the catch-22. *European Management Journal*, *10*(2).

Willcocks, L., & Griffiths, C. (1994). Predicting risk of failure in large scale information technology projects. *Technology Forecasting and Social Change*, *47*, 205-228.

Yin, R. K. (1994). *Case study research: Design and methods*. Beverly Hills, CA: Sage Publications.

Endnote

[1]   For confidentiality purposes, the organisations are referred to in code throughout the chapter.

Chapter X

Investing in Online Privacy Policy for Small Business as Part of B2C Web Site Management:
Issues and Challenges

Geoff Erwin, Cape Peninsula University of Technology, South Africa

Mike Moncrieff, Cape Peninsula University of Technology, South Africa

Abstract

"You have zero privacy anyway. Get over it." These words by Scott McNeally, CEO of Sun Microsystems, represent one pole of opinion on the privacy protection spectrum in the global world of the World Wide Web and Internet. At the other end, some authors identify privacy as "... perhaps the most contentious and serious issue facing information and communication technology (ICT) managers ..." Assessing these extreme opinions, how does a small business Web site operator determine a feasible and responsible course of action for handling personally identifiable information

collected in the course of business? Theoretical and practical frameworks must reinforce privacy treatment. Mishandling of the privacy issue can disrupt both the reputation and success of an e-commerce or other Web site, threatening the return on investment for the business. This chapter explores the current developments in privacy legislation in South Africa and examines the practical issues faced by a business-to-consumer (B2C) small business Web site owner implementing an online privacy policy.

Introduction

One of the risks associated with owning and operating a Web site is the contingent liability attendant on preserving confidentiality of personal information surrendered by an e-customer in the course of a transaction.

No matter how user-friendly and attractive a Web site is, the success of the Web site can be jeopardized by the casual or systematic mishandling of personal information by the Web site owner/operator as well as the Internet service provider (ISP). To protect the investment made by the Web site owner in developing and maintaining a Web site, management should ensure that the personal information volunteered by e-customers is securely and confidentially held. In the event that personal information is sold or passed on, accidentally or deliberately, without the direct consent of the e-customer, the Web site owner could face difficulties such as liability for damages, legal penalties, loss of existing customers, and reluctance by potential customers to use the Web site. The policies and methods of privacy protection can be a significant amount of Web site development and maintenance costs. In this chapter, the authors explore various issues associated with the management of personal information on a Web site associated with the protection of an e-customer's privacy.

Background

Privacy

Gauzente (2004) finds that there is no single generally agreed upon definition of privacy. For the purposes of this chapter, the authors have chosen a definition quoted by Gauzente from the Electronic Privacy Information Centre (EPIC) as follows: "… the right of individuals to control the collection, use, and dissemination of their personal information that is held by others."

Personally Identifiable Information

Personally identifiable information (PII) is personal information that can be linked back to an individual. Such information can form enough evidence to link it to a specifically named individual, hence the "personal" aspect. The Electronic Communications and Transactions Act (ECT Act, 2002) includes a comprehensive definition of PII. Romney and Romney (2004), among others, offer some examples of personal information: age, height, weight, medical records, and opinions. They state that publicly available information such as job title or address is not included in the definition of personal data (PII), although, in the opinion of the authors, data such as an address could help to narrow the possible individual involved.

Gauzente (2004) describes a "privacy concern continuum" of personal information ranging from gender, at the level of least concern, through credit card details at the highest level. Each B2C Web site owner must choose a level of privacy policy and implementation that affects concerns along this spectrum, usually in a phased approach. Goodburn and Ngoye (2004) assert that aggregate information compiled from PII does not enjoy the same protection under the law as PII, provided that the aggregate data is incapable of being related to specific individuals. Organizations that collate data from a collection of individuals into summary reports, such as opinion survey facilitators, would fall under this "aggregate information" category.

The issue of the availability of PII is increasingly contentious because of the ease with which an Internet connection can be used to disseminate such information, the multiple different opportunities each consumer has to provide PII to various Web sites, and the reports of so-called Spyware being used to gather PII without the user being aware of that activity.

The Issue of Privacy in B2C E-Commerce

E-customer concerns about privacy online are considered by many authors to be a key disincentive to shopping online (Hann, Hui, Lee, & Png, 2002; Schwaig, Kane, & Storey, 2005). PII can be used by a Web site owner/operator to customize the online shopping experience for a returning e-customer (e.g., by recommending products based on past purchases). The motivation for collecting PII need not be solely for in-house use, however, as it is highly valued by marketing organizations (Goodburn et al., 2004).

Privacy issues in business-to-consumer (B2C) e-commerce constitute a double-edged sword, which can inflict damage on both sides of the relationship. When privacy is compromised, the e-customer risks exposure of PII. This can have consequences ranging from the nuisance of receiving unsolicited marketing material through more insidious threats such as identity theft or discrimination. EPIC describes identity theft as "... the number one crime in the United States." EPIC attributes the rising incidence of identity theft to improper disclosure and use of PII (epic.org, 2005).

Ashley, Powers, and Schunter (2002) identify three reasons why organizations are concerned about PII viz. legislative penalty; brand and reputation erosion; lawsuits. Security breaches at online payroll service provider PayMaxx that exposed the PII of 25,000 people, forced closure of the site (news.com, 2005). Alexa, an Amazon.com subsidiary, was obliged to destroy some PII in its databases and pay up to USD 1.9 million to its customers in settlement of a class action lawsuit (news.com, 2001).

Relevance of Online Privacy Policies

Also referred to as a privacy notice, an online privacy policy (OPP) consists of statements informing an e-customer what information is collected during the course of a transaction and how it will be processed, stored, and used (Earp, Anton, & Jarvinen, 2002). Given the statement "Privacy concerns people, whereas confidentiality concerns data" (University of Kentucky, 2005), it could be argued that a privacy policy ought more properly to be called a "confidentiality policy."

Schwaig et al. (2005) observe that relatively few e-customers bother to read OPPs and those that do find them hard to understand. In light of this, these authors question a company's motivation to spend money on something of little use to the customer. In their view, companies may be more concerned about being seen to have a policy, creating a favourable, trustworthy image, than about the policy's content or enforcement.

The results of a survey conducted by the authors for a previous paper confirmed that many South African e-customers also experience difficulty in understanding an OPP (Moncrieff & Erwin, 2004).

Impact of Small Business Management on Privacy Policy

In the South African context, small, medium and micro enterprises (SMMEs) are defined in the National Small Business Act (Small Business Act, 1996) as owner-managed, having no more than 200 employees, total turnover not exceeding ZAR 64 million and total gross assets (excluding fixed property) of no more than ZAR 23 million.

Peslak (2005) reports that privately held companies are less likely to have privacy policies than public companies. They are also less likely to show consistency in the adoption of e-customer driven policies. Since SMMEs are by definition owner-managed, it is reasonable to expect that adoption of information technology (IT) and e-commerce will be significantly influenced by the attitudes of the business owners. It can be inferred that this influence will extend to the SMME's compliance with privacy practices.

It takes an organization more interested in preserving and enhancing customer relationships than in collected data to implement a comprehensive privacy management system (Ashley et al., 2002). In the case of SMMEs, the motivation for this must come from the business owner.

The relatively small size of an SMME usually means that the owner/manager(s) have multiple roles, such as accountant, lawyer, network operator, clerk, manager, financier, and more. This reduces the attention that can be paid to issues such as privacy, inter alia, compared with large organisations. A large organisation often employs a chief information officer (CIO) to marshal resources and policies to address privacy and other overarching concerns. Outsourcing of privacy compliance to a specialist service provider may be essential for SMMEs.

Legislation

One of the consequences of the advances in Internet technology has been an exponential growth in data flows unmatched by corresponding privacy protection technology (Ashley et al., 2002). These authors suggest that associated violations of privacy have prompted many countries to enact protective legislation. Rising concerns about data protection are confirmed in a South African Law Reform Commission Report (2003), "the Report," which states that over 30 countries have implemented data protection laws, and that the number of countries doing so is increasing steadily.

The expression of personal privacy legislation varies between countries. However, there are common underlying principles set out in the Report. The Report states that "personal" information must be:

1. Obtained fairly and lawfully
2. Used only for the specified purpose for which it was originally obtained
3. Adequate, relevant, and not excessive to the purpose
4. Accurate and up to date
5. Accessible to the subject
6. Kept secure
7. Destroyed after its purpose is completed

The Report discusses two seminal agreements issued in 1981, which have had far reaching influence on national laws around the globe. These are:

1.   The Council of Europe's 1981 Convention for the Protection of Individuals with Regard to the Automatic Processing of Personal Data

2.   The Organisation for Economic Cooperation and Development's (OECD) Guidelines Governing the Protection of Privacy and Transborder Data Flows of Personal Data

The durability of these documents may in part be ascribed to the fact they were expressed in terms of principles relating to gathering, holding, and usage of personal information rather than the technology of the era. In addition, the European Union enacted the Data Protection Directive in 1995 (European Union, 1995) with the aim of enabling the formulation of consistent privacy protection laws for citizens across member states of the Union. Articles 25 and 26 of the Directive are of particular significance to international trade in that they demand that there should be no cross border flow of personal data to a country "… which does not ensure an adequate level of protection …". The provisions of these articles have come to be known as the "safe harbour" principles.

In the United States, the Federal Trade Commission (FTC) is the arbiter of privacy regulation. Currently the FTC favours self-regulation by industry (Schwaig et al., 2005). Self-regulation is based on five principles—notice, choice, access, security, and enforcement detailed in the Fair Information Practices report (FTC, 2000).

The Report characterizes the European Union approach to data protection as based on legal protection of a political right. In the United States, the Report considers information privacy as being "… left to the marketplace …" and based on economic rather than political power. The Report characterizes the Australian and Canadian models as co-regulatory, where industry develops the rules, which are policed by an oversight agency. Canadian privacy legislation entitled Personal Information and Electronic Documents Act (PIPEDA) came into force in 2004. Fines for violation of PIPEDA can be up to CAD 100,000.

Privacy legislation in South Africa may be considered to be at a formative stage. Vecchiatto (2005) quotes South African Cyber Law expert Reinhardt Buys as stating that privacy is "… only dealt with on a voluntary basis …" in the ECT Act (2002). The South African Law Commission initiated a project entitled "Privacy and Data Protection" in 2002 which, when it comes to fruition, is expected to impact on the ECT Act (2002) and the Promotion of Access to Information Act (PROATIA, 2000) (South African Government Information, 2002).

The South African Law Reform Commission Report (2003) contains the following preliminary proposals:

- Privacy and data protection should be regulated by legislation.

- General principles of data protection should be developed and incorporated in the legislation.

- A statutory regulatory agency should be established.

- A flexible approach should be followed in which industries will develop their own codes of practice (in accordance with the principles set out in the legislation) which will be overseen by the regulatory agency.

The current fluid state of privacy legislation in South Africa in no way lessens the need for organizations to be aware of their obligation to preserve privacy.

Buys in Vechiatto (2005) points to the importance that EU countries attach to privacy and the key role that privacy plays in their trade relationships. The South African Law Reform Commission Report (2003) expresses similar sentiments, warning that privacy concerns can constitute an impediment to international trade.

Privacy Education

Many people believe that cryptography presents a complete solution to the online privacy and security conundrum (Orgill, Romney, Bailey, & Orgill, 2004). Cryptography plays a role in making transfers of data (largely) unreadable to an outsider or unauthorised snoop. However, this may only delay the availability of the clear text from becoming known if the Web site operator has inadequate controls in place to control such windows of opportunity as discarded backup discs and access points which are not protected.

A common approach is to recognize that unauthorised access to data (PII) will occur and make the content of the accessed data unusable. This approach is also used with security and confidentiality issues, as well as with privacy. Privacy refers to PII. Confidentiality often refers to organisational material such as business plans, salaries of directors and the like. Even when cryptography is used, there is still the aspect of the receiver/storer of PII knowingly disseminating that PII, either for monetary gain or in ignorance of the sensitivity of the data.

Orgill et al. (2004) describe human nature as the weak link in any security strategy. These authors identify shortcomings in education as one of the reasons a person may compromise the security with which they are entrusted. A practical illustration of the importance one e-commerce participant attaches to reinforcing the privacy message among its employees can be found in the following extract from the OPP of share-it!, a German software vendor:

Every quarter, as well as any time new policies are added, our employees are noti-
fied and/or reminded about the importance we place on privacy, and what they can
do to ensure our customers' information is protected. (share-it!, 2005)

Romney et al. (2004) point to the need for ICT professionals to be familiar with developments in privacy law because of the inevitable impact on the design and operation of databases. These authors conclude that instruction in the basis of privacy legislation is essential to an ICT education. It is commonly held that ignorance of the law is no excuse. Ignorance of the ramifications of privacy law on the part of an ICT professional carries the risk of serious consequences, economic and legal, for both the ICT professional and his or her employer (Romney et al., 2004). This can endanger the viability of the organization, threatening the whole of the ICT investment.

Operations and Systems Level Privacy Management

A Holistic Strategy

A holistic privacy management strategy should address both the information systems and operational environments of the SMME. Information systems must be capable of supporting the requirements defined by the OPP. At the operational level, management need to demonstrate commitment to policy, and employees need guidelines to ensure they are aware of the procedures to be followed in dealing with and protecting the privacy of PII.

A Systems Level Strategy

Ashley et al. (2002) state that there is no existing technological solution to the challenge of instituting enterprise-wide privacy management. In their view, the problem cannot be seen purely as one of data security. It is more a data management problem than one of security. Core to their thinking is that PII should be linked to the OPP in force at the time it was submitted by the e-customer. They advocate a "Sticky Policy Paradigm" (i.e., the policy should "stick" to the data and govern access to it). Table 1 below shows their framework for management of collected PII.

Ashley et al. (2002) call for creation of a privacy policy by a chief privacy officer (CPO), in consultation with people who can formulate it in terms of the legal requirements, the strategy of the business and the relevant legislation, if any. Elements

Table 1. Proposed framework for management of PII (Source: Ashley et al., 2002)

1	Define an enterprise privacy policy.
2	Deploy the policy to the IT systems containing privacy sensitive information.
3	Record consent of end users to the advertised privacy policy when they submit privacy sensitive data.
4	Enforce the privacy policy and create an audit trail of access to privacy sensitive information.
5	Generate both enterprise wide and individualized reports showing access to privacy sensitive information and their conformance to the governing privacy policy.

that the policy must address are *Data Users* (data subject users), *Data Operations* (who can do what to the data), *Data Types* (e.g., "Contact Information" as opposed to types in a database schema), *Purposes* (how the data will be used), *Conditions* (qualification of rules e.g., disclosure to statutory authorities), and *Obligations* (e.g., requirement to log certain types of access). Deployment of the privacy policy requires correlation of the *Data Types* in the privacy policy to PII in the organisation's databases; *Data Users* to roles in the organisation and *Purposes* to tasks and procedures performed in the course of business.

No PII should be collected without the explicit consent of the e-customer to the terms of the extant privacy policy including every stated use of the information. Stored information should be identifiable as belonging to the data subject, and linked to the currently effective policy and the data types within the policy. Enforcement of the policy can be implemented in real-time by means of a suitable application program interface (API) and through delayed monitoring of access log files.

Reporting facilities should be provided to permit an auditor to log and review breaches of policy. The data subject user should be able to request reports detailing the information held on file and indicating which private information has been compromised in terms of the agreement under which it was submitted. The data subject user must also be afforded means to correct the data.

Operational Aspects of Privacy Management

The search for practical methodologies for dealing with privacy concerns is not new. In a paper written before the advent of e-commerce, Smith (1993) prophetically describes information privacy as possibly "… the most important issue of the information age." The same organizational issues identified by Smith in the protection of PII remain relevant today.

Smith describes privacy policy development in the organizations studied as being intermittent, responding to outside threats such as adverse publicity or changes in legislation. A negative consequence of this approach was that in the periods between policy developments, employees had either to operate with policies inconsistent with actual practice, or without policy, at all when no new policy had yet developed for a changed environment. Smith advocates a proactive approach as the "... backbone of the privacy approach of corporations that use personal information ..." The author urges that business executives take an aggressive stance to the creation of privacy policies. Once a policy is established, the author argues that employee commitment must be ensured through education. A continuous monitoring process is essential to ensuring that practice adheres to policy.

Smith warns against reliance on implicitly inferred policies because this places employees in a position where they cannot produce officially endorsed procedures to support their actions. To avoid a situation where employees experience "value conflicts" resulting from inconsistencies between policy and practice, the author recommends that an environment is engendered in which employees can freely raise concerns about information privacy.

Discussion

E-commerce has matured and moved on from the heady days prior to the dot com meltdown in the early 2000s when the industry seemed to be driven more by catch-phrases than sound business principles. Whether genuinely motivated by customer concerns or simply to look good in the marketplace, all B2C Web sites will need to establish privacy policies made public in an OPP. The evolution of privacy law in South Africa will to a large degree determine the content of these organizational policies.

To avoid penalties resulting from violation of privacy laws, the onus will be on the operator of a Web site to ensure that the promises in the policy are made good in day-to-day operations. Achieving this will firstly require commitment to the OPP from the owner of the SMME. Explicitly stated in-house policies congruent with the OPP will need to be established and regularly reinforced with all employees. To avoid the "drift" described by Smith (1993), compliance with procedures must be audited regularly.

Conclusion

Few SMMEs are likely to have the infrastructure to support a full-time CIO. This does not mean that the privacy of data control function can be eliminated. Romney et al. (2004) quote Catherine MacInnes writing on compliance with PIPEDA in Computing Canada as follows:

... To comply with the legislation, some organizations will have to completely overhaul their process for collecting, using, and storing personal information...

South African B2C Web site operators are in a somewhat similar situation to their Canadian counterparts prior to the enactment of PIPEDA. Although the actual form of the final legislation is not known, it can be reasonably expected to be modeled on the proposals contained in the South African Law Reform Commission Report (2003). As such, it should be expected to have teeth in the form of significant legal penalties for violators. Web site systems will be subject to privacy laws, and management needs to factor that into their investment in the development, protection, and maintenance costs.

The requirement to manage PII responsibly cannot be ignored. Organizations involved in e-commerce have an obligation to cultivate awareness of emergent privacy legislation in their employees, to harness the appropriate skills (both technical and legal), to ensure that their procedures and systems are prepared for imminent changes. All these privacy considerations are now part of the normal management task of protecting the investment in the business.

References

Ashley, P., Powers, C., & Schunter, M. (2002, September 23-26). *From privacy promises to privacy management.* Presented at the New Security Paradigms Workshop '02, Virginia Beach, VA.

Earp, J. B., Anton, A. I., & Jarvinen, O. (2002). *A social, legal and technical framework for privacy management and policies.* Presented at the 8th America Conference on Information Systems (AMCIS 2002), Dallas, TX.

ECT Act. (2002). *Electronic Communications and Transactions Act 2002.* Retrieved March 29, 2005, from http://www.polity.org.za/pdf/ElectronicCommunications.pdf

epic.org. (2005). *Identity theft and data broker services*. Retrieved June 16, 2005, from http://www.epic.org/privacy/id_cards/testimony50905.pdf

European Union. (1995). *Data protection directive*. Retrieved June 16, 2005, from http://www.cdt.org/privacy/eudirective/EU_Directive_.html

FTC. (2000, May). *Privacy online: Fair information practices in the electronic marketplace: a federal trade commission report to congress*. Retrieved June 12, 2005, from http://www.ftc.gov/reports/privacy2000/privacy2000text.pdf

Gauzente, C. (2004). Web merchants' privacy and security statements: How reassuring are they for consumers? A two sided approach. *Journal of Electronic Commerce Research*, *5*(3), 181-198.

Goodburn, D., & Ngoye, M. (2004). Privacy and the Internet. In *Cyberlaw @ SA II* (2nd ed.). Pretoria: Van Schaik.

Hann, I., Hui, K., Lee, T. S., & Png, I. P. L. (2002, December 15-18). *Online information privacy: Measuring the cost-benefit trade-off*. Presented at the 23rd International Conference on Information Systems, Barcelona.

Moncrieff, M. J., & Erwin, G. J. (2004, September 1-3). e-customer perceptions of an online privacy policy. In *Proceedings of the 6th Annual Conference on World Wide Web Applications*, Johannesburg.

news.com. (2001). *Amazon unit settles privacy lawsuit*. Retrieved June 16, 2005, from http://news.com.com/2104-1017_3-256663.html

news.com. (2005). *Payroll site closes on security worries*. Retrieved June 16, 2005, from http://news.com.com/Payroll+site+closes+on+security+worries/2100-1029_3-5587859.html

Orgill, G. L., Romney, G. W., Bailey, G. B., & Orgill, P. M. (2004). The urgency for effective user privacy-education to counter social engineering attacks on secure computer systems. In *Proceedings of the 5th Conference on Information Technology Education*, Salt Lake City, UT (pp. 177-181).

Peslak, A. R. (2005). Privacy policies of the largest privately held companies--a review and analysis of the Forbes private 50. In *Proceedings of the 2005 ACM SIGMIS CPR Conference on Computer Personnel Research*, Atlanta, GA (pp. 104-111).

PROATIA. (2000). *Promotion of Access to Information Act 2 of 2000*. Retrieved June 12, 2005, from http://www.polity.org.za/html/govdocs/legislation/2000/act2.pdf

Romney, V. W., & Romney, G. W. (2004). Neglect of information privacy instruction – a case of educational malpractice? In *Proceedings of the 5th Conference on Information Technology Education*, Salt Lake City, UT (pp. 79-82).

Schwaig, K. S., Kane, G. C., & Storey, V. C. (2005). Privacy, fair information practices, and the Fortune 500: The virtual reality of compliance. *The Database for Advances in Information Systems, 36*(1), 49-63.

share-it! (2005). *Privacy statement of share-it!*.Retrieved June 17, 2005, from http://www.shareit.com/privacy_statement.html?sessionid=232599852&random=b6c6c21f4ae32176a699f6044d45f168

Small Business Act. (1996). *National Small Business Act, 1996.* Retrieved June 19, 2005, from http://www.polity.org.za/html/govdocs/legislation/1996/act96-102.html

Smith, H. J. (1993). Privacy policies and practices: Inside the organisational maze. *Communications of the ACM, 36*(12), 104-122.

South African Government Information. (2002, August). *Media statement by the South African Law Commission concerning its investigation into privacy and data protection.* Retrieved June 12, 2005, from http://www.info.gov.za/speeches/2002/02082614461004.htm

South African Law Reform Commission. (2003). *Privacy and data protection, Issue Paper 24: Summary of proposals and questionnaire.* Retrieved June 16, 2005, from http://wwwserver.law.wits.ac.za/salc/issue/ip24-sum-ques.pdf

University of Kentucky. (2005). *Privacy vs. confidentiality, what's the difference.* Retrieved June 19, 2005, from http://www.research.uky.edu/ori/ORIForms/Privacy%20vs%20Confidentiality.pdf

Vecchiatto, P. (2005). *SADC looking to harmonise cyber laws.* Retrieved June 12, 2005, from http://www.itWeb.co.za/sections/business/2005/0504111215.asp

Chapter XI

Examining the Approach Used for Information Technology Investment Decisions by Practitioners Responsible for IT Planning in Namibia

Karna Naidoo, University of KwaZulu-Natal, South Africa

Abstract

Despite the technological progress made by organisations in Namibia, the impact of IT has not been studied. The existing definition of IT is not comprehensive enough to include all relevant IT expenditures. No return calculations are made, though managers are showing growing concern at the increasing IT costs. The purpose of this article is to determine what organisations in Namibia use as basis for investing in IT. In interviews with six organisations in Namibia, it was determined how they define and manage their investment in IT. Some conclusions can be drawn, the first being that organisations need to look at their definition of IT to include all aspects of IT like communication systems, maintenance, etc. the second implication is that somebody must be appointed to take responsibility for managing the IT investment.

Introduction

Throughout history, progress in technological behaviour had profound social significance—regardless of whether it was based on mere intuition, trail-or-error, or scientific approach. Machiavelli as *cited* by Bass (1990) made the following comment about systems in general: "There is nothing more difficult to plan, more doubtful of success, nor more dangerous to manage than the creation of a new system. For the initiator has the enmity of all who would profit by the preservation of the old system and merely lukewarm defenders in those who would gain by the new one."

We now realise that information systems (IS) are the centre of a new business reality in the 1990s. The impact of the IT revolution is a phenomenon that is affecting every aspect of Third World societies. This revolution increasingly affects anything from the way organisations conduct business to the organisation of schools. The impact can even be stronger than the impact of gaining independence by drastically changing the course of economic development in a county. The major problem is that the use of IT is not fully understood nor studied in the Third World countries in order to yield meaningful insights.

Previous Attempts to Quantify IT Expenditure

Although there has been some growth in the usage of IT over the last couple of years, no analysis of the impact of IT on sales, costs, and profits of organisations has been made in Third World countries. It is, however, important that organisations inform themselves of the impact of IT usage on operating results and profitability. Strategies can then be developed in order to gain a competitive advantage.

Weill and Olson (1989) use case studies of organisations to determine how IT is defined, how IT investments are measured, tracked, and what other factors control IT investment decisions. Some important issues emerged from their study, namely that managers must adopt a broad definition of IT and that IT expenditures can be measured and tracked against a convenient base (revenues, total expenses, or management control costs). Weill et al. believe that attention must be paid to certain factors concerning any important IT investment, namely: managers' commitment to IT, previous organisational experience with IT, user satisfaction with systems, and the turbulence of the political environment of the organisation. A literature study based on a graphical cost/benefit approach to computer systems selection was presented by Shoval and Lugasi (1988). They note that stages, like analysing the needs of the system and defining its requirements and attributes, need attention.

Ahituv and Neumann (1990) state that any attempt to assess the value of information should be closely linked to the decision supported by the information. They noted that the selection of criteria to use in comparative analysis is the easier part in cost/benefit analysis. The complicated part is to identify all the elements which form part of cost and benefits, and determining how to measure (or estimate) all those elements.

Kwong and Mohammed (1985) suggest the use of a computerised index (CI) that can quantitatively evaluate the impact of computerisation on profitability and, in the process, develop an indicator to the extent and sophistication of computerisation. The organisations used show that an increasing degree of computerisation is generally associated with an increasing profitability margin as indicated by the CI—even in the short term.

In his study involving experienced users, Davis (1989) suggests the use of determinants, the most important one being that if potential users believe that a given application is useful, they may simultaneously believe that the system is difficult to use and that the performance benefits of usage are outweighed by the efforts of using the application.

In conclusion, it can be said that IT investment uses resources of organisations. There are no consensus of the definition of IT and the measurement of its tangible and intangible benefits. This makes IT investment difficult to manage.

Case Study Results

Six mini case studies were conducted to help understand how organisations define and manage their IT investments in Namibia. The six organisations compose of five large profit-making organisations, while the sixth organisation is a part of the educational system in Namibia. A lengthy, semi-structured interview was conducted with the senior representatives in information systems of each organisation. Every attempt was made to keep the identity of the organisation and sensitive information confidential.

Primary questions covered the following:

- What does the organisation regard as part of their IT?
- How do they manage and track IT investments?
- From where does the impetus for buying IT equipment start?
- What factors influence IT investment decisions?

Organisation 1—Education

Organisation 1 is in the field of tertiary education in Namibia. The interviewee is the director of the computer bureau. According to him IT is defined to include only hardware and software. During the past two years, the budget for purchasing IT equipment was drastically cut. All purchases of IT equipment were done from savings in department's budget. IT is tracked in a combined centralised and decentralised way, but no attempt is being made to include relatively small expenditures. IT equipment is not captured on the tracking of the investment if a department buys IT equipment from own savings. No ROI is calculated although departments are assessed on an output vs. input basis (output could be preparation for lectures while input could be space, equipment, number of persons in the department etc.).

The impetus to buy IT equipment originates from departments who identify a need, get top management's permission, and proceed to buy the equipment. Political considerations do play a significant part in decisions to invest in IT. The management of the IT investment is done on a partly centralised and partly decentralised basis. There is no link between the buying of IT equipment and the strategy and the strategy of the organisation.

Organisation 2—Transport

Organisation 2 is a large organisation in the transport sector. The interviewee is the chief clerk who controls IT. The interviewee noted that the process of investing resources in IT is the responsibility of individual divisions. IT is defined as all hardware and software. The productive capacity of the IT is planned in order to allow maximum advantage of their investment. The interviewee believes that investment in IT could be maximized but stated that no real attempt is being made to do so. No return calculations are made on the investment and there are decentralised tracking of the investment. He noted that political issues do play part in decisions to invest in IT. The impetus to invest in IT comes from a central point. If the need for II is recognised, he has to be notified. There is no link between investment in IT and the strategy for the organisation.

Organisation 3—Banking

Organisation 3 is a geographically dispersed commercial bank. The interviewee is a member of the management of the bank. The bank includes hardware and software in its general view of IT. No productive capacity planning for IT is being done in the bank. The bank keeps track on all levels of IT equipment in a combined centralised and decentralised basis. This is done as no simple measure is considered enduring enough in terms of accuracy. The bank's decision to invest in IT is done at corporate level the following inputs from base. Every department manages its own IT.

The interviewee stated that political considerations play a big part in the decision to invest in IT. According to him, there definitely is a link between the buying of IT equipment and the strategy of the organisation.

Organisation 4—Insurance

Organisation 4 is a local firm who handles all sorts of insurance for a large clientele basis. The interviewee is the manager of the financial department. Their definition of IT includes hardware and software. No productive capacity or any tracking of their IT equipment was done. They do not conduct return calculations on their IT investment because they consider it too complicated. All IT equipment in their possession is managed from a central position.

Political considerations do play a part in their decision to invest in IT and tat is why top management takes all decisions regarding IT investments. There is a link between the strategy the organisation employs and decisions to invest in IT or not.

Organisation 5—Consumer Products

Organisation 5 is a large manufacturing organisation in the consumer products industry. The interviewee is the manager of the information department. According to the interviewee, the definition includes all PC-hardware and software as well as all consumables. Productive capacity is planned in advanced as management wants to see IT equipment put to use. All IT equipment is managed in a centralised way. No return calculations are done on the investment in IT. The decision to invest in IT comes from management. He also said that political considerations play no part in decisions to invest in IT. There is a link the decision to buy IT equipment and the strategy for the organisation.

Organisation 6—Insurance

Organisation 6 is a large multi-national insurance organisation with three major businesses, namely individual insurance, group insurance, and investment. The interviewee is the computer consultant to the organisation. The definition of IT does not include consumables but encompasses all hardware and software. Decentralisation of the organisation is the reason why managers of the organisation decided to decentralise the management of IT. No return calculation is made on IT investments. Political considerations play a part in the decision to buy IT equipment. The impetus to buy IT usually comes from managers and the lower-hierarchy based on what their opposition is doing and how they define their strategy.

Analysis of Key Factors

The Definition and Tracking of IT

The majority of organisations viewed hardware and software as the only part of its investment in IT. There seems to be a trend to keep the definition of IT as narrow as possible.

IT Investment Management

Organisations track IT expenses with varying degrees of success. Tracking is done mainly on the basis of comparing it with budgeted amounts for the specific year and taking care not to exceed the budgeted amount. Another problem could be that It investments by departments are not captured on the overall picture of the organisation. No return calculations on investments are done as people tend to think it is too difficult. The total hardware appeared as assets in the asset register though some organisations did not keep track of software expenses at all.

Political and Other Influences

Political considerations are important factors in most organisations and have significant impact on the acquisition of IT equipment. These considerations sometimes overshadow the technical and economic considerations and are becoming more important. In most cases the impetus for investment was taken by managers. This was not necessarily connected to a decision to incorporate more IT into the organisation. In all (but two) organisations there was no link between IT and the strategy for the organisation.

Implications of the Findings

The implications from the findings are: (1) Define and track IT as IT expenditures increase the need for a definition for IT becomes an important issue. This must be broadened to include all cost aspects of IT; and (2) the calculation of the return on investments in IT can be complex as no real cash flow is available.

Recommendations

Organisations in a Third World country like Namibia must realise that they have to manage their IT investment by:

1. **Defining and tracking IT investments:** Redefine the definition of IT so that it includes all expenditures, such as hardware, software, people, consumables, training, and maintenance. There must be accurate recording of this expenditure over time against a convenient base such as revenues or staff employed, etc.

2. **Looking at IT investment and return:** To justify IT investment poses a problem for many organisations. Return on investment (ROI) calculations sometimes does not apply to certain IT investments because it is difficult to determine a definite income stream. Managers must, however, recognise that ROI calculations are not always relevant for all IT investments. They must remember that some IT investments could be essential to the organisation's survival. Lastly, managers must keep in mind that the total IT investment needs to be calculated if they want to see the effect of the IT investment on the organisation.

3. **Concentrating on organisational issues:** Issues that must be liked into are: Top management commitment to IT; previous experience with IT; user satisfaction with systems; and the political environment of the organisation.

Conclusion

It was found that IT definitions are not comprehensive enough. The problem could be that organisations do not sit down and constructively plan their investment in IT. I had the feeling that organisations in Namibia have no idea of the total amount of resources invested in IT. Another factor is that this investment is not managed satisfactorily and that nobody wanted to take responsibility for managing IT investment. My final conclusion is that workshops must be organised and people educated in the concepts of managing IT investment.

References

Ahituv, N., & Neumann, S. (1990). *Principles of information systems for management* (3rd ed.). Dubuque: WC Brown Publishers.

Bass, B. M. (1990). *Handbook of leadership* (3rd ed.). New York: The Free Press.

Davis, F. J. (1989, September). Perceived usefulness, perceived ease of use, and user acceptance of IT. *MIS Quarterly*.

Kwong, H. C., & Mohammed, M. Z. (1985). Profit impact of computerisation. *Hong Kong Computer Journal*.

Shoval, P., & Lugasi, Y. (1988). Computer systems selection. *Information and Management, 15*.

Weill, P., & Olson, M. H. (1989, March). Managing investment in IT: Mini case examples and implications. *MIS Quarterly*.

Chapter XII

A Case Study on the Selection and Evaluation of Software for an Internet Organisation

Pieter van Staaden, Media24 Ltd., South Africa

Abstract

The author conducted research to determine whether IT managers, IT auditors, users, management, etc. (all decision-makers) use a certain evaluation and selection process to acquire software to meet business objectives and the requirement of users. An argument was used that the more thorough the software evaluation and selection process, the more likely it would be that the organisation will chose software that meets these targets. The main objective of the research was therefore to determine whether Media24 uses evaluation methods and obtains the desired results. The results confirmed that Media24 uses suggested protocol as noted in the theory for software acquisition correctly during most stages.

Introduction

There is a wide variety of methods that can be used for selection of software in various fields of business (e.g., manufacturing, service providers, insurance, wholesale, retail, etc.). This software is used for a variety of purposes in businesses. However, selecting the software that meets organisational requirements and business objectives could prove to be a challenge considering the number of vendors and software available.

Choosing the right software for your company can be bewildering. There are thousands of titles to choose from, and programs and their functionality differ frequently. (Buyerzone.com, 2002)

A hurried, uneducated choice could lead to various problems in the company. Some of these are failing to support an important business process, supporting a process inaccurately or inefficiently, unhappy customers, disgruntled employees, loss of sales, and poor financial performance.

Competition in the Western Cape requires good performance in all aspects of the electronic publication industry. Bad judgments or decisions in terms of software acquisition could cause a company some losses and complications in their daily operations. Choosing the right software is therefore important and can be achieved by using pre-determined evaluation and selection guidelines.

Evaluation and Selection of a Commercial Software System

Decisions Made Prior to the Software Evaluation Process

As mentioned by Capterra's software selection methodology (2002), certain procedures should be completed before the actual evaluation is conducted. They suggest that the company should start off by interviewing some staff members, addressing corporate vision, analysing existing systems limitations and features, and looking at present policies and procedures. The company should also determine whether new software will help the business and if it will increase competitive advantage.

They argue that when the decision is made to purchase software, a project plan should be developed to evaluate and list the evaluation criteria that will be used during the process. A project team should also be selected to carry out the evaluation. This team must include representatives from all levels the organisation. If the proposed software incorporates financial aspects, the audit team should also be included.

Determine Requirements for the New Software Package

The purpose would be to create a comprehensive and prioritised list of requirements to help evaluate the software. Base Consulting Group (BCG) (2000) state that the requirements definition should consist of several processes (such as managerial requirements (budget/timing, reporting requirements), functional requirements (stated business needs, technical requirements), and IS standards (data flow diagrams, system interfaces, and hardware and network requirements with emphasis on capacity).

They also note that some companies do not develop detailed requirements and as a result may be dissatisfied with the final outcome. Romney and Steinbart (2000) support this statement and suggest that one or any combination of four strategies (listed below) should be used to determine requirements for the new software:

- Survey end-users to determine what their requirements for software is by using questionnaires, personal interviews, and focus group discussions.
- Analyse the existing system and eliminating requirements that have already been defined.
- Examine how the existing software is used, helping to determine the shortcomings of the system, and identifing any new requirements needed by users.
- Pilot demonstrations of applications/software systems could be utilised when there is a problem in identifying requirements.

Document the Requirements

The systems requirement document or software requirement specifications should be the starting point for measuring performance of the final system (Shelly, Cashman, & Rosenblatt, 1998). Users must understand the document to be able to improve the final version. The content of this requirements document will depend on the type of company and the complexity of the new system. BCG (2000) states that the requirements document is the cornerstone to evaluate the software and should be used to identify requirements. Capterra (2002) argues that there is a methodological approach available to help with requirement analysis. This is listed in Table 1.

Table 1. Capterra's methodology (2002)

COLUMN NAME	DESCRIPTION
Functional department, business processes, and process.	This creates the requirements hierarchy and ensures that all processes are covered (e.g., would be creditors department, cheque printing, approving cheques for printing, etc.)
Requirement type	This identifies the requirement as functional, technical, vendor related, or contractual.
Requirement description	This details the requirement itself and should be as descriptive as possible.
Priority and ranking	*This could be used during the evaluation.*
Objective addressed	This could be used to match the requirement to a business objective.
Comments	This can be used for any additional comments or justifications.

Selecting Vendors

Michell and Fitzgerald (1997) argue that the range of services offered by IT vendors is large and growing rapidly. They also note that while searching for the "best" vendor, it should be borne in mind that the process of selection and evaluation of a vendor is important. Base Consulting Group (2000) suggests that the project team's first step should be to identify the vendors who offer software solutions that could be used. It could be a high-risk approach not to properly evaluate vendor companies. The sources used to compile the list of vendors should be recent and reliable. These sources include software user groups, databases, industry groups, research firms, consulting firms, trade shows, seminars and conferences, current users, personal recommendations and contacts, competitors, IT, and business magazines, as well as Web sites.

Preliminary Evaluation of Vendor Companies and Their Product

Ward (2001) argues that selecting software from a vendor should be a simplified process. She suggests that vendors be invited to participate in a software demonstration because it reduces time spent on evaluations. Companies could work toward solving the business problems earlier resulting in faster return on investment. Base

Consulting Group (2000) states that inviting too many vendors to participate increases the costs and timelines of the project. Team members may also lose focus after seeing too many product demonstrations. In order to shorten the time of the process send the request for proposal (RFP) to a shortlist of 5 vendors, and do a preliminary evaluation of the vendors.

The evaluation team should look at things like:

- The standard functionality and key features of the product
- Technology requirements (hardware, additional software, database, operating system, network, development tools)
- Product considerations such as viability, stability, and cost
- Products targeting different, smaller, or much larger companies or industries should be eliminated
- Eliminate products that are in development or a recent release.
- Licensing and support costs are examined and products that are over/under priced should be eliminated (licensing escalation must be considered).
- Develop a request for proposal (RFP).

According to Levinson (2001), an RFP guides buyers through a process of tying business needs to technical requirements (e.g., as the particular platform on which the software needs to run on or the systems with which the solution must interface). It clarifies why they are undertaking a particular project. Schwalbe (2000) suggests that the RFP should include: statement of the purpose, background information on the company issuing the RFP, basic requirements for the products and/or services being proposed, HW and SW environment, description of the RFP process, statement of work (SOW), and other information added (as appendices). The SOW should describe the work required for the procurement of the software and help vendors determines if they can deliver required goods and services.

Evaluation Preparations

Gather and Organise Resources

Lars and Matthew (2002) note that a reason for not detecting errors early is because the inadequacy of the test used by the team. The quality assurance of the evaluation project is jeopardised. To prevent this, the test team should ensure they have the resources to detect errors present. The adequacy of resources gathered should be determined at the same time potential vendors are identified. Resources could be added or updated to support the evaluation.

Determine the Evaluation Approach/Technique

Restrictions on Evaluating Software

Dean and Vigder (2002) state that, while purchasing software, there are some unique constraints on the ability to conduct effective testing. In general, it should be assumed that there is no access to the source code. If the source code is available it could not be modifiable and it means that the executable part cannot be tested internally and this rules out white box testing. Documentation should consist of user manuals and advertising materials and is not directed at evaluating the software (e.g., it does not describe the behaviour of the software in response to abnormal input).

Evaluation Techniques and Methods

Romney et al. (2000) suggest benchmarking while processing times of software are measured. Software with the lowest time is normally judged the most efficient. Oberndorf, Brownsword, Morris, and Sledge (1997) engaged scenario-based testing methods to represent typical procedures for the software to be programmed and not the software undergoing tests. Test procedures are developed based on scenarios and each is evaluated against a set of criteria. In this case, the initial scenarios are established using preliminary operational definitions. The results of this will serve as confirmation that the software performed satisfactory against set parameters.

Romney et al. (2000) suggest a point scoring technique to evaluate the vendor. Each criterion is assigned a weight based on its relevancy. The vendor is assigned a score based on how their proposal measures up to each criterion. The vendor with the highest score is then judged the "best." They argue that "requirements" costing is an alternative where the total cost of the proposed software is calculated. This provides an equitable basis for comparison.

Another method suggested by Voas, Charron, and McGraw (1997) is the use of fault injection techniques. This is effective when buyers do not have access to the source code. The method consists of inserting erroneous values into the control stream and checking the results. This technique is an example of evaluating (for discovery) to determine unknown or unexpected reactions of the product under evaluation.

Beizer (1995) suggests *black box testing* to allow a tester to treat each module as a unit that can be defined by its inputs and outputs (the interfaces to the module) without considering the route by which an input is transformed into a particular output. Visibility into the internal workings of the code module is not necessary and source code not required. An example of black box testing is boundary value analysis where inputs are supplied to the software to be tested (these values represent valid, invalid and parameters). The outputs are measured and accepted if they fall within expected limitations. This type of testing is used during acceptance testing and is the basis of validation testing, confirming the software performed the required functions.

Other techniques (Hausen & Welzel, 1993) include analysing product documentation, presentations, using trial versions, scheduling demonstrations, or attending training of the software. They suggest that one or more of the previously mentioned techniques could be used to supplement the evaluation of software. The project team should use discretion when selecting evaluation techniques as a company's approach and resources may vary.

Evaluation Considerations

Hausen and Welzel (1993) mention that some of the following principles should be taken into consideration:

- Repeat testing of the same product using the same product specifications with the same testing techniques must deliver similar results (Repeatability).
- Repeat evaluation of the same product to the same product specifications by different parties must deliver similar results (Reproducibility).
- The evaluation is free from bias while achieving any particular result (Impartiality).
- The result is obtained with minimum subjective judgment (Objectivity).

Product Evaluation

Hausen and Welzel (1993) state that the evaluation process should consider software features (compared to the requirements document), product information (acquired from the RFP, product demonstration, information gathered from investigating vendors, etc.), evaluation techniques, and process information (e.g., results obtained from the testing techniques).

Capterra's methodology (2002) states that all software should be evaluated to determine if it meets requirements (functional and technical). Any additional (functional/technical) requirements should be listed and re-calculated. Missing requirements should be listed and cost incurred to add these features should be calculated. Price and maintenance levels of the product have to be evaluated by totalling cost and maintenance levels. Firms must consider initial product costs (also long-term costs (such as training, implementation costs, maintenance, and upgrading costs). Project teams should keep in mind that software is expensive and by picking the wrong one could have costly repercussions.

Final Evaluation of Vendor Companies Providing Possible Software Solution

Pollard (1999) suggested the evaluation of the support and maintenance staff of the vendor. He notes that it is necessary to know the number of people in customer support. The response time can be measured by calling the customer support department. The availability and quality of the implementation support also ought to be evaluated. The new software could have bugs and other problems (e.g., not meeting the required deadline). The vendor must provide training because users want to use the system properly.

He suggests following up on customer references, reviewing case studies and finding out how many companies are using the software. The financial stability of a vendor is an aspect to consider. Pollard (1999) supports this by suggesting the examination of the financial history and the long-term financial stability of the vendor.

Selecting the Software System

The total score of the software should be recorded on a scoring sheet when a point scoring technique is used. All the software must be listed from the highest to the lowest. The software with the highest score would represent the best fit for the organisation. Although the software with the highest score might represent the best solution for the company, there may be reasons unrelated to the requirements that could prevent an organisation from selecting software. Inconsistencies should be identified (also extremes in scoring that may influence it—or a competency or deficiency within a single business function). Criteria such as a business partnership, potential future business, or other intangibles, must also be included.

Notify the Vendor

Once the steering committee has approved the vendor, then the vendor should be notified and a contract drawn up. The diagram (on the next page) was derived from the theory to illustrate steps used during the evaluation and selection process.

Problem Statement

Brown and Wallnau (1996) state that organizations should recognize the importance of technology "refreshment":

- To improve the quality of their products and services
- To be competitive with organizations providing similar products and services
- To remain attractive to investors

Any organization should invest in appropriate software to stay in business. Careful decision-making on investment into software is therefore essential. Whether the release of an update, or the availability of new software, should force an organization to initiate an evaluation process that provides timely, balanced information on which decisions can be made.

The problem statement was thus stated as:

...the more thorough the evaluation of software, the greater the chances could be for the organization to select the software that will meet their business objective and the requirements of the users.

Research Methodology

Objective

The objective of the study is to determine whether Media24 uses the correct software evaluation and selection guidelines when purchasing software from a vendor as prescribed in the theory and whether these guidelines have obtained results. Based on the theory and the problem statement, the research questions were stated as follows:

- Is the software evaluation process of Media24 thorough enough to select software that fulfils their end-user requirements?
- Does the organisation pick software that meets the business objectives easily?

Limitations of the Study

The researchers had decided to exclude legal procedures and only focussed on the project from a technical viewpoint. Also they were not allowed to use the name of any software used by Media24 as it might discredit the vendor or Media24. The

Figure 1. Graphical summary of software selection

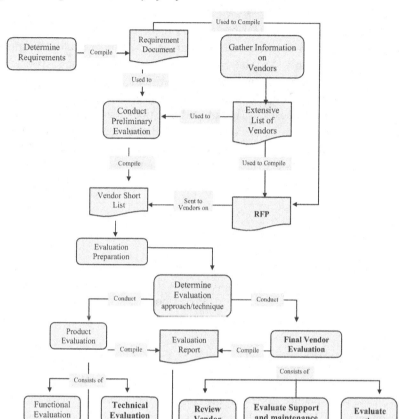

research scope also does not include the processes (e.g., contract negotiation) followed after a decision has been made.

Development of Questionnaire

The researchers compiled a questionnaire consisting of two sections (Section A and B). Section A contained seven sub-sections, covering aspects of evaluation and selection processes. Section B contains the user satisfaction survey. The questionnaire was handed to a Media24 IT manager who reviewed it. He also identified people responsible for evaluating and selecting software in Media24 to be respondents while he completed a questionnaire himself.

Section A was sent out to 15 decision-makers involved in acquiring software in Media24. The objective was to measure whether they used the evaluation techniques as prescribed in the theory. Section B was sent to 50 users of the software. The objective was to determine whether they were satisfied with present software. All questions where derived from the theory described earlier. A 5-point Lickert scale was used in most of the questions (it included questions that required respondents to pick more than one answer). The reason is to evaluate areas where answers from the respondent indicates an in depth approach to the evaluation process. At the end of each section, a section was dedicated to find out in more detail what respondents think.

Analysis of Data

The results of both sections were compared using cross tabulation. The data was captured and analyzed on an excel spreadsheet. Twelve "section A" respondents returned the questionnaires and 74% of the respondents who received section B returned the questionnaire.

Section A: Evaluation Process

Nearly all the respondents agree that the steering committee correctly directs the evaluation process (11). This indicates that people realise that there is a structure in place that could oversee the evaluation of software and is in agreement with a similar comment by Capterra (2002).

All the respondents agree that there are sufficient resources available to ensure that the evaluation process runs smoothly. Nine of the respondents indicated that the project team has enough expertise to conduct an evaluation. Three indicated that

Table 2. Project management structure

	SA	A	NDA	D	SD
There is a Steering Committee in place to oversee and direct the evaluation process	11	7	1	0	0
Sufficient resources are allocated to the evaluation process	4	8	0	0	0
A project team with the required expertise is assigned to conduct the evaluation and selection of the new software system.	3	5	1	3	0
AVERAGE	4	6	1	1	0

Table 3. Requirements definition

	SA	A	NDA	D	SD
Technical requirements are determined (e.g., the system interface)	5	7	0	0	0
The Functional requirements are determined (e.g., business objectives system has to fulfil)	5	5	2	0	0
Managerial requirements are determined (e.g., reporting capabilities, budget, timing)	4	8	0	0	0
Requirements are properly documented and easy to understand	2	7	1	2	0
AVERAGE	4	7	.5	.5	0

they disagree with this. There might be a problem that falls outside the scope of this study and needs to be addressed by management. The organisation therefore needs to assemble a project team that is representative of the people working in the organisation (see also Dean & Vigder, 2002). Nine of the respondents indicated that Media24 used the interview method to determine requirements. The same respondents have also used the present system to ensure that they meet the correct requirements (see Figure 4). Six respondents have indicated that they use questionnaires to collect requirements. It seems that project teams in Media24 prefer to use three methods to determine software requirements.

Table 4. Vendor identification and evaluation

	SA	A	NDA	D	SD
Various sources (e.g., Web sites) are investigated in order to identify the software available.	3	7	2	0	0
A preliminary evaluation is conducted to limit software that are going to be extensively evaluated.	3	7	0	1	1
The support and maintenance staff provided by the vendor is evaluated based on…					
…response time	4	7	1	0	0
…quality of support	1	9	2	0	0
…number of people	0	1	1	8	2
…cost	1	10	1	0	0
The company providing the software system is evaluated based on…					
…long term Financial stability	5	5	0	2	0
…customer References	4	7	1	0	0
…number of clients	4	5	3	4	0
…long and short term strategic planning	0	2	2	8	0
AVERAGE	2	7	1	.7	.3

All respondents have indicated that technical requirements are determined before-hand (systems interface). Ten of the respondents are happy that business objectives have been met while determining functional requirements. All agree that managerial requirements should be met when requirements are defined. Nine of the respondents noted that requirements are properly documented. Media24 needs to address this to ensure that people are in agreement otherwise it can become a problem.

Ten of the respondents agree that many sources should be investigated to identify correct software. The same number agrees that Media24 should ensure that software that meets requirements are evaluated. This is done to limit the number of products to be considered. On the other hand, 11 of the respondents agree that the support/maintenance staff provided by the vendor is evaluated on response time while the quality of support is rated high by 10 of the respondents. It seems to the authors that 'old fashioned' values are still important while looking at new IT investments. This is in agreement with the statement made by Capterra (2002) that end-users value help provided by the supplier.

The number of people working for the vendor is not regarded as important by the respondents; as long as their service is not affected by it (quality is rated higher). Eight stated that cost plays a role while maintenance is evaluated. Most of the respondents noted that the vendor should be evaluated on financial stability and customer references. The number of clients and long-term strategy of the vendors were not used when looking how reputable the vendor is. This is something that Media24 and similar organisations need to investigate.

Table 5 displays the data collected on the RFP. Most of the respondents agree that this is complied with by Media24. Many (10) stated that the evaluation processes

Table 5. Request for proposal

	SA	A	NDA	D	SD
A Request for proposal is sent to Vendors.	10	1	1	0	0
The RFP includes…					
…the purpose of the RFP	1	9	2	0	0
…all necessary background information of the company issuing the RFP	1	4	6	1	0
…the requirements for the new system	4	7	1	0	0
…the hardware and software environment currently being used	3	4	4	1	0
…instructions on how to reply and a description of how responses will be dealt with	9	2	1	0	0
…a statement of work (SOW) that includes the required work needed for the procurement of the new software solution.	1	9	2	0	0
AVERAGE	4	5	2.6	.4	0

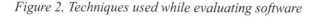

Figure 2. Techniques used while evaluating software

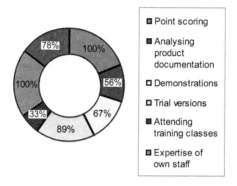

are properly documented while thought is given to objectivity (11) and impartiality (9). Most (10) of them agree that repeatability is lacking while reproducibility (7) is important and needs careful attention. Impartiality is an aspect that needs to be addressed as a third of the people noted that it is lacking. The averages for the request for proposal can be improved but because there are individual items that management of Media24 needs to pay attention to as stated. The common method used to evaluate the software is the point scoring technique (Figure 2). Trial versions of software have a better chance to be selected if it was analysed previously or used. The other method that Media24 uses to evaluate software is the expertise of their staff in a particular field.

Table 6 shows the evaluation process. The respondents were positive that the final score used to determine how well the software product meets the requirements is a good method. Nine respondents are in agreement that the documentation to do this

Table 6. Evaluation of the product

	SA	A	NDA	D	SD
The evaluation score of the product is determined based on how well it meets the pre-determined requirements.	1	11	0	0	0
The evaluation process and results are properly documented.	1	8	2	1	0
When conducting the evaluation thought, is given to…					
...Objectivity	7	4	1	0	0
...Repeatability	0	0	4	7	1
...Reproducibility	0	6	4	2	0
...Impartiality	7	2	2	1	0
AVERAGE	3	5	2	1.8	.2

Table 7. Results obtained from decision makers

	SA	A	NDA	D	SD	TOTAL
The final decision is not made solely based on the evaluation result, but also includes other intangible aspects (e.g., potential future business)	1	9	2	0	0	12
I am satisfied with the evaluation results obtained by our company.	4	7	0	1	0	12
AVERAGE	2.5	8	1	.5	0	12

evaluation is well laid out beforehand. Management needs to convince the three that does not agree to accept the documentation as presented. Objectivity is complied with but repeatability of the evaluation is not highly thought off (and the same for reproducibility). Nine of the respondents noted that the tests were impartial. Again, it would be a task for management to convince the remaining three that this is the case before problems are experienced (also supported by Shelly et al., 1998).

Most of the people agree that the final decision to acquire software is based upon the evaluation results. Eleven of the respondents agree that they are happy with the results achieved by Media24. Agreeing meant that they use the methods as prescribed in theory but there are some methods that are not used presently (e.g., benchmarking and black box testing). These should be investigated and used to ensure that the methods presently being used is still considered the best (Beizer, 1995).

User Satisfaction and Overall Effectiveness of Evaluation Process Used

Nearly all the respondents (11) at Media24 are satisfied with the software that was purchased by Media24. Eight of the respondents have agreed that it falls within the parameters set by the organisation. The respondents that do not agree (4) may be users that were not part of the project team. They should be convinced that the software is of benefit to Media24. Eleven of the respondents agreed that the software meet their requirements. This is supported in their article by Michel and Fitzgerald (1997) who stated that normally most of the users who were part of the process are happy with the software.

This could mean that the individual user requirements agree with Media24's requirements. However, seven of the respondents agree that there is room for improvement This should be investigated in another study as this falls outside the scope of this study. This does not agree with previous statements made by the respondents. Maybe the present evaluation procedure should be extended to inquire about reasons why

Table 8. User satisfaction

	SA	A	NDA	D	SD
I am satisfied with the software I am using.	2	9	0	1	0
The commercial software system fulfills the business objective it was assigned to.	1	7	3	1	0
The commercial software system adheres to my requirements.	2	8	0	1	0
There is no room for improvement for the commercial software system I am using.	0	4	2	5	1
AVERAGE	1.5	7	1.25	2	.25

Figure 3. Number of complaints from users

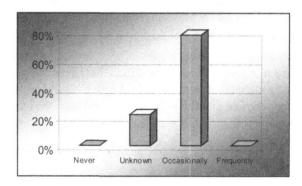

the respondents argue that there is room for improvement. This should be included as part of the evaluation.

The respondents (9) complain about the software occasionally to ensure that management pay attention. Seven of the users argue that there is room for improvement. This would require another survey to find out why users complain about the software and if there is room for improvement.

Section B: Assessment

The main objective of section B was to assess whether the users where satisfied with the software acquired by Media24. There are some complaints lodged by the respondents (e.g., the systems response time and redundant processes and procedures

Figure 4. Key area's average

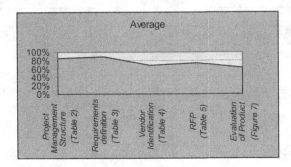

included in the current system and that the software does not integrate with other software). The figure on the next page illustrates the percentage respondents who agreed that they use the correct evaluation techniques. The results are summarized according to key areas.

An area of concern should be the evaluation of the product for management (only 63% average with some areas that were identified that needs attention). Eighty-six percent of users agreed that they where satisfied with the software obtained. Sixty-five percent of users verified that the software systems meet the business objective and 84% noted that the software they are using meets their requirements (also supported by Voas et al., 1997).

Discussion and Conclusion

From the findings, the researchers conclude that Media24 has identified and used the better suited evaluation techniques as described in the theory. End-users were generally satisfied with the software and agreed that the software meet their requirements and business objectives. The above-mentioned statement answers the first research question. It is evident that software that help Media24 achieve its goal has a better chance of being selected (answer to the second research question).

The researchers note that there were some complaints mentioned by end-users. They feel that this "unhappiness" could be because not all employees were actively involved in determining the requirements or because the requirements were not communicated to all users. A manager during an interview noted that the software he was using does not integrate with one of the sub-systems. This eventually leads to more work, as manual reconciliation has to be done between the sub-system and the software. This could be because the requirements or the software weren't described properly in the request for proposal. Most of the statements indicated that e-commerce organisations should be careful how they select software (Capterra, 2002; Hausen & Welzel, 1993; Lars & Methven, 2002). This was also supported by the research findings of this study.

Future Research

Further research might be needed to refine or redesign the evaluation approach used by Media24. The reason is that the current software will be outdated soon and with the rise of new technology, the evaluation and selection process might have to be adjusted. There were also some issues that were not picked up before the installation of the product (e.g., integration with sub systems). This indicates why the evaluation and selection process might have to be revised. Other studies could help place emphasis on the use of specific evaluation models. In order to speed up the process and to gather more data more respondents will have to be included in the sample before the next survey is conducted.

References

Base Consulting Group: Strategic Technology White Paper Series. (2000). *Software selection: A business-based methodology*. Retrieved August 2002, from http://www.baseconsulting.com/ assets/PDFs/BusinessBasedMethodology.pdf

Beizer, B. (1995). *Black box testing: Techniques for functional testing of software and systems*. New York: John Wiley & Sons Inc.

Buyerzone.com. (n.d.). Retrieved August 2002, from http://www.buyerzone.com/ software,internet_software/printable_bg.html

Brown, A.W., & Wallnau, K. C. (1996). *A framework for systematic evaluation of software technologies*. Software Engineering Institute Carnegie Mellon University. Pittsburgh. Scientific Literature Digital Library. Retrieved August 2002, from http://citeseer.nj.nec.com/cache/papers/cs/23040/http:zSzzSzwebfuse. cqu.edu.auzSzInformationzSzResourceszSzReadingszSzpaperszSzsoftware. evaluation.pdf/brown96framework.pdf

Capterra detail-level software selection methodology. (2002). Retrieved August 2002, from http://www.capterra.com/detailed_software_selection_methodology.pdf

Dean, J. C., & Vigder, M. R. (2002). *COTS software evaluation techniques*. National Research Council Canada: Software Engineering Group. Retrieved August 2002, from http://seg.iit.nrc.ca/papers/NRC43625.pdf

Hausen, H. L., & Welzel, D. (1993). *Guides to software evaluation scientific literature digital library*. Retrieved August 2002, from http://citeseer.nj.nec.com/cache/papers/cs/12053/ftp:zSzzSzftp.gmd.dezSzGMDzSzSW-QualityzSzEval-Guide746.pdf/hausen93guides.pdf

Lars, M., & Matthew, G. (2002). *Ten points for improving the testing process: White paper*. Retrieved August 2002, from http://www.tautester.com/download/ten_points.pdf

Levinson, M. (2001, July). Vendor management: Do diligence. *CIO Magazine*. Retrieved August 2002, from http://www.cio.com/archive/070101/vet.html

Michell, V., & Fitzgerald, G. (1997). The IT outsourcing market place: Vendors and their selection. *Journal of Information Technology, 12*(3), 223-237.

Oberndorf, P., Brownsword, L., Morris, E., & Sledge, C. (1997). *Workshop on COTS-based systems*. Retrieved August 2002, from www.sei.cmu.edu/pub/documents/ 97.reports/pdf/97sr019.

Pollard, W. E. (1999, July). Confessions of a software salesman. *CIO Magazine*. Retrieved August 2002, from http://www.cio.com/archive/070199/expert.html

Romney, B. R., & Steinbart, P. J. (2000). *Accounting information systems* (8th ed., pp. 638-641). NJ: Prentice Hall.

Schwalbe, K. (2000). *Information technology project management*. PA: Course Technology. 311, accessed August 2002.

Shelly, G. B., Cashman, T. J., & Rosenblatt, H. J. (1998). *Systems analysis and design* (3rd ed.). Cambridge: Course Technology.

Voas, J., Charron, F., & McGraw, G. (1997). *Predicting how badly "good" software can behave*. Reliable Software Technologies Corporation. Scientific Literature Digital Library. Retrieved August 2002, from http://citeseer.nj.nec.com/cache/papers/cs/743/ftp:zSzzSzrstcorp.comzSzpubzSzpaperszSzieee-gem.pdf/voas97predicting.pdf

Ward, S. (2001, December). Keep it simple when buying enterprise apps. *CIO Magazine*. Retrieved August 2002, from http://www.cio.com/analyst/051101_hurwitz.html

Chapter XIII

Internet:
A Right to Use and Access Information, or a Utopia?

Inban Naicker, University of KwaZulu-Natal, South Africa

Abstract

This study examines the impact of the Internet on a student society by investigating the effective use of the Internet at tertiary education. The main objectives of the studies were to determine whether the Internet is being optimally utilized at tertiary education, and to evaluate the level of utilization of the Internet. The study also identified problems experienced by students. A convenience sample of 95 undergraduate students was used at the University of KwaZulu Natal (Westville campus) (only information systems and technology (IS&T) students were included in the study because they had access to computers). The researcher compiled a questionnaire to collect the data. The study revealed that the activity that students mostly used was e-mail systems. The majority of the students (81%) have indicated there are insufficient computers for proper Internet usage. Fifty-eight percent of the students still use the library to access information. Seventy-four percent of the students have indicated that the Internet is easy to use.

Introduction

The Internet has been in a state of rapid evolution since its beginning in the late 1960s, and is currently evolving and growing faster than ever (Botha, Bothma, & Geldenhuys, 2004). Already the Internet has had an effect on the people who do business, study people who interact with each other, and how people live. However, one can expect to see more changes as society moves deeper into the 21st century. Cheung and Heung (1999) state that universities across the world are expanding their investment in Internet technologies and are promoting Internet usage in education. The study carried out by them showed that Internet usage was having a positive impact on students. The Internet can be a valuable tool at universities.

However, students are not optimally utilizing the Internet to its fullest advantage. They are not always using the Internet for academic use, and do not spend enough productive time on the Internet. An example of where students are misappropriating the Internet is the illegal downloading of music and games.

This study will therefore briefly discuss the Internet and the impact it has on available information for tertiary students. It also explains the research methodology on how the data was collected and handled and it will discuss the results as well. Finally, some recommendations will be made.

Literature Review

This article discusses what the Internet is, how it is used, and its implications for tertiary usage. Much like the Concord leaving the competition in its jet stream at twice the speed of sound, nothing else has come close to the growth experienced by the Internet—not the industrial revolution, not the electronics revolution, and not even the computer revolution (Bothma, 2000). Berkeley (2004) defines the Internet as a network of networks.

According to Berkeley (2004), the Internet is the transport vehicle for the information stored in files or documents on another computer. The Internet itself does not contain information but is a mechanism for information dissemination and a medium for collaboration and interaction between individuals and their computers without regard for geographic location (Singh, 2002). Content created on the Internet ranges from simple e-mail messages to sophisticated sites incorporating sounds, images, and words. The Internet is therefore arguably one of the most significant technological developments of the late 20th century (Jagbora, 2003).

History of the Internet

Botha et al. (2004) note that the first baby steps, which eventually lead to the Internet as we know it today, were taken in the early 1960s at the height of the Cold War. The U.S. government was looking for a way to maintain communications in the event of a nuclear attack. A team of engineers formed the Advanced Research Project Agency (ARPA), a part of the U.S. Department of Defense, teamed up with Rand Corporation to develop a network that could be used with confidence. Although the military did not decide to use this approach, it provided the basis of the Internet (Botha et al,. 2004).

ARPAnet initially connected major computers at the University of California at Los Angeles, the University of California at Santa Barbara, Stanford Research Institute, and the University of Utah (Macura, 2004). According to Hughes (1994), ARPAnet was an experimental network designed to support military research. The idea was that every computer on the network could talk, as a peer, with any other computer. This early network proved so successful that soon other computer sites located within universities, government, and large organizations began linking to this network. Furthermore, this form of communication and the type of information that was shared over this network was very computer-orientated and user friendly (Bothma, 2000).

The Internet Working Group (INWG) was the first body to take up this role under the leadership of Vinton Cerf (known as the father of the Internet). ARPAnet's original standard for communication, developed by Cerf and Bob Kahn, became known as the network control protocol (NCP). As time went by, the NCP was superceded by a higher level and more sophisticated standard, known as the transmission control protocol/internet protocol or the TCP/IP. All networks joined together became known as the Internet (Botha et al., 2004).

Growth of the Internet

Clark (2003) notes that the Internet is the fastest growing technology in the world. Current estimates indicate that over half the estimated 200 million Internet users are in the United States. South Africa was ranked 25th in the world in terms of Internet connectivity (Clark, 2003). According to Singh (2002), it has taken 7 years to reach a 25% market share, as opposed to the telephone that took 35 years, and the television that took 26 years. A report states that 414 million people had Internet access at the end of 2000 and predicts that figure will almost triple to 1.17 billion by 2005. About 730 million of those will be using wireless devices such as Web-enabled cell phones to go online. In countries with low Internet penetration, most wireless Internet devices will be the primary or only Internet access device (eTForecasts ..., 2001).

According to a survey undertaken by a Canadian newspaper (General social survey ..., 2001), the survey found that people who use the Internet tend to be younger, have higher incomes, and more education than those who don't. About 70% of individuals aged 25 to 29 used the Internet, compared with 61% of those aged 35 to 39, and only 13% of seniors aged 65 and over. Individuals with university education were much more likely to use the Internet than those with less than a high school diploma. Among individuals 20 or older, 13% of those with less than a high school diploma used the Internet, compared with 79% with University education.

As far as South Africa is concerned, a recent study undertaken by Arthur Goldstuck and Cathy Stadler of Acuity Media Africa *cited* by Bothma (2000), revealed that the number of Internet users in South Africa, rated within the top 30 Internet user countries in the world, is estimated to be 1.2 million, expected to rise to 2 million by 2000.

Services on the Internet

World Wide Web

The Web was created at CERN, Switzerland's nuclear research facility, by Tim Berners-Lee in 1989 (Bothma, 2000). He states that the term Web was coined by Berners-Lee in 1990 to describe information spanning the planet like a giant spider's Web, with threads linking knowledge and information from all over the globe, making it available to a worldwide audience. According to the article, the Web was originally conceived and developed to meet the demand for automatic information sharing between scientists working in different universities all over the world (What about CERN's ..., 2002). Hughes (1994) states that the initial project proposal outlined a simple system of using networked hypertext to transmit documents and communicate among members.

In 1991, an early WWW system was released to the high-energy physics community via the CERN program library. Early in 1993, the National Centre for Supercomputing Applications (NCSA) at the University of Illinois released a version of their browser. The world's First International World-Wide Web Conference was held at CERN in May. By the end of 1994, the Web had 10,000 servers, 2000 were commercial, and 10 million users (What about CERN's ..., 2002).

What is the World Wide Web?

According to Hughes (1994), the WWW is officially described as a wide-area hypermedia information retrieval initiative aiming to give universal access to a large universe of documents. It is basically a subset of the Internet and is a way of looking at and organizing the information on the Internet. The Web provides access to information on (Clark, 2003):

- Individuals, organizations, government (legal, commercial, and educational)
- Learning material
- Health services
- Journals and newspapers
- Virtual libraries, art galleries, and museums
- Virtual shopping malls
- Databases and archives
- Advertisements and promotional goods
- Pornography

The Web organizes information according to pages interlinked with each other using hypertext (Bothma, 2000). The current foundation on which the WWW functions is the programming language called hypertext mark-up language (HTML). Every document site, movies, sound file, or anything you find on the Web has a unique uniform resource locator (URL) that identifies what computer the thing is on, where it is within the computer, and its specific file name (Berkeley, 2004).

Web Browsers

The prerequisites for the WWW are a computer, a connection to the Internet, and a browser. The function of a Web browser is to interpret the programming language of the Web pages (HTML) and transform it into words and graphics. On each page, certain words, phrases, or even images are highlighted, and clicking on them causes the browser to go and find another page (What about CERN's ..., 2002). Berkeley (2004) describes a browser as a computer program that resides on your computer enabling the user to use the computer to view documents.

The first Web browser to become truly popular and capture the imagination of the public was NCSA Mosaic. Netscape is the browser that introduced most of all the remaining major features that define a Web browser as users know it. Boutell (2004), however, argues that Microsoft Internet Explorer is by far the most common Web browser in use. According to Bothma (2000), the most popular browser in use then was Microsoft's Internet Explorer with between 55-74% of the market share, followed by Netscape Navigator with between 26-35% of the market.

E-Mail

Lerner (2004) notes that e-mail is a message sent from one computer, known as a mail server, to travel over the Internet. Once it arrives at the destination mail server, it's stored in an electronic mailbox until the recipient receives it. To send e-mail, a connection to the Internet and access to a mail server, this forwards the mail. The standard protocol for sending e-mail is called simple mail transfer protocol (SMTP). The advantages of e-mail noted by Grant and McBride (2000) as: It's fast, cheap, and reliable.

File Transfer Protocol (FTP)

File transfer protocol (FTP) is the simplest and most secure way to exchange files over the Internet. The most common use for FTP is to download files from the Internet (Grant et al., 2000).

Internet Relay Chat (IRC)

Internet relay chat (IRC) is one of the most popular and most interactive services on the Internet. IRC lets people all over the world to participate in real-time conversations and was written by Oikarinen in 1988 (IRC, 2004).

Newsgroups

Newsgroups are a collection of messages pertaining to a particular subject. They are a combination of bulletin boards and newsletters, with each dedicated to a specific interest, hobby, profession, or obsession (Grant et al., 2000).

Barriers of Entry to Internet Usage

According to Goble (2002), the barriers of entry to Internet usage are *telecommunication costs, ISP costs, equipment costs, training and computer literacy*, and *language*. These are discussed next (Goble, 2002):

- **Telecommunication costs:** South Africa has only one authorized telecommunications company, Telkom. It has a monopoly and is the sole supplier of the country's telecommunication infrastructure.

- **Internet service provider (ISP) costs:** Internet access to users is provided by local ISPs. An ISP is a company that provides individuals or companies with access to the Internet, as well as other related services such as Web site development and/or the hosting of Web sites. It is usually a commercial organization that maintains a direct and permanent connection with the global Internet via the Telkom telecommunications infrastructure (Bothma, 2000). The initial cost is the purchase of a subscription and then a monthly charge for that subscription.

- **Equipment costs:** Access to the Internet implies that the correct equipment is available and configured. The majority of computer hardware is imported into South Africa from abroad. A&T *cited* by Goble (2002) recommends the following:

  o   PC with a Pentium 90 processor or faster, Windows 95, 98, Me, NT 4.0 2000, or XP, Microsoft Internet Explorer 5.0 or higher

  o   128MB RAM

  o   40gB of unused hard disk space

  o   A 32-bit colour display

This makes the cost of entry into this medium high for the average South African.

- **Training and computer literacy:** The Internet is a complex network of Web sites and Web pages developed independently and without any pattern. Users should be able to use the Internet, and tools such as e-mail, as effectively and efficiently as possible. Training in both the use of an Internet browser and the use of a PC is integral to being able to access the Internet (Goble, 2002). The average illiteracy rate in South Africa in 1999 was 15% of the total population. South Africa has a computer literacy percentage of 8% of the population (Goble, 2002).

- **Language:** The Internet was founded and based using the English language to send and receive information. Therefore, people who are unable to read, write, or speak English are excluded from communicating in this medium.

The Impact of the Internet in Tertiary Education

In most universities, the Internet is already an important medium of communication, a way of enhancing access to educational resources and a means of creating interactive communities of learning (Pickering, 2000). Cheung et al. (1999) state that many universities across the world are expanding their investment in Internet technologies and are actively promoting Internet usage in university education. The study carried out by Cheung et al. (1999) showed that the Internet usage was found to have positive impacts on students learning. The potential role and use of the Internet in the provision of information services for both research and study in South Africa's tertiary institutions is no longer a highly debatable issue (Kaniki, 1999).

Fleck and McQueen (1999) argue that the Internet revolution arrived faster and with more complications than many institutions expected. They further state that the rapid development of search engines and the expanded use of the Web increased the demand for Internet-related services at universities. However, the Internet is unorganized and Web sites appear, disappear, move, or mutate on a daily basis. While the Internet is difficult to search, it is even more difficult to search it well. Moreover, the information found on the Internet has both useful and useless information co-existing (Jagbora, 2003). The rapid growth of some of the following places a real burden on institutions (Fleck et al., 1999):

- Pornography and hate sites, and downloading of useless information
- Interference with legitimate research and academic use
- Hacking, security
- Cost, growth
- Legal issues related to fair use, harassment, and so forth
- Chat rooms
- Access by non-students
- Competition with ISPs

There are thousands of Internet "home pages" which serve as information sources for institutions and organizations. Most Universities throughout the world have established their presence on the Internet, thereby making it possible for researchers to access past and current research publications. Prospective students can also access information on courses being offered by institutions as well as their admission requirements. Journals, magazines, newspapers, books, and archives provide another important avenue for the construction, publication, and circulation of texts (Jagbora, 2003).

Due to poor funding, university libraries ability to acquire new books and to subscribe to journals have been badly affected (Chifwepa, 2002). Academic libraries in South Africa are and will therefore increasingly come under pressure to provide Internet-based information services (Kaniki, 1999). While traditional library resources and services are suited for particular kinds of research and study information needs within the academia, the Internet is suitable for other needs and it can supplement traditional library services. The question for academic libraries, should be not so much as to when will the Internet replace the library or how best will librarians counter the challenge but rather, as how best to incorporate the Internet into services offered by the library (Kaniki, 1999).

According to Dos Santos (1998), technological advances and explosive growth of the Internet are rapidly eliminating the time and space constraints inherent in the existing model. Dos Santos gives an example of where one can easily have students view a video of an instructor's lecture from anywhere and at their leisure, and students can chat (using text, audio, or video) without getting together physically (Dos Santos, 1998).

The Internet provides an educational discourse in which learners can interact widely with other members of a learning community. Their interaction for learning can be immediate, prompt, widely shared, and resource supportive, which may not be possible in a traditional mode of teaching, confined by the classrooms physical condition (De Villiers & Cronje, 2001). Irdus and Latch *cited* by Katz and Yablon (2002) state that through the Internet, learning has become significantly more flexible and content sources much more accessible.

Taylor and Cohen (2001) note that the primary institutional processes where the Internet can have an impact on tertiary education are *communication, information and research, teaching and learning, and services and commerce.*

- **Communication:** Communications solutions available via the Internet include e-mail, instant messaging, individualized Web portals, video conferencing, listservs, and group calendaring.

- **Information and research:** The Internet has revolutionized the process of accessing and retrieving information.

- **Teaching and learning:** How an institution employs the Internet to facilitate teaching and learning depends heavily upon its mission, vision, competition, and positioning. Examples of teaching and learning tools include: software such as WebCT, Blackboard, and Prometheus); online class content; audio/video capabilities; instructional chat rooms; and distance education.

- **Services and commerce:** Many services and commercial transactions benefit in terms of timeliness, accuracy, cost, convenience, and customer satisfaction.

Information Overload

Since the advent of the printing press, there has been increasing pressure on individuals to keep abreast and in control of information. The Internet has compounded the situation by increasing the volume of available information and the speed at which new knowledge becomes accessible (Rochat, 2002). He defines information overload as large quantities of varied sources of information received on a regular basis at a rate that limits assimilation and increased by unsolicited information. Lyman and Varian (2000) notes that 2.1 billion unique, publicly accessible Web pages are on the Internet, while 7.3 million are added per day. The "deep" or "invisible "Web (information generally inaccessible to software spiders, for example databases) is 500 times larger than the visible Web. Butcher et al., cited by Rochat (2002), list the factors that contribute to information overload:

- Information is collected to illustrate a commitment to rationalize and competence while information is sought to verify the information collected.
- Vast amounts of unsolicited information is received.
- Managers require information to support decisions made.
- Information is collected in case it is useful.
- Managers play it safe and obtain all information possible.
- When the person does not understand available information he/she feels overwhelmed by the information.

In an attempt to deal with the quantity of information, people have developed the following adaptive mechanisms (Rochat, 2002):

- **Chunking:** Gathering information on the basis of generic terms
- **Omission:** Skipping of information
- **Queuing:** Deferment of processing at peak times
- **Filtering:** Neglect or irrelevant information
- **Capitulation:** Escape from the task

Information overload is a problem in an evolving society. Similarly, there is no solution to handle the vast quantities of information that are faced with on a daily basis. The solution is summarized by Lyman et al. (2000) as the challenge is to learn to swim in that sea (of information), rather than drown in it.

Internet Addiction

Since the advent of high quality, low-cost hardware, and software, the development of a graphically based, easy-to-use method of accessing remote computer sites (i.e., the WWW), use of the Internet by students has increased dramatically. Institutions find that students cultures are created via e-mail, Web surfing, multiple user dungeons (MUDS, which are interactive, role-playing games), spending time in chat rooms, and homepage production. Students provide e-mail addresses as the preferred code of contact rather than telephone numbers. Although the Internet can be a powerful tool for academic study and personal communication, for some people, Internet access can prove to be a temptation that is hard to resist. Pathological or problematic use of the Internet, also called "Internet addiction," is a behaviour pattern that appears to be affecting more and more people, including students (Kandell, 1998). Kandell describes Internet addiction as a psychological dependence on the Internet regardless of the type of activity once logged off.

In research conducted over the past four years, psychologists have theorized that it is possible to become addicted to the Internet. The addiction has been named Internet Addiction Disorder (IAD). To be diagnosed with IAD, an individual must meet some of the criteria. These criteria include developing a tolerance to the Internet and increasing Internet usage steadily, developing withdrawal symptoms, and surfing the Internet for longer that was intended and socially isolating oneself from friends or family members (Kovach, 2001). Research, according to Friedenberg (2002), estimates that about 3% of those who go online may suffer from problematic usage.

Kandell (1998) argues that university students as a group appear more vulnerable to developing a dependence on the Internet than most segments of society. Use of the Internet in society and on institutions is growing at an exponential rate. Although the Internet is a tool for gathering information and for interpersonal communication, dangers exist for those who make it the central focus of their lives. Research in this area is just starting, but more is needed to understand the full scope of Internet addiction and the most effective modes of treatment (Kandell, 1998).

Plagiarism on the Internet

Although plagiarism has been around as long as students have, the Internet has dramatically increased the ease of and opportunities for plagiarism. "Cyber-plagiarism" is the term used to describe the process by which students either copy ideas found on the Internet without giving proper attribution, or the process by which students download research papers from the Web, in whole or in part, and submit it as original work (Guide to plagiarism ..., 2004).

Plagiarism has never been easier than it is today. The Internet now makes it easy to find thousands of relevant sources in seconds, and in the space of a short time, plagiarists can find, copy, and paste together a term paper, article, or even a book. Because the material online is produced by writers of varying levels of quality and professionalism, it is often difficult for educators and editors to identify plagiarism. Even when an educator does suspect plagiarism, the sheer size of the Internet seems to work in the plagiarists favour (Plagiarism.org, 2004). According to Harris (1996), the most often plagiarized works on the Web are "links" sites, such as "Yahoo."

Reasons for Plagiarism

The reasons for plagiarism are (Why students plagiarize ..., 2004):

- **Lack of research skills:** Many undergraduate students do not know how to search the library catalogue, search databases for journal articles, or use other reference sources.

- **Problems evaluating Internet sources:** Many students do not know how to critically evaluate Internet sources and this can impact on the students writing.

- **Confusion between plagiarism and paraphrasing:** Studies indicate that up to 60% of students cannot distinguish between paraphrased and plagiarized text. The problem is magnified when students need to paraphrase unfamiliar vocabulary and technical terms.

- **Confusion about terminology:** Terminology is another problem that perplexes students and compounds their confusion and anxiety. Many students do not understand the difference between a report and an essay, between exposition and argumentation.

- **Confusion about how to properly cite sources:** The lack of consistency among the different style guides compounds the problems that students experience when citing sources.

- **Poor time management and organizational skills:** Undergraduate students often do not have the time management or organizational skills necessary to complete a large research paper.

Strategies to Avoid Plagiarism

In order to avoid plagiarism, students should (Harris, 1996):

- Give credit whenever you use another person's idea, opinion, or theory.
- Put in quotations everything that comes directly from the text.

- Paraphrase.
- Check your paraphrase against the original text.

Another option would be to use a plagiarism-detection service. Turniton offers a plagiarism-detection service that addresses this growing problem of plagiarism. In an Australian study, Turnitin.com detected 166 of the essays, or 9% of the total, had more than a quarter of their material pilfered from electronic sources. Fourteen percent of the essays had 5% or more of the material plagiarized (Foster, 2002).

Internet Abuse

Cyber-Crime

The Internet remains an open network that offers users no guarantee of security, privacy, or integrity (Schoeman, 2000). Botha et al. (2004) defines cyber-crime as the use of the Internet and its technologies to commit crime on individuals or organizations. Security on the other hand, is the means by which crime can be reduced or eliminated. The increase in Internet security breaches can be attributed to the following aspects (Botha et al., 2004) such as: The Internet is an *open system*, and the communication path is inherently unsecured.

Hacking

Conlin cited by Botha et al. (2004) describes hacking as the obsessive use of computers to gain unauthorized access into corporate systems. There are two types of attacks (i.e., passive attack and active attacks). In a passive attack, the perpetrator simply monitors the traffic to try and learn secrets. In an active attack, the perpetrator tries to break through the defences (Schoeman, 2000).

E-Mail Abuse

Watson (2003) defines spam as simply unsolicited and bulk mail. Unsolicited means that the recipient didn't give consent to receive the e-mail. The content could be commercial such as advertisement or company newsletter, or non-commercial such as joke e-mails or chain letters. Flame mail is hate mail that is transmitted over the Internet. Hate mail is used to incite employees against each other, or against the organization. For example, in 2002, a member of staff sent an e-mail around the then University of Durban-Westville campus purporting to be from another member of staff, making comments about colleagues and the management of the University (Botha et al., 2004).

Viruses

Viruses are programs that have the ability to destroy computer files, programme files, and sometimes computer hardware. Virus scanners are necessary as they have caused a lot of damage over the past few years. According to experts, viruses represent a much bigger problem than hackers (Schoeman, 2000).

Privacy

Customers are often expected to fill in detailed forms when accessing certain sites. Unsecured sites expose the customer to abuse from cyber attackers. The attacker can very easily obtain the personal information of the customer, such as residential addresses, account numbers, and passwords. These could be used to send the customer spam, flame mail, or even personal abuse such as stalking and assault (Botha et al., 2004).

Downloading Music Off the Internet

Over the past few years, there have been many technological developments granting people the ability to download music off the Internet. By law, downloading a digital song violates the intellectual property rights of the artist, or in most cases, of the record companies who contracted those rights from the artist (Choi, 2002).

Universities need to make every effort to educate students about what they are doing when they download music from the Internet. Institutions need to monitor student shares on computers and electronic storage systems that belong to the Universities. They must ensure that MP3s and other copyright-protected materials are not readily available for download to users either on or off campus (Powell, 2003).

Pornography

Pornography is defined as pictures, writing, or other material that is sexually explicit and sometimes equates sex with power and violence. Adult-orientated sites make up less than 2% of all content on the Web. While sexually explicit material comprises only a small fraction of online content, that fraction is highly visible, controversial and accounts for a significant amount of Web traffic (Wright, 2004).

Summary

The literature has shown that problems exist on the Internet. The following research questions were not answered:

1. Is the Internet usage at tertiary education moving towards less learning efficiency and more time spent for non-study purposes?
2. Are students spending enough "productive" time on the Internet?
3. Does the university have enough computers for Internet usage?
4. Does the Internet help students with their studies?

This section has discussed the review of the Internet and issues that aft students and their application of Internet searches for information. The next section will discuss the various methods used to collect the data.

Methodology

The main aim of this study is to determine whether the Internet is being optimally utilized in tertiary education for information purposes, and to evaluate the level of utilization of the Internet using the University of KwaZulu-Natal (Westville).

Sampling

Convenience sampling is used in exploratory research where the researchers are interested in getting an inexpensive approximation of the truth. As the name implies, the sample is selected because they are convenient. This non-probability method is often used during preliminary research efforts to get a gross estimate of the results, without incurring the cost or time required to select a random sample.

The sampling method used was convenience sampling. A sample of 95 was drawn from the institution for the study. The 95 respondents were compromised of:

- 40-first year students
- 30-second year students
- 25-third year students

Only information systems and technology (IS&T) students were used for the study, as they were easily accessible. Furthermore, information systems and technology students have access to computers to use the Internet readily. Postgraduate students were not included in the study as they were not readily available.

The study was conducted at the University of KwaZulu Natal (Westville campus). Also, there is no known documentation of studies done at the University of KwaZulu Natal (Westville campus) after an extensive search was done at the library.

The Instrument

The researchers compiled a questionnaire to collect the data and were handed out to students during their self-study sessions. According to Walonick (1997), questionnaires are special purpose documents that allow the researchers to collect information and opinions from respondents. Questionnaires allow the researchers to collect data from a large number of respondents while maintaining uniform responses.

The researchers decided to use a combination of both open format and closed-ended questions The questionnaire compromised of dichotomous scale questions such as yes or no type of questions, tick the correct box, and one ordinal scale question, where respondents were required to use ranking. The researchers will use the questionnaire to collect the data and will do a correlation analysis using SPSS after collating the data on an EXCEL spreadsheet.

Presentation of Results

This section deals with the presentation and analysis of data collected. The aim of this is to obtain a measure of association between each of the given variables. The majority of the respondents (59%) fell into the age group between 18 to 20, followed by the 20 to 22 age group, which made up 27% of the sample. Respondents aged 22

Figure 1. Age distribution

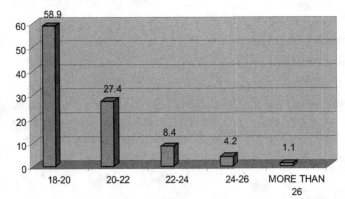

to 24 accounted for 8%, followed by 4% in the 24 to 26 age category. The smallest group was older then 26 years (one respondent). The reason why this age group is so small is because tertiary education students are young and the majority of them starts university at an early age and often completes their degrees/diplomas within three to four years. This is probably the reason why majority of the respondents fell into 18 to 20 category.

The first large group (64%) spends less than 3 hours on the Internet. The second largest group (24%) spends 3-6 hours on the Internet. Nearly 10% of the respondents indicated that they spend between 6-12 hours using the Internet. The smallest group comprising of only one respondent uses the Internet more than 12 hours per week. It is evident that students are not spending a lot of time on the Internet. The reason why 64.2% of students spend less than 3 hours on the Internet is probably because of lectures or other activities/commitments. Only one respondent shows that if a student uses the Internet for more than 12 hours, he or she could have an addiction problem. This agrees with the statement made by Kovach (2001) that students develop a tolerance to the Internet, and has an inherent desire to surf the Internet for longer periods of time. Psychologists have theorized, according to Kovach (2001), that it is possible to become addicted to the Internet.

Nearly 50% of respondents have made the attempt to learn the Internet on their own, and it can be stated that they are Internet literate. This finding substantiates the statement by Katz and Yablon (2002) that through the Internet, learning will become more flexible, and will be a way of enhancing educational resources. This finding also shows that lecturers are not assisting students on how to use the Internet since they only constitute 21% of the respondents. Nearly 19% of the respondents indicated that they were taught by friend/s to use the Internet. Ten percent of respondents have indicated that they were exposed to the Internet by means such as computer magazines, newspapers, etc.

Figure 2. Period taken for ease of Internet usage

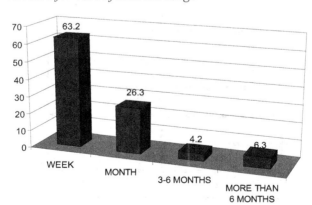

Ease of Internet Usage

Figure 2 depicts how long students took before they were comfortable using the Internet. The majority of respondents (63.2%) indicated that they took a week before they were comfortable using the Internet. Goble (2002) notes that for the beginner, the process of "surfing the net" is both taunting and difficult. Training in both the use of an Internet browser and the use of a computer is an integral part of being able to use the Internet. It is important for students to quickly get accustomed to using the Internet.

Reasons for Using the Internet

Table 1 illustrates the various uses of the Internet by the students. Students were asked to select what activities they do online such as surfing the net, sending e-mails, SMS, chatting, etc. The activity that the students rated as the most constantly used was e-mail (mean of 1.6), followed closely by academic use (mean of 1.4). Many students according to Kandell (1998) provide e-mail addresses as the preferred contact rather than the telephone numbers. Since Internet access is free at university, students have access to free Web-based e-mail systems such as yahoo and Webmail.

The Internet is a tool that can be used to encourage and help students with their studies. This is in agreement with De Villiers and Cronje (2001), who stated that the Internet is one of the most powerful tool for providing learners and lecturers with independent and interactive learning. They further state that the Internet provides an

Table 1. Rating of online activities

Description	Mean
E-mail	1.6
Academic use	1.4
Surfing	1.3
SMS	0.8
Chatting	0.6
Downloading	0.3
Online games	0.3

educational discourse in which learners can interact widely with similar members of a learning community.

According to Clark (2003), the WWW is a network of interlinked pages, displaying text, hypertext, images, sound, video, and data. The Internet provides online presence and information such as learning materials, health services, journals and newspapers, virtual libraries, virtual shopping malls, music, game centres, advertisement and promotional goods, software, pornography, junk, and the list goes on. Therefore, students have a variety of sites to surf from. However, research according to Friedenberg (2002) estimates that about 3% of those who go online may suffer from problematic usage, and these users fall into one or more of four categories. The first group has a lack of impulse control, showing difficulty in controlling their inherent desire to stay for long periods of time. The next group goes online when they are lonely or depressed. The third group seeks social comfort on the Web. The last category, the one that university students are most likely to fit in, goes online to avoid coping with stress.

Sending SMSs via SMS sites was rated as the fourth most used activity (mean of 0.8) when students go online, followed closely by chatting (mean of 0.6). Today, SMS is a fast and popular way to send text based messages, especially amongst the youth. There are many SMS sites that allow users to send SMSs free of charge. The activity that students rated as seldom used was downloading of music and playing online games (mean of 0.3). There are several Web sites students can use to download music for free. Choi (2002) is of the opinion that downloading a digital song violates the intellectual property rights of the artist. Kandell (1998) states that although the Internet is an excellent tool for gathering information and for interpersonal communication, dangers exist for those who make it the central focus of their lives.

Time Constraints

Nearly 90% of the students indicated that they are being restricted to use the Internet because of time. From analyzing the results, the researchers are of the opinion that the reasons for students having insufficient time to utilize the Internet is probably because of lecture time and due to computer laboratories closing early.

The questionnaire included a final question where respondents could express their opinions on what problems they encounter when using the Internet. The question was phrased as follows: "List 3 problems that you encounter when using the Internet?" Fourteen respondents have indicated that they do not have sufficient time to spend on the Internet because the computer laboratories close early (at 4:30 pm). One of the questions that were posed to students was how much extra time they would recommend for Internet usage at University.

The majority of the respondents (39%) indicated that they require 2-4 hours, followed by 25% of the respondents who have indicated that they require 1-2 hours. Twenty percent of the respondents have indicated that they require more than 4 to 6 hours. The smallest group of respondents (15%) indicated that they require more than 6 hours. It is evident from that the University should allow students adequate time for using the Internet.

The majority of the respondents (97%) indicated that they access the Internet mostly at the university. This is quite a high percentage, and the reason for this is that because university provides the student free access to the Internet. This is in agreement with the statement by Cheung and Haung (1999) who argued that a high percentage of university has an Internet presence and these institutions provide students with the ability to access the Web as well as e-mail and other related Internet activities.

In other first world countries, students have 24 hours access to the Internet. This is in agreement with Cheung et al. (1999) who stated that the Internet is available 24 hours a day in most first world countries. Furthermore, students who pay their fees may feel that they have to take advantage of the free Internet usage offered by the university. Only one student indicated that they use the Internet at home. None of the respondents have indicated that they use the Internet at an Internet café. This is probably because of the cost factor involved.

From the correlation analysis of where the respondents mostly access the Internet and the overall hours spent on the Internet per week, the data showed significance at the 0.01 level. The correlation analysis demonstrates the strength of the association between the two variables (i.e., where students access the Internet and the number of hours spent on the Internet (.41)). This result proved that there is a strong relationship between theses two variables and it is impacting positively on the outcome of the study. The researchers find it difficult to comprehend how 3 hours can be adequate for efficient use of the Internet to be achieved. When reviewing the group that spent more than 12 hours, it raises much concern because this group could lead to Internet addiction. To re-iterate and support the researchers viewpoint, the study done by Kovach (2001) also suggests that if students have an inherent desire to surf the net for longer periods of time, it could lead to Internet addiction.

Availability of Computers and Usage of the Library

More than 81% of the respondents have indicated that there are insufficient computers. Goble (2002) recommends the following computer equipment as a market entry requirement for effective Internet usage at tertiary education:

- Pentium 4
- Windows 98, ME, NT 4.0 2000, or XP
- Microsoft Internet Explorer 5.0 or higher
- 128 MB RAM
- 20 GB of unused hard disk space
- A 32-bit- colour display

Nearly 58% of the respondents have indicated that they still use the library to access information. Jagbora (2003) states that printed materials in libraries have a certain fixity and finitude and this is probably the reason why students still use the library to access information.

The correlation analysis of whether there are adequate computers at the university and if respondents are still using the library for information showed a significance at the 0.01 level (.412). This result shows that because of the inadequate number of computers, students are using the libraries. There are not sufficient computers in the labs because of equipment costs. This is in agreement with the statement made by Goble (2002). According to him, one of the barriers of entry for proper Internet usage is equipment expenses such as hardware and software, network cables, etc, and ISP (Internet service provider) costs. Goble (2002) noted that access to the Internet implies that the correct equipment is necessary and must be available.

Another reason why there are not enough computers in the labs is probably because of telecommunication costs. South Africa has only one authorized telecommunication company, Telkom. According to Goble (2002), it has a monopoly and is the sole supplier of the country's telecommunication infrastructure. Goble further notes that since there is no competition, normal market effects prevalent in first world countries such as the USA and UK cannot play any role in bringing down the cost of telecommunication, and this fundamental flaw in government policy has a ripple effect on all goods and services produced in this country as consumers absorb the non-competitive costs. Telkom's pricing is also not competitive with the rest of the world.

A large percentage of students (58%) still use the library as their primary source of information. This implies that students are not fully utilizing the Internet for information. The students are turning to the library for information rather than the Internet. Today university libraries have suffered serious setbacks in terms of funding. Chifiwepa (2002) supports this statement by noting that due to poor funding, the libraries ability to acquire new books and to subscribe to journals has been badly affected. Jagbora (2003) states that libraries have become crammed with millions of printed materials. So, looking for any kind of material in the library can be time consuming. Kaniki (1999) states that academic libraries in South Africa are increasingly under pressure to provide Internet-based information services. He goes on further to state that while traditional library resources and services are best suited for meeting particular kinds of research and study information needs within the academia, the Internet is best suited for other academia information needs and in other cases, it can supplement traditional library services. In the near future, the Internet could replace libraries. Therefore, students need to be taught the necessary skills on how to use the Internet before this conversion can take place.

The correlation analysis demonstrates the strength of the association between the use of the library to access information and the restriction due to time constraints. The correlation analysis showed significance at the 0.01 level (.166-not high). This is an important observation as the researchers feels that the fact that there is inadequate number of computers would therefore impact on the fact that the majority of students are still using the library.

The correlation analysis demonstrates the strength of the association between the two variables i.e. the adequate number of computers and the time constraints (.402). From the results, eighty one percent of the students indicated that the computers were inadequate for proper Internet usage. The result is important as it shows a direct relationship between these two variables. The inadequate number of computers results in the students waiting their turn and thus becomes a time constraint. This can possibly have a negative impact by discouraging students to use the Internet.

Search Engines, Online Databases, Library Catalogues, and E-Journals

Eighty-four percent of the respondents have indicated that they know how to use search engines. A low percentage of the respondents (30%) indicated that they are familiar with online databases, library catalogues, and e-journals. Universities must therefore take the necessary measures to educate students, especially final and postgraduate students how to use online databases, library catalogues, and e-journals. Rochat (2002) notes that the Internet has revolutionized the process of accessing and retrieving information. One method of achieving this is through online databases, library catalogues, and e-journals.

The correlation analysis of whether the respondents know how to use search engines or online databases, library catalogues, and e-journals showed significance at the 0.01 level (.28). The correlation analysis demonstrates the strength of the association between the two variables (i.e., the use of search engines and online databases, library catalogues, and e-journals). From the analysis of the data in Table 4.9, it would appear that the majority of students (84%) know how to use search engines. Therefore, the researchers is of the opinion that the large percent (70%) not familiar with online databases, library catalogues, and e-journals is possibly due to the fact that they have to pay for this service.

Jagbora (2003) supports this statement by stating that information found on the Internet has both useful and useless co-existing. Therefore, it is good that a large portion of students (84%) know how to use search engines because knowledge of how to use search engines will eventually reduce the time that the student spends in finding the appropriate information that he or she is looking for. Kaniki (1999) states that a user must have the knowledge and skills necessary to conduct complex searches and sieve through the vast information to choose the most appropriate he or she needs.

Nearly 38% have indicated that they depend on the Internet. This shows that the students are not using the Internet mainly for academic purposes. This illustrates a correlation at the 0.01 (.268) level between the dependency on the Internet to assist students with their studies and how much more time students require to use the Internet. The association does not display any casualty. These results indicate that students need to start using the Internet to assist them with their studies. Digital classrooms, supplemented with telecommunications media according to De Villiers and Cronje (2001) are currently being used in tertiary institutions world wide in the form of Web-based courses. If these digital classrooms are implemented in the near future at South African tertiary institutes, it could have a major impact on students by encouraging and improving their learning efficiencies.

Nearly 74% of the respondents have indicated that the Internet is easy to use. The Internet is not easy to use for some students probably because they don't have a basic knowledge of computers. Therefore, to use the Internet properly, students need to be both computer and Internet literate. Eighty six of the respondents have indicated that information from the Internet is easy to read and understand with a correlation of .666.

From the correlation analysis of where the respondent felt that the Internet is easy to read and understand, the data showed a high significance at the 0.01 level. This is in agreement with the statement by Goble (2002) who stated that although modern applications use picture icons and multimedia applications, information is still primarily text based and communication, especially e-mail requires the user to read and write. Jagbora (2003) stated that hypertext publications, incorporating live or moving images and real sounds defy easy classification, and multiple links to other documents and sites encourage new patterns of reading activity.

The Internet was founded and based using English language to send and receive information. English dominates the world of computing and Information Technology today. It is the most widely used computer language, being used by both developers and end-users. Most Web pages are written in English (Goble, 2002). Therefore, students who are unable to read write or speak English will find difficulty in using the Internet. The correlation analysis demonstrates the strength of the association (.725) between the two variables (i.e., use of search engines and the ease of using the Internet). The researchers are of the opinion that a greater percentage of the respondents (74%) find the Internet easy to use and therefore they are encouraged to use search engines.

Conclusion and Summary of the Results

The results that were obtained from the data and presented in tables and graphs were discussed. The study aimed to find out how effectively students are using the Internet at tertiary education. The study revealed that students are not using the Internet responsibly i.e. for educational purposes only. They are using the Internet for their own personal uses such as surfing the net, sending SMSs via SMS sites, chatting, etc. A number of problems were identified regarding adequate computer equipment availability in the computer labs; and students being restricted to use the Internet because of time constraints. The study has also revealed that students are not utilizing the Internet to assist with their studies.

Research Questions

The following questions were presented in the literature review:

1.   *Is the Internet usage at tertiary education moving towards less learning ef-ficiency and more time spent for non-study purposes?*

The study revealed that students are using the Internet for other purposes rather than for academic usages but there was no conclusive evidence from the study that indicates that Internet usage at tertiary education is moving towards less learning efficiency. The study has revealed that the majority of students use e-mail as the most used activity when going online. Therefore, the university should implement a monitoring policy, which is discussed thoroughly in the recommendations.

2.   *Are students spending enough productive time on the Internet?*

The findings from the study revealed that students are not spending enough time utilizing the Internet because of time constraints. Nearly 90% of the students have indicated that they are being restricted to use the Internet and 10% have indicated that time is not a problem. The majority of the students have indicated that they require 2-4 hours more. Therefore, UKZN should allow students sufficient time for using the Internet.

3. *Does the university have enough computers for Internet usage?*

It is evident from the study that the university clearly has a shortage of computers for proper utilization of the Internet. The majority of the students (80%) have indicated there are insufficient computers for proper Internet usage. One of the reasons why UKZN has a shortage of computers is because of equipment costs, student's negligence, and not taking care of the equipment. The University can reduce this problem with the help of sponsorship programs.

4. *Does the Internet help students with their studies?*

The study has revealed that students are utilizing the library as a source of information more often than the Internet. The researchers strongly beliefs that the main reason for this result is that there is a lack of computers available to the students. This problem will need to be addressed if the university intends moving forward and keeping in line with international levels of other universities.

Recommendations

Responsibility of University and Students

The University provides access to various computer resources such as the Internet. These resources are available to enhance the learning process and to achieve quality learning outcomes for students. It is the responsibility of the university to encourage students to become familiar with the Internet. Students should be taught the proper way to use the Internet and not to abuse e-mail, the WWW, and so forth. Students, particularly first years should be made aware of Internet abuse. Students must also use the Internet and computers responsibly. They must comply with the rules and regulations of the computer facilities in the university labs. System administrators must also be responsible for the correct and reliable operation of the network and computers.

Monitoring

It was revealed from the study that students are wasting time on the Internet by surfing the net, sending SMSs, chatting, downloading music, playing games, and so forth. There is a large amount of offensive material from the Internet. The most common type of offensive material is pornography and hate sites. Visiting or downloading of this offensive material is considered overuse, and Internet usage is therefore being wasted. Given that there is no guaranteed means of preventing student's exposure to this kind of material, strategies needs to be adopted. University needs to adopt a monitoring strategy.

The university must monitor student's activities when going online. They can achieve this with the assistance of Web monitoring software, which records which sites the student has visited. According to Grant et al. (2000), companies are using Web monitoring software that records an employee's e-mail sent and received and the sites visited. Grant et al. further state that some of the software is capable of ringing "alarm like" bells to alert management when employees are visiting pornographic sites.

Computer Equipment

The study has revealed that the university has a shortage of computers, and some of them are not in proper working conditions. Every effort has to be made by the university to insure the stability, performance, and reliability of the equipment. University should repair the computers that are not working properly.

Technicians should be available when a PC or other equipment is damaged and must try and rectify the problem immediately. Therefore at least one technician needs to be placed in the various computer laboratories. Students should be responsible. They must take care of the equipment in the computer laboratories. They should adhere to the following rules and guidelines:

- Clean up after finishing using a laboratory computer.
- Do not bring food or beverages into the computer laboratories.
- Do not steal or remove any piece of equipment from the computer laboratories.
- Do not swap around any equipment such as changing of keyboards, mouse, or other equipment from one computer to another.
- Do not alter data, software, or directories.
- Report all equipment faults immediately.

- Students should properly shut down their workstations.
- Report suspected viruses to the systems administrator.

In order for the equipment to be functioning properly, both university and students must be responsible for the equipment.

Sponsorships

The university can promote Internet usage via sponsorships programs. They can either apply for funding or new equipment. In 2003, the university built the Govan Mbeki lab via a sponsorship, but this is only one facility. There should be about three to five computer laboratories in university. The only way this can be achieved is through sponsorships. There should be more available computers in the library since students use the library as their primary source for information. Funds coming from sponsorships could also be used to upgrade existing computers.

Computer Laboratories

Students are being restricted to use the Internet because of time. The computer laboratories should be opened at 8:00 am and close at 18:00 pm instead of 16:30 pm. The laboratories should also be opened on weekends. However, this privilege should only be granted to third year and postgraduate students. When a student enters a computer laboratory, university must ensure that each student has a computer available at his/her disposal. Only authorized users must be allowed into the computer laboratories.

E-Mail Usage

E-mail is a tool used for communications, in which users must have a responsibility to use in an efficient, ethical, and lawful manner. Students must adhere to the following guidelines when using e-mail systems at university:

- Do not send messages that are offensive, harassing, obscene, or threatening.
- Do not send, create, or forward advertisements, chain letters, and other unsolicited mail (spam).
- Do not send excessive e-mail messages to recipients, either on or off campus.

- Do not send e-mail containing warnings or virus alerts to other university users.
- Do not flood another system, network, or user account with e-mail.

Downloading of Music and Other Large Graphic Files

Sites such as IMESH, Kazaa, and other download sites needs to be restricted from students. Downloading music form the Internet is considered copyright infringements and is illegal. Therefore, university needs to ensure that students are aware of the consequences of downloading music off the Internet. Powell (2003) recommends that universities need to monitor student's shares on computer and electronic storage systems that belong to the universities. Limits should also be placed on file sizes and the types of files that are downloaded.

Web Filtering Software/Firewalls

Installed on a computers server, this Web filtering software is able to filter inappropriate Web sites (such as online chatting, SMS sites, etc.) while still allowing useful ones to be accessed. A firewall is an access control gateway and determines what type of acceptable traffic may flow through it.

Policies

The university needs to implement policies, which are designed to regulate day-to-day online activities. Policies give users guidelines of what constitutes appropriate and inappropriate use of university computer resources. Policies outline in very clear terms what kind of Internet usage is permitted, what kind is not, and the consequences for violating the rules. Having a clear designed policy will enable the university to protect against wrong doings such as engaging in behaviour that impedes normal use of the network, Internet, or other resources, overloading the network with excessive data, pornography, etc.

If students are in breach of these university policies, the user's account or computer access including access to the computer labs must be suspended and students will be subject to the normal disciplinary procedures of the university.

Future Research

- Future research needs to be conducted concerning the reasons why students are misusing the Internet at UKZN (Westville campus). These findings could identify some important factors that can improve Internet usage among university students.

- A comparative study should be conducted between other South African universities and even the Technikons. The study would be able to identify which institutions have a better Internet usage.

- Further research must be conducted with regards to the reasons why students are turning to university libraries rather than the Internet.

- The activities of university staff when they utilize the Internet should also be researched to determine whether they are abusing Internet facilities.

Conclusion

The study proved to be beneficial to both the researchers and the students. The aim of the study was to assess the effective usage of the Internet at tertiary level. The study explored the various aspects and factors relating to efficient Internet usage in terms of how this was perceived by the students. It was evident that the Internet is not being utilized efficiently and effectively by the students. This has raised much concern with the researchers in terms of what steps need to be taken in order to improve on this result. The researchers recommends further research in this field in order to improve on higher standards of education through the Internet, which will be beneficial to future students.

References

Berkeley, C. U. (2004). *What are the Internet, the World Wide Web, and Netscape?* Retrieved April 3, 2004, from http://www.lib.berkeley.edu/teachinglib/guides/internet/whatis.html

Botha, J., Bothma, C., & Geldenhuys, P. (2004). *Managing e-commerce*. Pretoria: Juta & Co.

Bothma, C. H. (2000). *E-commerce for South African managers*. Pretoria: Interactive Reality.

Boutell, T. (2004). *What was the first Web browser?* Retrieved July 19, 2004, from http://www.boutell.com/newfaq/history/fbrowser.html

Cheung, W. M., & Huang, W. (1999, August 13-15). An exploratory investigation of Internet usage and its impact in University education. In *Proceedings of the America's Conference on Information Systems*, Milwaukee (pp. 903-905). Retrieved April 1, 2004, from http://aisel.isworld.org/pdf.asp?spath=/amics/1999/316.pdf

Chifwepa, V. (2002, April 10-12). Internet and information provision: The promises and challenges in African university libraries. In *Proceedings of the NetLab and Friends of Conference*, Lund, Sweden. Retrieved April 7, 2004, from http://www.lab.lu.se/netlab/conf/chifwepa.html

Choi, S. (2002). *The ethics of downloading music.* Retrieved August 3, 2004, from http://members.rogers.com/mrbuddy/ethicspaper.html

De Villiers, G. J., & Cronje, J. C. (2001, June). Longitudinal comparison of two presentations of an Internet based course for adult learners: A university case study. *SAJIM, 3*(1). Retrieved April 7, 2004, from http://www.sajim.co.za/default.asp?to=peer1vol3nr1

Dos Santos, L. B. (1998, August 14-16). *Internet-based instruction: Experience with multi-university cooperative learning.* Presented at AMCIS 1998. Retrieved April 1, 2004, from http://aisel.isworld.org/pdf.asp?spath=/amics/1998/t26_02.pdf

Fleck, R. A., & Mcqueen, T. (1999). *First monday. Internet access, usage, and policies in colleges and universities.* Retrieved April 7, 2004, from http://firstmonday.org/issue4_11/fleck/index.html

Foster, L. A. (2002). *Up to 14% of Australian university students may be plagiarizing from Web, study suggests.* Retrieved July 29, 2004, from http://chronicle.com/free/2002/11/2002/12001t.htm

General social survey: Internet use. (2001). Retrieved July 14, 2004, from http://www.statscan.ca/daily/english/010326/d010326a.htm

Goble, R. C. (2002, September). The Internet—an enlist luxury or the people's necessity? *SAJIM, 4*(3). Retrieved April 7, 2004, from http://www.sajim.co.za/default.asp?to=student2vol4nr3

Grant, D., & Mcbride, P. (2000). *Guide to the Internet: Getting your business online.* London: Butterworth-Heinemann.

Guide to plagiarism and cyber-plagiarism. (2004). Retrieved July 29, 2004, from http://www.library.ualberta.ca/guides/plagiarism/index.cfm

Harris, P. K. (1996). *Copyright issues on the Web.* Retrieved July 29, 2004, from http://iteslj.org/articles/harris-copyright.html

Hughes, K. (1994). *A guide to cyberspace.* Retrieved April 3, 2004, from http://www. sr.net/srnet/enteringwww/guide.toc.html

IRC. (2004). Retrieved July 19, 2004, from http://www.Webopedia.com/TERM/ I/IRC.html

Jagbora, K. O. (2003). *First monday. A study of Internet usage in Nigerian Universities, Ille-Ille, Nigeria.* Retrieved April 1, 2004, from http://firstmonday. org/issues/issue8_12jagbora/index.html

Kandell, J. J. (1998). *Internet addiction on campus: The vulnerability of college students.* Retrieved July 29, 2004, from http://www.inform.umd.edu/CC/ personal/~kandell/iacpbart.htm

Kaniki, M. A. (1999). *Internet use and training needs of staff of the ESAL consortium, KZN, SA: Partnership between historically disadvantaged and advantaged institutions (HDI's and HAI's).* Retrieved May 18, 2004, from http://www. ifla.org/IV/ifla65/papers/041_115e.htm

Katz, J., & Yablon, B. (2002, March). Who is afraid of university courses? *Educational Media International, 39*(1), 69-73. Retrieved July 29, 2004, from http://search.epnet.com/direct.asp?an=6895099&dp=aph

Kovach, N. (2001). *Internet addiction a threat to college students.* Retrieved July 29, 2004, from http://www.thepost.baker.ohiou.edu/archives3/jan01/012501/ news1.html

Lerner, M. (2004). *Harness e-mail: How it works.* Retrieved July 19, 2004, from http://www.learnthenet.com/english/html/20how.htm

Lyman, P., & Varian, H. R. (2000). *How much information?* Retrieved July 29, 2004, from http://www.sims.berkeley.edu/how-much-info/

Macura, J. K. (2004). *Internet for you: Part 1: History of the net.* Retrieved August 3, 2004, from http://www.rsna.org/tech/internet/internet1-1.html

Pickering, J. (2000). *The Internet in universities: Liberation or desensitisation?* Retrieved June 11, 2004, from http://www.csv.warwick.ac.uk/~psrev/geosci. html

Plagiarism.org. (2004). Retrieved July 29, 2004, from http://www.plagiarism. org/plagiarism.html

Powell, D. W. (2003). *P2P and MP3s: Staying out of the middle.* Retrieved August 4, 2004, from http://www.educause.edu/ir/library/pdf/CRM0345.pdf

Rochat, C. (2002, June). Possible solutions to information overload. *SAJIM, 4*(2). Retrieved July 29, 2004, from http://www.sajim.co.za/default. asp?to=student4vol4nr2

Schoeman, J. (2000, September). Web site security? Is the threat real? *SAJIM*, *2*(2/3). Retrieved July 14, 2004, from http://www.sajim.co.za/default.asp?to=student2

Singh, A. M. (2002). *The Internet-strategies for optimal utilization in South Africa*. Retrieved April 1, 2004, from http://www.sajim.co.za/default.asp?to=peer4vol4nr1

Taylor, F. D., & Cohen, M. B. (2001). *Untangling the World Wide Web*. Retrieved July 26, 2004, from http://www.kaludisconsulting.com/pdf/KAL_Web_rev3.pdf

Walonick, S. D. (1997). *Survival statistics*. Minneapolis: Statpac Inc.

Watson, J. M. (2003, September). What is spam? *SA Computer Magazine*, 41-42.

What about CERN's greatest achievements? (2002). Retrieved July 19, 2004, from http://public.Web.cern.ch/public/about/achievements/www/www.html

Why students plagiarize? (2004). Retrieved July 29, 2004, from http://www.library.ualberta.ca/guides/plagiarism/why/index.cfm

Wright, B. (2004, April). Fighting child pornography. *SA Computer Magazine*, 49-51.

Chapter XIV

Information Security in Small Businesses

Kishore Singh, University of KwaZulu-Natal, South Africa

Abstract

This chapter discusses the impact of security in small and medium enterprises. It views the development of a security policy in serious light and come up with some recommendations on how this can be handled.

Introduction

The management of information security and security related events has become an issue commanding ever-increasing attention from the various professions attending to the information needs of organisations using ICT[1] (Von Solms, 2001). The basic need of developing secure information systems (IS), however, continues to remain unfulfilled. This is because the focus continues to remain on the means of delivery of information (i.e., the technology (Galliers, 1993)). Management continues to believe that information security and related problems can be solved by technical means (Vermeulen & Von Solms, 2002). The responsibility of information security is entrusted to the technical department without proper, direct, and continuous support from executive management. The net result is that technology is used to solve the information security problem without a total, comprehensive solution (Von Solms & Von Solms, 2004).

This chapter describes the contribution made by small businesses[2] to the South African economy, reviews some of the current literature in information security, and examines some of the more recent (2002 to 2004) survey statistics describing the state of information security in organisations. This chapter is aimed at academics, information security researchers, information security practitioners, and owners of small businesses that make use of computer-based information systems. Additionally, any student of information security that needs to understand the fundamentals of effective information security implementation in small businesses will find this chapter useful.

Small Business Profile

South Africa has a thriving small business sector supported by a network of financial and non-financial service providers. By enabling people to meet their basic needs for survival, small businesses play an important role in economic development. It has been proven in many parts of the world that the small business sector stimulates economic growth, redistributes wealth, and creates jobs. The latter being particularly important within the context of the reality that large corporations' demand for labour does not increase in proportion to their growth (Ntsika, 2002).

According to Ntsika (2002), some of the reasons why small businesses in South Africa have become an important target for policy makers are: (1) they can easily absorb excess labour capacity as compared to other sectors, (2) the cost of creating a job is lower than in the large businesses, (3) they create more competitive markets, (4) they can easily and quickly adapt to changing consumer tastes and trends, (5) they often use local recycled resources, (6) they provide opportunities for entrepreneurs, and those who are unemployed, under-employed, or retrenched, (7) they allow workers with limited or no skills or training to learn these on the job, (8) they are often sub-contracting by large enterprises thereby providing flexibility to production processes, and (9) they play an important role in innovation.

Classification and Distribution of Small Businesses

For the purpose of this chapter, enterprises in South Africa have been categorized according to the definitions provided in the National Small Business Act (NSBA, 1996). Table 1 summarises the NSBA (1996) classification of small businesses.

The National Small Business Act (NSBA, 1996, p. 34) additionally distinguishes a small business using the following three criteria: (1) total full-time equivalent employees (<100, with the exception of mining and quarrying; and manufacturing (<200), (2) total annual paid turnover (figures vary according to sector), and (3) total gross asset value (figures vary according to sector).

Growth of Small Business Sector

During his State of the Nation Address (2004), the South African president stated that South Africa would continue to focus on the growth and development of a modern "first economy" in order to generate resources to meet the challenges of its underdeveloped "second economy." He added that further expansion of small and

Table 1. Classification of small businesses source (Adapted from the National Small Business Act 1996)

Category		Characteristic
1.	Survivalist	income generated is less than the poverty line, there are no paid employees and the asset value is minimal
2.	Micro	turnover is less than the VAT registration limit, they are not formally registered and employ between 1- 4 people, excluding the entrepreneur
3.	Very small	operate in the formal market and have access to modern technology
4.	Small	a secondary co-ordinating management structure is in place with some form of managerial level coordination
5.	Medium	further decentralization of decision-making, a more complex management structure and further division of labour are evident

medium enterprise will be a contributing factor and promised to help increase the market share of small businesses (Mbeki, 2004).

Prior to the official launch of the Small Enterprise Development Agency (SEDA), the Deputy Minister of Trade and Industry commented that small businesses have an important role to play in the economy. The minister added that further development of the small business sector will assist in economic growth, job creation, and reduction of poverty in South Africa (SEDA, 2004).

Contribution to Economy

South Africa's small business sector is the backbone of the national economy and currently employs over 50% of the workforce and accounts for over 35% of the GDP (Ntsika, 2004). According to Ntsika (2002), the contribution of small businesses in 2001 to GDP was 36.1%, up from 32.7% in 1995. Small businesses accounted for at least half of GDP in the agricultural and construction sectors and more than 40% of GDP in the trade, catering, and accommodation, as well as the transport, storage, and communication sectors.

In 2002, small businesses employed 68.2% of people employed in the private sector, as opposed to 44% in 1995 and 53.9% in 2001. Small enterprises constituted the most significant small business employer, (accounting for 21% of total small business employment), followed by medium-sized (18% of total small business employment) enterprises and micro enterprises (17% of total small business employment).

The largest provinces in economic terms are Gauteng, Kwazulu-Natal, and Western Cape, which jointly account for 69% of South Africa's GDP. Some 60% of all enterprises and 70% of all small businesses are concentrated in these three provinces. Small business distribution in these three provinces is Gauteng (38.4%), Kwazulu-Natal (18.4%), and the Western Cape (13.4%) (Ntsika, 2002).

Small Businesses and Technology

According to Pratt (2002), small businesses have benefited from new technologies that have decentralized computing and telecommunications. In the past only large corporations could acquire the sizable capital required for commerce that depended upon mainframe computers and other costly business equipment. However, since the 1980s, the advent of inexpensive personal computers have enabled small firms to compete with larger businesses. First, the cost of equipping a home office has dropped significantly and the capabilities of business tools have improved. Second, the Internet, is transforming the way people work, live, and conduct business. E-mail, the Internet, and the cell phone offer connections that extend globally from any location--an office building, a home office, a car, or boat (e.g., Amazon.com, initially started out in a home basement, has since taken over the online book market from Barnes and Noble). Individuals now have access to information and to markets on a 24×7 basis (Pratt, 2002).

Small businesses, by their very nature, are able to adapt to change faster than large businesses. Small businesses are the fastest changing sector of business (SBA, 1999a). Small businesses are embracing the use of Internet technologies and e-commerce as a way to leverage their limited resources and to reach an expanded customer base. According to SBA (1999b), small home-based businesses represent more than 18% of all homes with personal computers, and of all home-based businesses in the United States, 60% use personal computers to conduct their business activities (Pratt, 2002).

According to SBA (1999b), the rate of Internet connectivity among small businesses rose from 21.5% in 1996 to 41.2% in 1998 to 61% in 1999. The percentage of small businesses with a World Wide Web (WWW) presence was 35% in 1999. Of those small businesses with a Web site, 78% were motivated to develop one in order to reach new and potential customers. One third of small businesses currently perform business transactions using their Web site. Small businesses that use the WWW have higher annual revenues than those that do not, averaging about one million U.S. dollars per year more (SBA, 1999b).

Small businesses often initiate technological innovation, the use of business applications, the use of personal computers, and the Internet (Oliver, 2000). The personal computer and Internet support smaller businesses and allow them to match big-business efficiencies, thereby enhancing their ability to communicate with suppliers and customers, lower costs, and expand markets (Oliver, 2000). Innovative entrepreneurs (early adopters) use technology and the Internet as a way to market niche products and reach distant customers in ways that were not available in the past. As a result, of this adoption of technology, structural changes are required industrial organization.

Petkov, Fry, Petkova, and D'Onofrio (2003) state that small businesses need technology in order to succeed. Some of these technologies could be used to solve the problems of smaller businesses and to accumulate knowledge for improvement of their services. Lubbe (2004) states that investment in IT has an impact on the competitiveness of small and medium organisations. As a result, small businesses are beginning to spend a higher percentage of their turnover on IT; however Lubbe (2004) goes on to state that the biggest limitation to ICT implementation in small businesses was that 80% of them did not know how to use ICT correctly. Additionally, the biggest mistake that small businesses made in implementing ICT was that they did not understand that they cannot do everything themselves.

From the discussion in the preceding paragraphs, the author concludes that ICT adoption and an Internet presence are emerging as powerful tools for business success. As more small businesses show successful use of ICT, other small businesses will be motivated to adopt these technologies and practices. Embracing ICT and the Internet are critical factors that will determine a small businesses market share in the future. Those small businesses that ignore or hesitate to implement new technologies will be doing so at their own risk (Pratt, 2002).

Small Businesses and Crime

Berger (1981) affirms that security, in general, is a problem for small businesses. A small business does not have the business base across which to spread the cost of security personnel or technologies. Additionally, he concludes that businesses with more than 100 employees are better able to afford a security officer or manager on staff. Chelimsky, Jordan, Russell, and Strack (1981) recognize that small businesses suffer more from crime than larger businesses and bear a greater proportion of loss as a result of crime than other businesses. The author therefore concludes that those least able to protect themselves—the small business sector—are targeted more often, and the consequences are often more serious.

According to Chelimsky et al. (1981), insurance companies attribute approximately 30% of business failures to internal theft. A 20-year old analysis of white collar crime conducted by Berger (1981) confirms that internal theft by employees surpasses the incidents of shoplifting, hold-ups, and burglary collectively.

Small businesses continue to embrace new technologies resulting in the computerization of many business processes (Pratt, 2002). As a result, they have become potentially more vulnerable to internal theft. This is particularly true with regards to theft of money, which is the most threatening crime to small business (Doney, 1998). Most small businesses aren't large enough to have security experts on staff (Keogh, 1981), yet the potential result of computer-based crime can be catastrophic (e.g., business failure, financial, and personal liability). Studies described in Doney (1998) indicate that the average loss experienced by a business is about ten times higher when a crime is committed with the assistance of a computer as compared to when committed without it.

According to Pratt (2002), the issues that arise in the move of small businesses to electronic commerce include the cost of establishing and maintaining an Internet presence and security issues associated with online transactions. Of the security-related concerns, the predominant one is that of fraud. The concern over fraud is expected to be amplified by security concerns related to digital cash, as that medium becomes common.

Most small businesses are managed by the owner with only basic management structures (if any) in place (NSBA, 1996). A survey conducted by Lubbe (2004) established that one-half of small business owners do not have any idea of what ICT entails nor how it should be used. It is therefore a reasonable conclusion that by embracing new technologies without correct investigation, implementation, or incomplete understanding of the technology itself, small business owners are exposing themselves to a risk environment and are unable to set up and maintain a suitable level of information security without expert assistance. Additionally, a survey conducted by PriceWaterHouse Coopers (ISBS, 2004) determined that, more than 50% of businesses in the United Kingdom think that information security incidents will continue to increase in the future, despite their high confidence in existing security controls. How then can small business practitioners deal with the ever-increasing threat to information security?

Initial attacks of computer-based information systems were aimed at specific organisations, primarily large corporate enterprises. Although smaller firms were attacked, most small firms could somewhat depend on "security through obscurity" (Panko, 2004, p. 10). Today, most attacks are equivalent of firing guns into the crowds. This implies that every computer attached to a telecommunications network has an equal opportunity of being compromised (Panko, 2004).

Lubbe (2004) verifies that a security gap exists between current and required security practices in small businesses. This gap did not appear as a result of the absence of a shared vision. Instead, according to Lubbe (2004), there was an agreement between big business and small business respondents about the importance of certain security tasks and security skills. Many of these security tasks, however, received low importance scores from small business practitioners.

Review of Information Security Literature

This section reviews some of the current literature in the subject of information security and provides a background to the problem of information security in small businesses.

Definition of Information Security

Security relates to the protection of valuable assets against loss, misuse, disclosure, or damage (ITGI, 2001). Security related problems occur because of the need to balance two important yet conflicting goals viz. (1) the goal of providing access to resources and (2) the goal of preserving confidentiality, integrity, and availability (Mehta & George, 2001).

Tsujii (2004) defines information security as a process for establishing a complete system of social fundamentals that links and coordinates technologies, administration, and management techniques, legal and social systems, and information morals. This, he states, will improve usability and efficiency, enhance security and privacy, and lead to a reduction in monitoring and surveillance over system users. Finne (1998) suggests that when information is misused, lost, or threatened it is as a result of insufficient information security.

The United States National Institute of Standards and Technology (NIST, 1995, p. 5) offers the following definition of information security

"The protection of information system assets (including hardware, software, firmware, information/data and telecommunications) against various threats and attacks in order to preserve the integrity, availability, and confidentiality of these systems."

A desirable outcome of security is thus the reliability and preservation of system conditions and functions. Confidentiality, integrity, and availability (CIA) are regarded as the three components of information security (Tsujii, 2004). These concepts are summarized in Table 2.

Williams (2001) states that the concept of security relates to the protection of valuable information assets. The data or information must be protected against harm from threats leading to its loss, inaccessibility, alteration, or wrongful disclosure. The main objective of information security is to protect the interests of those relying on information, and the systems that deliver the information, from damage resulting from failures of availability, confidentiality, and integrity (Williams, 2001).

The IT Governance Institute (ITGI, 2001) confirms that information security objectives are met when: (1) information is observed by or disclosed to only those who have a right to know (confidentiality), (2) information is protected against

Table 2. Confidentiality, integrity, and availability (Adapted from Tsujii, 2004)

	Component	Description
1.	Confidentiality	Only a person who has permission to access particular information can access it.
2.	Integrity	Information and its associated processing methods are authentic and complete.
3.	Availability	The ability of authorised users to access information and related assets reliably whenever necessary is preserved.

unauthorised modification (integrity), and (3) information is available and usable when required, and the systems that provide it can appropriately resist attacks and recover from failures (availability).

The COBIT security baseline (COBIT, 2004) ascertains that the relative priorities and significance attached to confidentiality, integrity, and availability varies according to the value and type of information and the context in which it is being used. For example, integrity of management information is important to a business relying on critical strategy-related decisions, and integrity of online shopping is very important to a home user. Furthermore, the amount of protection afforded to a system depends on the likelihood of a security incident occurring and the level of impact the incident will have should it occur (COBIT, 2004).

The definition of information security adopted in this chapter is as specified in NIST (1995), for example:

Information security is the protection of information system assets[3] against various threats and attacks in order to preserve the confidentiality, integrity, and availability of these systems.

Importance of Information Security

COBIT (2004) establishes that ICT has become an integral part of everyday business and private life, and dependency on information systems is constantly growing. New technologies have emerged that allow unprecedented functionality but introduce new risks and environments that are harder to control (e.g., wireless technology, mobile computing, and integration of technologies (i.e., multimedia). Increased dependency on ICT by individuals and organisations alike implies that the impact of system failures is magnified. Whether the incident happens to a home user (e.g., relying on online banking) or an enterprise (e.g., relying on online customers), security incidents have a real impact. With the proliferation of communication networks, individuals are justified in being concerned about the privacy of their personal information and organisations need to protect the confidentiality of corporate data, while promoting electronic business (COBIT, 2004).

According to ITGI (2001), ICT can generate many direct and indirect benefits, and as many direct and indirect risks. These risks have led to a gap between the need to protect systems and the degree of protection applied. The gap is caused by (1) extensive use of technology, (2) increased interconnectivity of systems, (3) elimination of distance, time, and space as constraints, (4) rapid technological change, (5) decentralized management and control, (6) increase in unconventional electronic attacks against organisations, and (7) external factors such as legislative, legal, and regulatory requirements, or technological developments.

New risk areas that could have a significant impact on critical business operations, have emerged. These include: (1) increasing requirements for availability and robustness, (2) growing potential for misuse and abuse of ICT affecting privacy and ethical values, and (3) external dangers from hackers, leading to denial-of-service and virus attacks, extortion and leakage of corporate information (ITGI, 2001).

New technology provides the potential for dramatically enhanced business performance hence, improved and demonstrated information security can add real value to any organisation (small or large) by contributing to interaction with trading partners, closer customer relationships, improved competitive advantage, and protected reputation (ITGI, 2001). Technology can also enable new and easier ways to process electronic transactions and generate trust (ITGI, 2001). However, the ensuing increase in technical complexity has led to new and more complex risks (COBIT, 2004).

Von Solms (1998) notes that in the early days (pre-personal computer period), securing computing environments required few technical and physical mechanisms. With the advent of the personal computer (PC) and multi-processors, a number of additional technical security measures became necessary (e.g., user identification, authentication, authorization, and access control to data). Nevertheless, a precise information security policy ensured that the entire environment was controlled and secured, to an acceptable level, by the organisations personnel (Von Solms, 1998).

As organizations connect their communication networks to the Internet or to the networks of their business partners, it is no longer possible to maintain precise control over their ICT systems and users, and consequently information security in general. The information security policy, which dictates the behaviour of users within an organization, has no influence on any users outside the organization. Therefore, it is imperative for individual organizations to protect their own ICT environments satisfactorily since technologies such as EDI,[4] the Internet, and EFTPoS[5] enable organizations to exchange information electronically, and inadequate protection on one side may have negative consequences on the other side (Von Solms, 1998). It can be potentially harmful to any organisations reputation if business partners or potential business partners label the organisation as having inadequate information security.

Blatchford (1998) notes that severe business uncertainty can result from systems that are vulnerable and that poor information security can have adverse economic impacts on individuals, organizations, and society in general. Von Solms (1996) suggests that a stage is being reached where an organisations potential business partners will require proof of adequate information security. Failure to provide such evidence may result in the inability to attract new business and the potential loss of some existing business partners. Mitchell, Marcella, and Baxter (1999) confirm this by stating that information security breaches can have a devastating effect on an organisation. He notes that the loss of confidential information (proprietary product information, client data, and business plans) can result in the loss of customers and credibility and eventually reduced profitability. He goes on to say that while management processes, policies and technologies exist to protect corporate information, evidence continues to suggest that companies are either unaware of the scale of the threats, or are not taking steps to protect information.

As businesses begin to increasingly adopt and depend on the Internet and ICT to increase their bottom lines, concerns over security and related issues will continue to be listed as top challenges hindering increased earnings potential and expansion of market shares (Garg, Curtis, & Halper, 2003). In addition to the growth of e-commerce, laws such as the Electronic Communications and Transactions Act (ECT, 2002) stipulate that comprehensive safeguards must be deployed in order to protect the security, privacy, and confidentiality of personal and corporate information.

Thomson and von Solms (1998) claim that even though technological progression has contributed to the development of information security management, an emerging issue in information security is the change in the profile of the end-user. End-user tasks are no longer limited to simple data capture. Due to increasing competition from rival businesses, managerial end-users require access to information on a "must have now" basis. Additionally, these end-users often develop their own small systems to interpret and manipulate data. This increase in sophistication of the end-user combined with the need to grant them access to the information they require means that it is no longer possible to maintain effective information security with physical and technical controls only (Thompson et al., 1998).

A partial review of information security survey statistics (AusCERT, 2004; BCMS, 2003; E-Crime, 2004; ISBS, 2004) was conducted next in order to offer evidence to support (1) the importance of ensuring effective information security and (2) the increasing incidence of information security breaches in organisations. The results of the review are stated in the following paragraphs.

The 2004 E-Crime Watch Survey (E-Crime, 2004), conducted by *Carnegie Mellon University Software Engineering Institute's CERT® Coordination Centre*, showed a significant number of organizations reporting an increase in electronic crimes (e-crimes) and network, system or data intrusions. Forty-three percent of respondents reported an increase in e-crimes and intrusions when compared to the previous year (2003) and 70% reported that at least one e-crime or intrusion was committed against their organization. Respondents declared that e-crime cost their organizations approximately US$666 million in 2003. This increase in electronic crimes over the previous year demonstrates the need for organizations to develop coordinated efforts between their ICT and information security departments to maximize defence and minimize e-crime impact.

The Australian Computer Crime and Security Survey (AusCERT, 2004) conducted by the *Australian High Tech Crime Centre* and the *Australian Federal Police* showed a definite increase in the number of organisations experiencing electronic attacks (49%) in the last 12 months, when compared to the previous year (42% in 2003). The survey also indicated that a considerably higher percentage of organisations experienced harmful externally sourced attacks (88%) than harmful internally sourced attacks (36%). This trend continues to demonstrate that organisations connected to the Internet are at a higher risk than those that are not and these organisations appear to be finding it more difficult to prevent externally sourced attacks.

The Information Security Breaches Survey (ISBS, 2004) conducted by the *UK Department of Trade and Industry* and *PriceWaterHouse Coopers* highlighted the continuing increase in the number of UK businesses suffering a security breach. Seventy-five percent of all companies and almost all large companies had at least one security incident in the last year (2004). Overall, 33% of all UK businesses and 66% of large businesses had a serious security breach. This was an increase from just under 50% in 2002. The survey results also suggested that large businesses were more successful at repelling attacks. For the smaller businesses, 1 probe in 50 resulted in a breach of their defences as compared to less than one probe in a hundred for the larger businesses.

No comparable survey data exists that uniquely profiles the entire spectrum of South African businesses. However, in the first ever Business Continuity Management Survey ZA (BCMS, 2003) conducted by *KMPG* and *BMI-TechKnowledge,* 74% of the respondents indicated that their biggest concern was information security breaches. It must, however, be noted that this survey only sampled South African businesses with an annual turnover of between R100 million to R30 billion.

In the preceding paragraphs, a partial review of information security survey statistics was conducted. The year-on-year figures provide substantial evidence that information security breaches are on the increase. These figures provide conclusive evidence that (1) provision of effective information security is essential for an organisations continued existence, and (2) information security continues to remain a problem for many organisations. Witman (2004) supports this conclusion when he states that information security is a difficult task that requires complex interdependencies between organisations and work units in order to establish and maintain a systems security.

The foregoing discussions have offered evidence that reiterates the importance of information security. The benefits accruing from providing adequate and effective information security include (but are not limited to) increased profitability, larger market share and, most importantly, trust amongst business partners.

Definition of Threats and Vulnerabilities

An overview of the risk environment in which information systems operate in presented next. Information systems are susceptible to many threats and vulnerabilities that can cause various types of damage resulting in significant losses. The effects of these threats vary considerably: some affect the confidentiality or integrity of information while others affect the availability of a system (NIST, 1995).

A threat is the potential for a particular threat-source to successfully exercise a particular vulnerability. A threat-source is defined as any circumstance or event with the potential to cause harm to an ICT system. A vulnerability is a weakness that can be accidentally triggered or intentionally exploited. A threat-source does not present a risk when there is no vulnerability that can be exercised. In determining the likelihood of a threat, one must consider threat-sources, potential vulnerabilities, and existing controls (Stoneburner, Goguen, & Feringa, 2002). It is the author's conclusion that protection should be against threats that can exploit vulnerabilities. If vulnerabilities exist but there are no threats to exploit them, then little or nothing is gained by providing the protection.

Cisco (2001) identifies several threat-sources and provides some motivations why security crimes are committed. According to this white paper, sources of threats to information security include; organized criminals, cyber terrorists, industrial spies, foreign countries in conflict with targeted nations, disgruntled employees, and amateur hackers. Each of these groups has different motivations and poses a different type of threat and the damage caused can range from simple file integrity errors to total destruction of entire information systems. Some of the reasons why hacking and intrusions occur are: (1) organized criminals are economically motivated and seek information that can be sold or used to extort money from victims, (2) terrorists are politically and/or religiously motivated, (3) industrial spies are seeking competitive information, (4) disgruntled employees want to do damage to systems or obtain information to embarrass their employer or former employer, and (5) amateur hackers are attempting to prove their abilities (Cisco, 2001). Figure 1 gives a typical list of the threats experienced and the cost (US$) incurred by each type of threat in 2004 (CSI, 2004).

According to Figure 2, virus infections accounted for the largest portion of losses (approx. $55.05 million). In ISBS (2004), 70% of organisations surveyed suffered a virus infection, thus confirming the CSI (2004) finding. These results are further confirmed by MessageLabs (2005) where the finding is that at least one in every 34.95 email messages (during January 2005) contained a virus and this number continues to rise. This number is disturbing as 99% of all firms surveyed by CSI (2004) implement antivirus software.

Figure 1. Categories of security threats and associated costs (U.S. dollars) (Adapted from CSI, 2004)

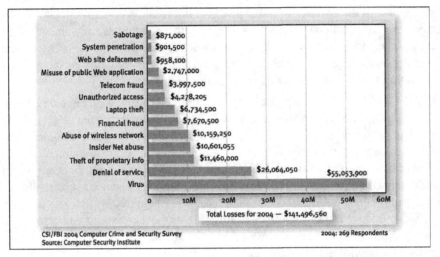

Other incidents identified by CSI (2004) were denial-of-service (approx. $26.06 million); theft of proprietary information (approx. $11.46 million); insider net abuse (approx. $10.6 million); abuse of wireless network (approx. $10.16 million); financial fraud (approx. $7.67 million); laptop theft (approx. $6.74 million); unauthorized access (approx. $4.28 million); telecom fraud (approx. $3.98 million); misuse of public Web application (approx. $2.75 million); Web site defacement ($958,100); system penetration ($901,500); and sabotage ($871,000). Although these statistics pertain to U.S.-based organisations, it is a reasonable conclusion that worldwide trends will follow similar patterns. A review of some information security survey statistics (AusCERT, 2004; BCMS, 2003; E-Crime, 2004; ISBS, 2004) was undertaken and this confirmed the author's conclusion.

Protecting ICT systems has never before been more important. Organisations today are facing a wide range of threats to their information assets. Any organisation that suffers an information security incident must be able to identify *who* did *what* and *when* they did it. By better understanding the potential threats and vulnerabilities, an organisation can implement a number of procedures in order to raise the level of its information security and reduce the likelihood of security related incidents.

Information Security Investment

The concept of investment has one purpose and that is to generate a return. This return is seen in the form of capital, time, and both tangible and intangible benefits (Tsiakis & Stephanides, 2005).

In support of Tsiakis et al. (2005), in 1995, Murray, (cited in Anttila, Kajava, & Varonen, 2004, p. 1), declared that *"information security should pay, it should not cost"*; as the common belief at the time was that information security was unproductive and only incurred an extra financial burden on organisations.

Prior to making information security investment decisions, facts about assets (i.e., information, software, hardware, and systems), vulnerabilities, and the probability of breaches (and damages) need to be analysed. An evaluation needs to be done in order to find the best possible security solution (Tsiakis et al., 2005). Lubbe (1997) supports this conclusion by declaring that the evaluation of technology investments is imperative due the increasingly strategic nature of the impact of technology on organisational performance.

A key factor in getting value from security is to ensure that technology investments protect the right assets. The financial returns gained from a successful implementation of security should justify the cost of security in terms of enabling the business. An organisation needs to assess security investment against the probability that a loss producing security incident will occur and multiply that by the impact that the problem will create (Tsiakis et al., 2005). Pipkin (2000) notes that the costs of implementing information security measures must be compared to the value of the information being protected and the consequences of incurring a security breach due to non-implementation of adequate security measures.

Investment decisions regarding information security should consider (1) the frequency of security breaches, (2) the cost of security breaches, and (3) investment in information security measures. Gordon and Loeb (2002) proposed a model to determine the optimal amount an organisation should invest in information security mechanisms. In their model, the amount to invest in security is taken as an increasing function of the level of vulnerability of the information being protected. The results of their research are summarised next:

- The optimal amount to invest in information security depends on the specific form of the security breach but should not exceed 37% of the expected loss due to the breach.

- There are no simple procedures to determine the probabilities of threat and their associated vulnerabilities.

- There are no simple procedures to determine the potential loss from information security breaches.

Cavusoglu, Mishra, and Raghunathan (2004) suggested the following additional approaches to determine the optimal investment in information security:

- The fear, uncertainty, and doubt (FUD) strategy. This approach is used by information security vendors to sell security solutions.
- The cost of deploying security. This approach asks the question, "What is the most I can get for $X,[6] given that I am going to spend $X?"
- Indirect estimation of dollar value costs associated with security breach announcements, such as the loss in market value (e.g., share price).
- Traditional risk or decision analysis framework. In this approach, the expected loss is computed once risks, potential risks and their likelihood of occurrence are identified.

Managers responsible for information security are increasingly required to justify their budget requests in purely economic terms. There has been considerable interest in using financial metrics used to justify and evaluate investments in information security (CSI, 2004). Figure 2 confirms this assumption.

Figure 2 illustrates that 55% of organizations use return on investment (ROI)[7] as a metric, 28% use internal rate of return (IRR) and 25% use nett present value (NPV). Although numerous metrics are available, ROI has emerged as the method preferred by most organisations.

Figure 2. Percentage of organisations using financial metrics to quantify information security investments (Adapted from CSI, 2004)

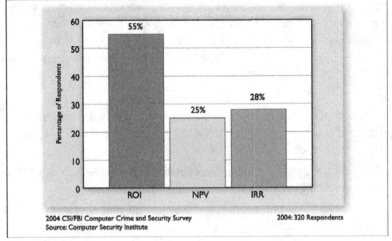

2004 CSI/FBI Computer Crime and Security Survey   2004: 320 Respondents
Source: Computer Security Institute

Return on security investment (ROSI) is the most recent catchphrase that economists are using to characterize the value of security investments. Despite the fact that defining ROSI is difficult, security practitioners need to understand the variables that define ROSI and assign dollar values to quantities that are inadequately defined (SBQ, 2001).

It is apparent that information security management is a demanding task; however assessing the value of security technologies is an essential requirement in effectively managing information security. Various techniques and tools are available to the practitioner of information security. However, the economic perspective stresses that, while some investment in information security is good; more security is not always worth the cost. Hence, it is the author's belief that, the amount that an organisation spends on information security will typically be far less than the expected loss from a security incident.

Impact of Information Security Breaches

No information security breach is good, but the impact of some incidents is considerably worse and more difficult to measure than that of others. There's always some financial aspect to security related incidents and organisations intent on not being victimised must pay a price as information security measures come at a price (Gordon & Richardson, 2004).

Every organisation (small or large) must understand the costs associated when information security is breached. Farahmand, Navathe, Sharp, and Enslow (2003) notes that the cost of an information security incident must be measured in terms of the impact on the business and, identical incidents in different organisations of the same industry could have different costs. The impact may be financial, in the form of immediate costs and losses, but the more serious incidents are those that have hidden costs associated with them. Furthermore, they (Farahmand et al., 2003) associate the following losses with information security breaches: (1) the brand image, public reputation, and the goodwill in the market place, (2) the financial value of business transactions, (3) public and customer confidence in the accuracy and fraud-resistance of business transactions, (4) the ability to maintain revenue cash flow in a timely manner, (5) the ability to resolve disputes beyond reasonable doubt, and (6) the ability to meet the requirements of regulators.

Cavusoglu (2002) states that public announcement of information security breaches are negatively associated with the market value of the affected organisations. He notes that compromised organisations lose approximately 2.1% of their market value within two days of the security incident and smaller organisations appear to be penalised more than larger ones when a security breach occurs. This means that smaller organisations must keep in mind the importance of information security for their survivability.

Campbell, Gordon, Loeb, and Zhou (2003) examined the market reaction to newspaper reports of information security breaches at publicly traded U.S. corporations. Potential costs identified with security breaches were (1) lost business (immediate and long term as a consequence of negative reputation effects), (2) activities associated with detecting and correcting breaches, and (3) potential legal liability. They observed that survey data on the cost of information security breaches was limited since many organisations are unwilling or unable to quantify their losses. They concluded that there is some evidence of an overall negative stock market reaction to announcements of information security breaches and these announcements affect the future economic performance of the affected organisations. They also found that all types of information security breaches did not have similar economic impacts. There was no significant market reaction to breaches not relating to confidentiality (e.g., denial-of-service attacks); however, a significant reaction to violations of confidentiality (e.g., breaching a customer database) was noted. It was also noted that many of the non-confidential incidents (e.g., virus attacks) received more publicity and affected more organisations than the confidential incidents. Nevertheless, stock market reaction was not determined by the level of media publicity.

Garg et al. (2003), conducted a study that extended to include investor reactions to information security incidents on security vendors. They concluded that the share price of security vendors responded positively to information security breaches, with increases of 0.9% to 3.3% on average for all incidents. The reason given for this situation was the perception of investors that attacks would result in an overall increase in security spending by all organisations (and not just the affected ones).

Many information security surveys (e.g., AusCERT, 2004; BCMS, 2003; CSI, 2004; E-Crime, 2004; ISBS, 2004) also use the cost of a security incident as a measure of its overall impact. However, it is evident that this is a difficult question to answer (e.g., Campbell et al., 2003; Garg et al., 2003; Farahmand et al., 2003; Cavusoglu, 2002). It has been shown that security breaches can have many different impacts. Direct cash expenditure is only one of these. Other costs, such as time spent investigating and responding, also need to be included. Some, such as the cost of business disruption or damage to reputation, are hard to quantify. The author concludes that every organisation (small or large) must understand the costs associated when their information security is breached and that breaking down the cost of security breaches into its component parts can assist in this process.

Information Security Management

A fundamental issue that arises in discussions about information security is that of responsibility. A reasonable answer is that information security ought to be the responsibility of anyone who can affect the security of the system although specific duties and responsibilities of individuals and business units may vary (NIST, 1995).

Birman (2000) states that information security is more than a technical issue, and could even have strategic as well as legal implications. It is therefore important that information security is evaluated at management level and is integrated into the processes of the business. An organisations' executive management must be involved in and be constantly informed of the effectiveness of the information security strategies implemented as they (management) are ultimately responsible (1) to the shareholders and (2) for compliance with applicable laws and regulations (Posthumus & von Solms, 2004; Von Solms, 1996). Entrust (2004) encourages the implementation and acceptance of an information security management framework. These actions, according to Entrust (2004), protect business information, improve the efficiency of the business and ensure that the business meets its legal requirements. Hong, Chi, Chao, and Tang (2003) state that an organisation should establish and maintain a documented information security management system. Organisations should examine the environment, familiarise themselves with security standards, define the scope of information security and assess the risk and control in order to develop an information security management system.

Straub and Welke (1998) declare that information security continues to be ignored by executive management and despite the seriousness of risk from security breaches; many organisations are either completely or insufficiently protected. If the threat is so clear then why is this so? Information security needs executive management support in order to succeed and to create a security-oriented culture in any organisation (Kankanhalli, Teo, Tan, & Wei, 2003; Siponen, 2001; Whitman & Matford cited in Witman, 2004; Williams, 2001). Goodhue and Straub (1991) note that managerial concern about information security is a function of (1) risk inherent in the industry, (2) the extent of the effort already taken to control these risks, and (3) individual factors such as awareness of previous system breaches.

In a study conducted by Mitchell et al. (1999), in 50% of the companies' surveyed, responsibility for information management was placed with the IT department while in only 25% responsibility was with senior management. Only 5% had a dedicated information security manager responsible for corporate information and most (57.5%) had the same person responsible for information security and information management. This study highlights the fact that in most organisations the management of information security continues to be placed within the IT function. IT managers continue to be responsible for managing and securing electronic information and it appears that information security is viewed as a technology problem to be dealt by the technology people. It is this attitude that is responsible for gaps in an organisations information security chain of defences.

In most organisations information security is the result of an evolutionary process and although a proliferation of technology has been implemented to provide security, the approach used does not appear to have been systematic (Anttila et al., 2004).

If an organisation does not have clear guiding principles or ideas for information security, the measures applied are very likely followed mechanically, leading to an ineffective implementation of security. Information security must be related to business performance and the final responsibility lies directly with the organisations' executive management.

Philosophy for Developing Information Security

NIST (1995) describes eight principles that are essential to developing an effective information security program in any organisation (small or large). These principles (see below) assist the information security practitioner in understanding how information security supports the mission of the organisation. Support for the NIST (1995) principles is provided in (e.g., DTI, 2004; OECD, 2002; Posthumus & Von Solms, 2004; Swanson & Guttman, 1996).

The eight principles that are essential to the development of an effective information security program are (NIST, 1995):

- **Information security must support the mission of the organization:** By selecting and applying appropriate techniques, information security aids the organization's mission by protecting its physical and financial resources, reputation, legal position, employees, and other tangible and intangible assets. Occasionally, information security may be seen as counter productive due to rules and procedures imposed on users, however, it must be emphasized that these (rules and procedures) do not exist for their own sake but to protect important assets. Information security should, therefore, be viewed as a means to an end and not the end itself.

- **Information security is an integral element of business management:** ICT assets are often crucial to supporting the mission of an organization (refer to the previous) and protecting them can be as critical as protecting other organizational resources, however, including security considerations in the management of ICT does not completely eliminate the possibility that these assets will be harmed. Ultimately, business managers must decide on the level of risk they are willing to accept (taking into account factors such as the cost of security controls and whether an organisations ICT assets are linked to an external partner).

- **Information security must be cost effective:** The costs and benefits of security should be carefully examined in both monetary and non-monetary terms to ensure that the cost of controls does not exceed expected benefits. Security should be appropriate and proportionate to the value of and degree of reliance on the information systems and to the severity, probability, and extent of potential harm. Security must be seen as *smart business practice* and by investing in security measures; an organization can reduce the frequency and severity of information security-related losses.

- **Information security responsibilities and accountability must be made explicit:** Depending on the size of the organisation, assignment of responsibilities may be internal or may extend across organisational boundaries. However, every organisation (small or large) can prepare a document that states organisational policy and makes explicit information security responsibilities.

- **System owners have information security responsibilities outside their own organizations:** If a system has external users, its owners have a responsibility to share appropriate knowledge about the existence and general extent of security measures so that other users can be confident that the system is adequately secure.

- **Information security requires a comprehensive and integrated approach:** Providing effective information security requires a comprehensive approach that considers a variety of areas both within and outside of the information security field. This comprehensive approach extends throughout the entire information life cycle.

- **Information security must be periodically reassessed:** Computers and the environments they operate in are dynamic. Security is *never* perfect when a system is implemented, procedures become outdated over time, new ways are constantly being discovered to intentionally or unintentionally bypass or subvert security, and changes in the system or the environment can create new vulnerabilities. All of these issues make it necessary to periodically reassess an organisations information security.

- **Information security is constrained by societal factors:** Security measures should be selected and implemented with recognition of the rights and legitimate interests of system users. This many involve balancing the security needs of information owners and users with societal goals. However, rules and expectations change with regard to the appropriate use of security controls. These changes may either increase or decrease security.

As more organizations share information electronically, a common understanding of what is needed and expected in securing information assets is required. The principles discussed in the preceding paragraphs address information security from a high-level viewpoint. These principles are intended to guide security practitioners in developing effective information security programs for organisations (small & large).

Designing and Implementing Information Security

As organisations develop, previous methods of communication can become less effective. Informal understandings and discussions can prove insufficient. Legal and regulatory pressures increase as companies expand. Providing the entire company with clear, concise, internal governance can bring real benefits in terms of efficiency as well as a means of reducing information risk (DTI, 2004b).

A policy is an expression of intent. An information security policy must provide clear direction and be supported by management for the implementation and maintenance of information security. To be effective the policy must be relevant, accessible, and understandable to all intended users throughout the organisation (DTI, 2004b).

According to DTI (2004b), Lichtenstein (1997), Microsoft (2005), and WatchGuard (2004), an information security policy is an important document to develop while designing an information system. The security policy begins with the organization's basic commitment to information security formulated as a general policy statement. The policy is then applied to all aspects of the system design or security solution. The policy identifies security goals (e.g., confidentiality, integrity, availability) that the system should support and these goals guide the procedures, standards and controls used in the design of the information security architecture. The policy must also define critical assets, perceived threats, and security-related roles and responsibilities.

Although each organization's security needs are unique, most security policies address common elements. Due to the dynamic nature of the ICT environment an information security policy is never set in stone, rather it is a living document. The SANS Institute (SANS, 2005) recommends that the following elements be included in a security policy:

- **Objectives:** Clearly states the reason the security policy exists
- **Scope:** Identifies the people and systems affected by the policy
- **Protected Assets:** identifies the assets that the policy protects (e.g., e-mail servers, databases, and Web sites)
- **Responsibilities:** Identifies the groups or individuals responsible for implementing the conditions of the policy
- **Enforcement:** Discusses the consequences of violating the policy
- **Remote access policy:** Outlines acceptable methods for remotely connecting to the internal network (e.g., whether employees are allowed to connect to the network from their home computers)

- **Information protection policy:** Provides guidelines to users on the processing, storage, and transmission of sensitive information
- **Virus protection policy:** Provides requirements for the use of antivirus software as well as guidelines for reporting and containing virus infections
- **Password policy:** Provides guidelines for how user-level and system-level passwords are managed and changed
- **Firewall security policy:** Describes, in general, how firewalls are configured and maintained, and by whom

Once the organisational security policy has been created, the next step is to establish the information security plan. While the policy defines the goals, the plan determines the steps that need to be taken to implement information security. Information security is not a separate task but an overlapping association of technologies, people, policies, and processes. The plan coordinates the whole security effort to match the organisations' security policy and ensures that there are no gaps (Microsoft, 2005).

The four steps in developing an information security plan (Lichtenstein, 1997; Microsoft, 2005; WatchGuard, 2004) are:

- **Assess:** The current state of security, identify critical assets, predict threats, and determine exposure for each asset
- **Plan:** For risks, noting that the objective is not to eliminate all risk regardless of cost but to minimise risks
- **Execute:** Check for adequacy, obtain participant feedback, modify plan if required and implement the plan
- **Monitor:** Research new threats as they become evident, modify the plan when changes occur (e.g., personnel changes) and perform ongoing maintenance (e.g., antivirus definition updates)

There is no silver bullet to the information security problem. Modern information systems are complex and dynamic and no simple solutions exist to completely protect organisational information assets. To be effective, security solutions must work together, and in harmony, to secure the critical assets of the organisation. Implemented solutions should be powerful, scalable and adaptable in order to effortlessly incorporate new functionality to meet emerging threats.

Review of Information Security Survey Statistics

Kabay (2001) notes that no one can be expected to give reliable answers pertaining to questions on information security. He adds that the two fundamental difficulties preventing the development of accurate statistics are: (1) the problem of detection and (2) the problem of reporting. The first problem is that an unknown number of crimes (of all kinds) are undetected because some frauds are discovered long after they have occurred. The second problem deals with reporting of security related crimes. Even if crimes are detected, few are reported in a way that allows systematic data collection. This belief is based in part on the un-quantified experience of information security professionals who have conducted interviews of their clients, and it turns out that only about ten percent of the attacks against computer systems revealed in such interviews were ever reported to any kind of authority or to the public.

On the basis of Kabay (2001), it follows that, even though the methodology used by information security surveys (e.g., AusCERT, 2004; BCMS, 2003; CSI, 2004; E-Crime, 2004; ISBS, 2004) may be imperfect and should not be taken as the absolute representation of the state of information security; they do however provide valuable data on the relative frequencies and severities of various security threats.

This section reviews ten of the more recent (2002 to 2004) information security surveys in order to determine the state of information security in organisations (small and large). Performing a meta-analysis of the surveys would be difficult because the questions asked differ both in content and method from survey to survey and because the results were developed and reported in different ways. Nevertheless, it was apparent that there were several common findings, which form the basis of this review.

The size of the organizations represented in each of the surveys, as measured by the number of employees, is given in Table 3. The table gives the total respondents for each survey and divides the organisations into small and large businesses as per the definition of small businesses adopted for this research.

Each of the surveys specifically asked if the respondents had experienced any security breaches in the previous year. Table 4 shows the specific survey data, with the numbers ranging from 39% to 74%. When examined chronologically, the overall trend is that security breaches are increasing.

Another frequently asked question related to the monetary loss resulting from information security breaches. Nine of the ten surveys provided some quantification of the monetary losses associated with information security incidents. Table 5 shows the survey results.

As can be seen by the reported data, the ability or willingness of the respondents to quantify losses is limited at best. Most of the surveys approached this area of questioning from the point of view of how much damage had been done in aggregate.

Table 3. Summary of respondents from small and large businesses

Survey	Respondents	Small Businesses (aggregate % employees)	Large Businesses (aggregate[1] % employees)
1. CSI 2004	494	19%	81%
2. ISBS 2004	1001	52%	48%
3. AusCERT 2004	240	15%	85%
4. E-Crime 2004	500	15%	85%
5. CSI 2003	530	18%	82%
6. AusCERT 2003	214	52%	48%
7. Deloitte 2003	175	none	100%
8. CSI 2002	503	16%	84%
9. ISBS 2002	1000	80%	20%
10. AusCERT 2002	95	39%	61%

Table 4. Survey comparison: Summary of security breaches experienced (Source: Compiled from each of the listed surveys)

Survey	Security Breach Experienced
1. CSI 2004	53% experienced a security incident in the past 12 months.
2. ISBS 2004	74% experienced a security incident in the past 12 months.
3. AusCERT 2004	49% experienced a security incident in the past 12 months.
4. E-Crime 2004	70% experienced a security incident in the past 12 months.
5. CSI 2003	56% experienced a security incident in the past 12 months.
6. AusCERT 2003	42% experienced a security incident in the past 12 months.
7. Deloitte 2003	39% experienced a security incident in the past 12 months.
8. CSI 2002	60% experienced a security incident in the past 12 months.
9. ISBS 2002	44% experienced a security incident in the past 12 months.
10. AusCERT 2002	67% experienced a security incident in the past 12 months.

As a result, the losses reported include average costs per serious incident (ISBS, 2004) to total losses per annum (CSI, 2004).

Nine of the surveys asked respondents what their most important security concerns were. These concerns are viruses, denial-of-service, some form of theft (ranging from data to equipment), misuse of systems and unauthorised access (hacking) appear in almost all of the top five rankings.

Table 5. Survey comparison: Financial loss

Survey	Amount of Loss Reported
1. CSI 2004	Total losses for the 54% able to quantify: $141,496,560
2. ISBS 2004	The average cost of a serious security incident was approximately £7,000 to £14,000. For large companies, the equivalent cost was approximately £65,000 to £190,000.
3. AusCERT 2004	Total losses for the 57% able to quantify: AU$15,921,064
4. E-Crime 2004	Of the 68% that tracked monetary losses the following breakdown was given: 3% - $10 million 5% - $1 million to $9.9 million 5% - $500,000 to $999,999 11% - $100,000 to $499,999 26% - Less then $100,000 50% - Don't know amount
5. CSI 2003	Total losses for the 48% able to quantify: $201,797,340
6. AusCERT 2003	Total losses for the 58% able to quantify: AU$11,800,783
7. CSI 2002	Total losses for the 44% able to quantify: $455,848,000
8. ISBS 2002	The average cost of a serious security incident was approximately £30,000
9. AusCERT 2002	Total losses for the 80% able to quantify: AU$5,781,300

The statistics confirm that information security breaches continue to rise annually. The data examined provides evidence that: (1) information security continues to remain a problem for many organisations and (2) the provision of effective information security is essential for an organisations continued existence. As more organisations continue to suffer from information security incidents and the associated financial losses, understanding the information security problem becomes essential in security planning and development of effective information security, especially for small businesses.

Chapter Summary

Information security is defined as the protection of information system assets against various threats and attacks in order to preserve the confidentiality, integrity, and availability of these systems. Modern society is significantly dependent on IT and there is little likelihood that this will change in the future. As globalization continues to advance and electronic civil disobedience increases in volume and efficacy, the implementation of effective information security continues to become an area of concern for academics, information security researchers, information security practitioners and management of organisations (small and large). It is essential that all stakeholders are aware of security threats and trends and take appropriate steps to provide adequate protection of information system assets.

Early research in information security (1970s and 1980s) treated information security as something tangible and concrete. Security was seen as a means to protect tangible assets and consisted purely of providing a security fence around information processing activities. However, security cannot be viewed as a disjoint sequence of activities nor is it just a sequence of "locks and keys" in the prevention of adverse events. As organisations have evolved and organisational structures are becoming more flat and decentralised in nature, a new vision for addressing information security concerns has emerged. This vision, which is the key to effective information security in the new millennium, must be aligned with social groupings and behaviour and include a substantial human component. This paradigm shift provides an excellent motivation and platform for holistic research into the information security crisis.

Information security research has predominantly been positivist in its approach. Phenomenological or interpretivist research is almost entirely absent. Historically, much of the analysis into the problems of, and solutions to, information security has been quantified against highly structured questionnaires. This method has bounded the discussion and preconditioned the answers and the resulting metrics are often given a factual status that they do not deserve. The fundamental limitation on the applicability of these findings is that generalisations in the field of information technology and security are difficult to justify due to the diversity of systems installed in organisations. A phenomenological approach to information security research would certainly be advantageous as it would attempt to bridge a gap between man and machine and in doing so would provide a holistic view of the problem domain, rather than a simplistic and one-dimensional explanation.

Studies conducted by Kotulic and Clark (2004) involving diverse organisations (small and large) indicate that information security research is one of the most intrusive types of organisational research, and that there is a general mistrust of anyone attempting to gain data about information security practices in organisations. It is nearly impossible to extract information of this nature from businesses without a major supporter.

A critique of several non-academic surveys on information security was done in order to create some baseline of data from which to perform this research. The findings of the critique were that: (1) information security breaches continue to rise annually, (2) the surveys were entirely quantitative in their approach, (3) the targeted audience were primarily large businesses with only a small percentage (if any) of small businesses participating, (4) information security continues to remain a problem for many organisations, and (5) the provision of effective information security is an essential aspect of a organisations (small and large) success and continued existence. Historically, some small businesses have been included in surveys on information security (see Table 2-3) however; South African small businesses are noticeably absent. Even though this is the case, the researcher believes that the reported findings are also applicable to small businesses in South Africa. Support for this belief is provided by Kabay (2002) who states that the basic reasons why we care about information security remain the same in every organisation (small or large).

Some concerns uncovered by the author during the literature search are: (1) small businesses are trying to do everything by themselves (without enlisting expert assistance) and (2) small businesses are frequently exposed to crime, (especially technology related crimes). The rationale is that they (small businesses) do not have the base across which to spread the costs of hiring security experts or implementing expensive security-related technologies. Additionally, the researcher has discovered that academic and non-academic studies in information security have concentrated primarily on large organisations. Possible reasons for this state of affairs are that: (1) large businesses can make a greater contribution to the economy and (2) that large businesses have bigger budgets and therefore can spend more on information security and security research. Many researchers are of the opinion that what is good for large businesses is also applicable to small businesses. This view is based on the incorrect assumption that research conducted in large businesses can be applied directly to small businesses. Consequently, this biased viewpoint has resulted in small businesses being excluded from information security research. Although information security attacks and breaches make no distinction in the size of the organisation (small and large are equally at risk), the small business practitioner has to recognise and manage information security risks without the resources available to larger businesses. Throughout this literature search, however, it has been found that models of information security developed for large businesses are simply forced onto small businesses without recognising the fact that small businesses are not just little big businesses.

With regard to small businesses, the findings reveal that this sector is rapidly growing and is making significant contributions to the economy. Furthermore, small businesses are embracing ICT and the Internet to gain competitive advantage, market share, and access to new markets, solve business problems, and to accumulate knowledge for improvement of services. Innovative entrepreneurs are also using technology and the Internet as a means to market niche products and to reach distant customers. The above-mentioned reasons provide excellent justification for developing and building capacity regarding academic research into the information security crises facing small businesses.

There is no silver bullet to the information security problem in small businesses. Information security requires a firm grounding in academic theory in order to be effective. Security cannot be gained by installing a gadget, no matter how good it is. Security is a process that must be woven into the corporate culture of every organisation (small or large), with due attention to the ever-changing landscape of threats, vulnerabilities and risks. Any models or guidelines developed must be relevant and take cognisance of the fact that small businesses are unique and that they have their own focus and drivers when dealing with the information security problem.

Conclusion

The contribution of this chapter is twofold. First, it presents the current research directions in information security. It identifies the trend that information security research is moving away from a narrow technical viewpoint to a broader managerial perspective. Although a multitude of research and data exists in the field of information security, the literature indicates that information security research is restricted to large organisations. While academic research has investigated different perspectives of information security, it has been found that most of the studies looked at specific issues with little or no attempt being made to obtain a complete view of information security. Additionally, academic researchers have concentrated on information security in large organisations and presume that these findings are compatible with small businesses. Most researchers also rely on standards bodies (e.g., ISO,[8] BSI,[9] NIST[10]) to develop frameworks on which information security research is based.

Second, this chapter recognises the fact that the use of a phenomenological approach for understanding information security is still at a theory building stage. The literature search found practically no case studies that used a qualitative approach for evaluating information security. Almost all the studies on information security were based on the positivist paradigm. This highlights the need for interpretivist empirical research to develop a set of management guidelines for investigating and implementing effective information security practices in small businesses.

References

Anttila, J., Kajava, J., & Varonen, R. (2004, August). Balanced integration of information security into business management. In *Proceedings of the 30th EUROMICRO Conference* (pp. 558-564).

AusCERT. (2004). *Australian computer crime survey 2004*. Retrieved February 17, 2005, from http://www.auscert.org.au/download.html?f=114

Berger, D. L. (1981). *Security for small businesses*. Woburn, MA: Butterworth Inc.

Birman, K. P. (2000). The next generation internet: Unsafe at any speed. *IEEE Computer, 33*(8), 54-60.

Blatchford, C. (1998, December). Computer controls—diffusion into the smaller firm: (A qualitative research study: Part 1). *Computer Fraud & Security, 1998*(12), 13-17.

Blatchford, C. (1999, January). Computer controls—Diffusion into the smaller firm: (A qualitative research study: Part 2). *Computer Fraud & Security, 1999*(1), 14-19.

Business Continuity Management Survey (BCMS). (2003). *Business continuity management survey ZA 2003*. KPMG. Retrieved February 1, 2005, from http://www.kpmg.co.za/download/bcssurvey_03.pdf.

Campbell, K., Gordon, L. A., Loeb, M. P., & Zhou, L. (2003). The economic cost of publicly announced information security breaches: Empirical evidence from the stock market. *Journal of Computer Security, 11*(2003), 431-448. IOS Press.

Cavusoglu, H. (2002). *The economics of information technology (IT) security.* Presented at the 8th Americas Conference on Information Systems. Doctoral Consortium.

Cavusoglu, H., Mishra, B., & Raghunathan S. (2004, July). A model for evaluating IT security investments. *Communications of the ACM, 47*(7), 87-92.

Chelimsky, E., Jordan, F. C., Russell, L. S., & Strack. J. R. (1979). *Security and the small business retailer*. Washington DC: Government Printing Office.

Cisco Systems (Cisco). (2001). *Economic impact of network security threats*. White paper. Cisco Systems Inc. Retrieved April 16, 2004, from http://www.cisco.com/go/security

COBIT Security Baseline (COBIT). (2004). *COBIT security baseline—an information security survival*. Retrieved February 17, 2005, from http://www.isaca.org

Computer Security Institute (CSI). (2004). *CSI/FBI 2004 computer crime and security survey*. Retrieved January 27, 2005, from http://www.gocsi.com/forms/fbi/csi_fbi_survey.jhtml

Dhillon, J., & Backhouse, G. (1999). *Working towards principles for information security management in the 21st century.* Research paper. London: LSE Computer Security Research Centre.

Doney, L. D. (1998, May-June). The growing threat of computer crime in small businesses. *Business Horizons, 41*(3), 81-87.

DTI. (2004). *Information security: A business guide to using the Internet*. UK Department of Trade and Industry. Retrieved March 18, 2005, from http://www.dti.gov.uk/bestpractice/technology/security.htm

DTI. (2004b). *How to write an information security policy*. UK Department of Trade and Industry. Retrieved March 18, 2005, from http://www.dti.gov.uk/bestpractice/technology/security.htm

E-Crime Watch Survey (E-Crime). (2004). *2004 e-crime watch survey*. Retrieved January 31, 2005, from http://www.cert.org/archive/pdf/2004eCrimeWatchSummary.pdf

Electronic Communications and Transactions Act (ECT). (2002). *Electronic Communications and Transactions Act No. 25 of 2002*. South Africa Government Online. South African Parliament. Retrieved January 15, 2005, from http://www.info.gov.za/gazette/acts/2002/a25-02.pdf

Entrust. (2004). *Information security governance: An essential element of corporate governance*. Retrieved January 17, 2005, from http://itresearch.forbes.com/detail/RES/1082396487_702.html

Farahmand, F., Navathe, S. B., Sharp, G. P., & Enslow, P. H. (2003). Managing vulnerabilities of information system to security incidents. *Communications of the ACM,* 348-354.

Finne, T. (1998). A conceptual framework for information security management. *Computers & Security, 17*(4), 303-307.

Galliers, R. (1993). Research issues in information systems. *Journal of Information Technology, 8*(2), 92-98.

Garg, A., Curtis, J., & Halper, H. (2003). Quantifying the financial impact of IT security breaches. *Information Management & Computer Security, 11*(2), 74-83, MCB UP.

Glaser, B. G., & Strauss, A. L. (1967). *The discovery of grounded theory*. Chicago: Aldine Inc.

Goodhue, D. L., & Straub, D. W. (1991, January). Security concerns of system users: a study of perceptions of the adequacy of security measures. *Information & Management, 20*(1), 13-27.

Gordon, L. A., & Loeb, M. P. (2002, November). The economics of information security investment. *ACM Transactions on Information and System Security, 5*(4), 438-457.

Gordon, L. A., & Richardson, R. (2004, January). Infosec economics new approaches to improve your data defenses. *Network Computing, 4*, 67-70.

Hong, K., Chi, Y., Chao, L. R., & Tang, J. (2003). An integrated system theory of information security management. *Information Management & Computer Security, 11*(5), 243-248. MCB University Press.

Information Security Breaches Survey (ISBS). (2004). *Information security breaches survey 2004.* PriceWaterHouse Coopers and UK DTI. Retrieved February 3, 2005, from http://www.pwc.com/images/gx/eng/about/svcs/grms/2004Technical_Report.pdf

IT Governance Institute (ITGI). (2001). *Information security governance: guidance for boards of directors and executive management.* Retrieved February 2, 2005, from http://www.isaca.org/Content/ContentGroups/ITGI3/Resources1/Information_Security_Governance_Guidance_for_Boards_of_Directors_and_Executive_Management/infosecurity.pdf

Kabay, M. E. (2001). *Studies and surveys of computer crime.* Retrieved February 1, 2005, from http://www.securitystats.com/reports/Studies_and_Surveys_of_Computer_Crime.pdf

Kabay, M. E. (2002). *What's important for information security: A manager's guide.* Retrieved February 1, 2005, from http://www2.norwich.edu/mkabay/infosec-mgmt/mgrguidesec.pdf

Kankanhalli, A., Teo, H., Tan, B. C. Y., & Wei, K. (2003). An integrative study of information systems security effectiveness. *International Journal of Information Management, 23*, 139-154.

Keogh, J. E. (1981). *The small business security handbook.* Englewood Cliffs, NJ: Prentice-Hall.

Kotulic, A. G., & Clark, J. G. (2004). Why there aren't more information security research studies. *Information & Management, 41*, 597-607.

Lichtenstein, S. (1997). Developing Internet security policy for organizations. In *Proceedings of the 30th Annual Hawaii International Conference on System Sciences.* Computer Society.

Lubbe, S. (1997). *The assessment of the effectiveness of IT investments in South African organizations.* PhD dissertation. University of Witwatersrand.

Lubbe, S. (2004). *The use of IT in small businesses: Efficiency and effectiveness in South Africa.* (Paper submitted to SAJEMS for publication).

Mbeki, T. (2004, February 6). *State of the Nation Address of the President of South Africa, Thabo Mbeki.* Houses of Parliament, Cape Town.

Mehta, M., & George, B. (2001). *Security in today's e-world.* Presented at the 8th Americas Conference on Information Systems.

MessageLabs. (2005). *E-mail threats (virus intercepts)*. Retrieved March 23, 2005, from http://www.Messagelabs.Com/Emailthreats/Default.Asp

Microsoft. (2005). *Security guide for small business*. Retrieved March 18, 2005, from http://www.microsoft.com/smallbusiness

Mitchell, R. C., Marcella, R., & Baxter, G. (1999). Corporate information security management. *New Library World, 100*(5), 213-227.

National Small Business Act (NSBA). (1996). *National Small Business Act No. 102 0f 1996*. South Africa Government Online. South African Parliament. Retrieved January 15, 2005, from http://www.info.gov.za/acts/1996/a102-96.htm

Ntsika Enterprise Promotion Agency (Ntsika). (2002). *State of small business development in South Africa Annual Review 2002*. Retrieved January 21, 2005, from http://www.ntsika.org.za/publications/AnnualReview2002.pdf

Ntsika Enterprise Promotion Agency (Ntsika). (2004). *Ntsika study series: Small business training case studies* (Vol. 1). Retrieved March 2, 2005, from http://www.ntsika.org.za/publications/studyseries1.pdf

OECD Guidelines (OECD). (2002, July 25). *OECD guidelines for the security of information systems and networks: Towards a culture of security*. Recommendations of the OECD Council, 1037th session.

Oliver, R. W. (2000). *The future of small business: Trends for a new century*. Sponsored by American Express, IBM, and National Small Business United in cooperation with RISEbusiness.

Panko, R. R. (2004). *corporate computer and network security* (International ed.). Prentice Hall.

Petkov, D., Fry, G. S., Petkova, O., & D'Onofrio, M. (2003). *Assisting small information technology companies identify critical success factors in Web development projects*. Presented at the 9th AMCIS.

Pipkin, D. (2000). *Information security: Protecting the global enterprise*. Prentice-Hall.

Posthumus, S., & Von Solms, R. (2004). A framework for the governance of information security. *Computers & Security, 23*, 638-646.

Pratt, J. H. (2002). *E-biz: Strategies for small business success*. Retrieved March 9, 2005, from http://www.sba.gov/advo/research/rs220tot.pdf

Remenyi, D., & Williams, B. (1995). Some aspects of methodology for research in information systems. *Journal of Information Systems*, (10), 191-201.

Secure Business Quarterly (SBQ). (2001). Return on security investment. *Secure Business Quarterly*, (Q4).

Siponen, M. T., (2001, June). Five dimensions of information security awareness. *Computers and Society,* 24-29.

Small Business Administration (SBA). (1999a). *Small business administration frequently asked questions.* Retrieved March 9, 2005, from http://www.sba.gov

Small Business Administration (SBA). (1999b). *E-commerce: Small businesses venture online.* Retrieved March 9, 2005, from http://www.sba.gov/advo/stats/e_comm.pdf

Small Enterprise Development Agency (SEDA). (2004). *Establishment of Seda on December 13, 2004 marks new era in small enterprise sector.* South African Government, Department of Trade and Industry. Media release. Retrieved January 21, 2005, from http://www.dti.gov.za/article/articleview.asp?current=1&arttypeid=1&artid=779

Stoneburner, G., Goguen, A., & Feringa, A. (2002, July). *risk management guide for information technology systems. Recommendations of the National Institute of Standards and Technology* (NIST Special Publication 800-30). US Dept of Commerce.

Straub, D. W., & Nance, W. D. (1990, March). Discovering and disciplining computer abuse in organisations: A field study. *MIS Quarterly,* 45-60.

Straub, D. W., & Welke, R. (1998, December). Coping with systems risk: security planning models for management decision making. *MIS Quarterly,* 441-469.

Swanson, M., & Guttman, B. (1996, September). *Generally accepted principles and practices for securing IT systems* (NIST Special Publication 800-14). US Dept of Commerce.

SANS Institute (SANS), The. (2005). *The SANS Institute Security Policy Project Web Site.* Retrieved March 28, 2005, from http://www.sans.org/resources/policies

Thomson, M. E., & Van Solms, R. (1998). Information security awareness: Educating your users effectively. *Information Management & Computer Security,* 6(4), 167-173, MCB UP.

Tsiakis, T., & Stephanides G., (2005). The economic approach of information security. *Computers & Security, 24*(2), 105-108.

Tsujii, S. (2004, November). Paradigm of information security as interdisciplinary comprehensive science. In *Proceedings of the 2004 International Conference on Cyberworlds (CW '04).*

U.S. National Institute of Standards and Technology (NIST). (1995). *An introduction to computer security: The NIST handbook* (NIST Special Publication 800-12). U.S. Department of Commerce. Retrieved January 31, 2005, from http://csrc.nist.gov/publications/nistpubs/800-12/handbook.pdf

Warren, M. J. (2003). Security practice: Survey evidence from three countries. *Logistics Information Management, 15*(5/6), 347-351, MCP UP.

WatchGuard. (2004). *A practical guide for better security.* Retrieved April 16, 2004, from http://www.watchguard.com

Webster, J., & Watson, T. (2002). Analyzing the past to prepare for the future: Writing a literature review. *MIS Quarterly, 26*(2).

Vermeulen, C., & Von Solms, R. (2002). The information security management toolbox—taking the pain out of security management. *Information Management and Computer Security, 3*(10), 119-125, MCP UP.

Williams, P. (2001, September 1). Information security governance. *Information Security Technical Report, 6*(3), 60-70.

Witman, P. D. (2004). Information security and shared leadership. In *Proceedings of the 7ᵗʰ Annual Conference of the Southern Association for Information Systems.*

Von Solms, B. (2001, May 1). Corporate governance and information security. *Computers & Security, 20*(3), 215-218.

Von Solms, B., & Von Solms, R. (2004). The 10 deadly sins of information security management. *Computers & Security, 23*(5), 371-376.

Von Solms, R. (1996). Information security management: The second generation. *Computers & Security, 15*(4), 281-288.

Von Solms, R. (1998). Information security management (1): Why information security is so important. *Information Management and Computer & Security, 6*(4), 74-177, MCB UP.

Endnotes

[1] Information and communications technology (ICT) represents all application and support systems *including* computer hardware, software and communications networks.

[2] A definition of small businesses is provided in the National Small Business Act (NSBA, 1996).

[3] Information system assets include hardware, software, firmware, information/data and telecommunications.

[4] EDI refers to *electronic data interchange.*

[5] EFTPoS refers to *electronic funds transfer at point of sale.*

6   $ refers to US$. The author uses US$ (and not localized currency values) in order to provide an international perspective on costs.

7   The terms ROI and ROSI are taken to have the same meaning in the context of this research.

8   International Standards Organisation

9   British Standards Institute

10   National Institute of Standards and Technology

Chapter XV

E-Learning:

An Investigation into Students' Reactions to Investment into IT at Tertiary Institutions

Solitaire Maherry-Lubbe, Dolphin Coast Enterprises, South Africa

Abstract

Constructivist theories and modern pedagogical concepts emphasize that an activation of students is one of the most influential factors for learning effectiveness. The implementation of those educational concepts in e-learning, especially in distance learning contexts, is a rather difficult challenge. Systems that assist lectures in this intention are required. In this study, a student's reaction towards e-learning is observed. The focus is on student's demographics in order to analyze their reaction towards e-learning. Solving tasks and observing and critiquing this solution process, instead of merely assessing the end product of e-learning processes. A sample of 105 students from the University was drawn and the findings suggest that e-learning investment can help address a need for this type of support.

Introduction

Technology is developing at a high speed and it has an impact on people's lives, especially the way one shops or does banking online. Gone are those days when one had to stand in long lines to cash money or pay transactions. Students need to study and work at the same time and the answer for that is e-learning. e-learning involves the use of a computer or electronic device (e.g., a mobile phone) in some way to provide training, educational, or learning material. e-learning can involve a greater variety of equipment than online training or education, for as the name implies, "online" involves using the Internet or an Intranet. CD-ROM and DVD can be used to provide learning materials.

The value of this research lies in the fact that it emphasises the importance of technology in teaching. It was therefore with this in mind that the researcher investigated why people need to invest into IT for teaching purposes. The researcher used Google and EBSCO host to look for articles, using the keywords e-learning, investment into IT and digital teaching as basis for searches for relevant literature. This chapter introduces the reader to the study focusing on the establishment of e-learning at a University in South Africa.

Literature Review

Much of the focus in e-learning today—from analysts, industry observers, consultants, and technologists—is on e-learning in the corporate world. But the biggest impact and opportunity for e-learning may be in education. Governments want to raise the skills and education level of its population, but to date e-learning has had little impact in this area.

e-learning can potentially transform education at every level. It can make high-quality educational experiences available to those whose location, economic, and personal constraints have prevented them from pursuing their educational goals. These learners also represent a wider student market for universities and other education establishments (Mkhize et al., 2005).

Much of the focus in e-learning today from analysts, industry observers, consultants, and technologists is on e-learning in the corporate world. But the biggest impact and opportunity for e-learning may ultimately be in education. Governments want to raise the skills and education level of its population, but to date e-learning has had little impact in this area. e-learning can potentially transform education at every level. It can make high-quality educational experiences available to those whose location, economic, and personal constraints have prevented them from pursuing their educational goals. These learners also represent a wider student market for universities and other education establishments.

Callaghan (2001) notes that much of the literature on the subject of e-learning extols the potential of the technologies for enhancing the learning experience. As has been mentioned, however, there is little evidence regarding learners' attitude to online learning, their responses to online as opposed to traditional classroom learning, their future use of online learning in their lives and the particular elements in online learning which learners find useful. Much of the literature also notes that traditional educators for their slow take-up of online learning elements in their teaching. Most commentators attribute this to teachers' lack of ability and enthusiasm for incorporating e-learning into the traditional classroom experience. Many of the dot.com e-learning ventures stress the importance of incorporating a wide range of communicative elements within the e-learning environment without producing the empirical evidence for their usefulness for learners (Callaghan, 2001).

Problems, Plagiarism, and Access

University Resistance

One issue is that universities don't see themselves merely as educational "content providers." Universities have a proud tradition of combining learning, research, teaching, and professional development. If one looks at higher education as a whole, it's not obvious how to implement e-learning. A second reason higher education resists e-learning is the absence of many of the technical skills needed as well as the experience in marketing and customer service necessary to support and develop this new market. Many universities are attempting e-learning initiatives, but on a limited scale. To have a chance of expanding the programs, they recognize the need for the right base of skills. Funding for such initiatives at the university level is another challenge.

A number of private ventures, especially in the United States, are attempting to tap into this potentially lucrative market. To date, these ventures have focused on the specific skills and technical capabilities needed. Where they fall short is in the area of access and sponsorship from universities, which resist giving up control, perceived or real. The result, again, is limited success. The organization needed a great deal of time and resources to become sustainable.

The government has to play a role in e-learning education. It has only recently entered this dialog, and initial results are promising. Governments show an interest in leveraging e-learning to create more widespread and cost-effective delivery of education from most levels, such as literacy training, all the way up to postgraduate degrees. The benefit of governmental support is that it can provide sponsorship and commitment. Universities need a development model that provides a common capability backed by government, allowing universities and other educational bodies to exploit e-learning and focus on content and teaching.

A model has emerged in the United Kingdom where the department for education and skills launched an initiative in 2001 called UK Universities. It was organized as a separate commercial enterprise that was expected to become self-funding and profitable over the next few years. With this organization, universities benefit because they can continue to focus on and own the content on the educational side, while UK Universities provides the capabilities and skills in marketing, sales, learning design, content development, and platform operation and support. All parties shared benefits and costs.

Salopek (2001) notes that accessibility is a buzzword that's been on the lips of people involved with e-learning for many months now. Optavia Corporation defines it as "the ability to use the Internet even when functioning under constraints." Those constraints can be of two types: functional limitations, also known as disabilities, and situational limitations, constraints caused by the devices a user is attempting to use. Salopek notes that one can expand Optavia's definition to embrace not only the Internet but all electronic and IT, as indeed the U.S. government has done.

Smart Force e-learning complied with new government standards for accessibility. Adkins *cited* by Salopek (2001) states that Smart Force's goal is to provide user experience to all users and they are making investments to integrate accessibility across [its] entire product line (Salopek, 2001). Smulders (2003) states that people can increase the learning potential of Web courses by following simple principles. Instructors and course developers are well versed in the art of instructional design. Despite this expertise and experience, many Web-based courses suffer from weak Web design and poor usability. Often, learners can't take advantage of good instructional design because the Web environment is too problematic: content is difficult to find, course tools don't work, and navigation is inconsistent.

Plagiarism

Major (2002) argues that universities have vowed to clamp down on businesses offering forged degree certificates. It came to light that a Liverpool based businessman is flouting the law and continuing to sell fake degrees over the Internet. Fakedegrees. co.uk claims to be the largest degree template library available in the world and sells degree certificates for £135. The site offers degree certificates that appear to come from universities based in the UK, USA, Australia, and New Zealand. The site is produced by Peter Leon Quinn, who calls himself a designer of impressive authentic looking certificates. Universities obtained a court injunction stopping.

New measures to help detect cheating students are being demonstrated at a conference in Newcastle. A survey of around 350 undergraduates found nearly 25% had copied text from another source at least once. A service that can scan 4.5 billion Web pages is now online so that lecturers can check the originality of the work submitted by students. The software was demonstrated at a meeting of the Plagiarism Advisory Service at North Umbria University (Major, 2002).

Hi-Tech Answer to Student Cheats

The Plagiarism Advisory Service notes that cheating is not a new phenomenon but the Internet has led to concerns within the academic community that the problem is set to increase dramatically. Service manager Fiona Duggan said:

The software has four databases that it checks students' work against and produces an originality report, which highlights where it has found matches. It demonstrates where the student has lifted text from, and it also takes you to the source where the match was found.

The software has been developed in the USA and the Plagiarism Advisory Service hopes it will go some way to stamping out the practice. Ms. Duggan noted that there are other things that can be done, like the way you set assignments so each student has something individual to put into the assignment so it is not so easy to copy (BBC News, 2002).

Accessing IT Education

Wood (2003) notes that people from ethnic minorities use their computers for education more than their richer neighbours, according to a DfES-commissioned survey into deprived areas of the UK. The study—which surveyed more than 1,500 people in deprived areas showed more than three-quarters of whom were from an ethnic minority—showed that, while 8 in 10 people in such areas recognised that IT skills were essential for their children, nearly two-thirds had beginner-level skills or none at all. Respondents were significantly less likely to own a PC or use the Internet than others in their communities, they found. Just 31% of blacks owned a PC, compared to 37% of whites, 42% of south Asians, and 44% from Chinese and other backgrounds. Some 40% of black people had used the Internet, compared to 38% of South Asians, 45% of whites, and 54% of Chinese and other respondents.

Literacy in English was a problem for South Asian people, with one quarter who did not use a computer citing language problems as the main factor preventing them from using a PC. There were also indications in interviews that gender may also act as a barrier for some Muslim women. South Asian people were less likely than other groups to use public facilities than other groups. Six in ten white non-users cited a lack of interest or need for computers, compared to only a third from black, South Asian, and mixed groups. The DfES welcomed the report. They note that they have a good understanding of the barriers that different groups face. Access to ICT, and the skills for using it, is critical to individuals' learning and employability (Wood, 2002). The Commission for Racial Equality said:

Public authorities need to be alert to the differences between ethnic groups in methods of learning and access to IT and the Internet in terms of messages and information they want to disseminate.

A total of 1,182 black and ethnic minority and 391 white households were surveyed in inner and outer London, Birmingham, Leeds and Bradford, Cardiff and Glasgow.

Wood (2003) argues that the following need to be looked at when preparing eco-systems:

1. **Environment:** Students need a certain environment (PC, connection, software) and some preparation needs to be done to make sure that the student has that.

2. **Technical skills:** Students need to know something about how to use whatever learning system exists. There has to be a way to impart this knowledge.

3. **Subject matter skills:** Students need to have some pre-requisite knowledge in the discipline to take the course.

4. **Study skills:** Students need to have the discipline and learning skills to benefit from the course.

5. **Support:** When students run into problems with any of these there has to be a mechanism to (a) find out and (b) help them through it.

6. **Content:** Designed for interaction—to keep students engaged—page clicking won't necessarily motivate students.

7. **Learner:** Disciplined, motivated to learn, has a need for learning, self-directed.

8. **Instructor:** Aware of students needs/concerns and involvement levels, attempts to draw students in to discussions early, organized schedule, provides resources for learners in need of additional learning (remedial).

9. **Technology:** Should play a servant role. Tools should be selected that involve learners and help them to connect with each other/content/instructor (e.g., chat, discussion questions, voice over IP are useful for connecting students and can be seen as student-cantered technologies).

10. **Organization:** Focused on learning, time, and resources made available, learners supported (through help desks etc.).

Many of these areas are outside of the instructors influence, but still need to be considered or if an area is weak (i.e., limited organizational support), other areas may have to play a more prominent role to ensure learners are prepared and succeed.

Rural and Urban Access

Conventionally, providing access has been defined as ensuring that rural communities can be wired up. For instance, Hudson (1994) advocates that the following be made available in rural and remote regions, to ensure equitable access:

- Universal single-party touchtone service (digital switching)
- Service quality sufficient for voice, fax, and data
- Rates based on community of interest (i.e., flat rate plans such as extended area service)
- Universal enhanced 911 (emergency services)
- Access to optional information services (local or toll-free calls for gateways to e-mail and databases in rural and remote areas)
- Mobile services

Just as salient, however, is ensuring that urban environments, where a majority of the new, visible, and minority immigrants tend to congregate, are able to get connected. A 1995 report by the U.S. Office of Technology Assessment (OTA) concerned the complex problems faced by urban cores with the increasing digitization of our knowledge sector. Given that much of the technological growth is taking place in the outer suburbs, edge cities, and high-tech parks, where there are often tax incentives, and a congruence of higher amenities, central and inner city urban areas are facing population losses and a lack of serviceable amenities (OTA, 1995).

Hvorecky (2004) argues that one of big expectations tied to e-learning speaks about its ability to introduce equal education to everyone. He claims that the possibility of e-courses to reach any corner of our planet will lead to the opportunity of delivering same high-quality education everywhere. The biggest optimists have a vision of top-ranking universities acting over the Internet using ready-made courses for huge amounts of students in third world countries. In accordance to well-known practices of e-learning, the students would study on their own pace by self-learning.

1. **Language barrier:** The World's population speaks several thousand different languages. Teaching and learning at the K-12 level can hardly be performed in any other language but in the children's native one. They must reflect social and cultural specifics so it can hardly cover more than the particular region.

Consequently, most of materials have to be produced locally. Such geographical limitations minimize chances for applications of e-learning.

2. **Absence of prerequisites:** At all education levels in countries behind the digital divide, the total absence of qualified teachers is much bigger problem than the distance from them. There are not enough human resources for preparing appropriate courses in any form, regardless whether on-ground or online.

3. **Technology hurdles:** Some teaching materials can be exploited as they do not require any knowledge of the foreign language or can be understood using limited language abilities. Broadband connection, high-resolution screens, and other course producers' expectations are often difficult to achieve in many countries. Slovakia for example belongs to OECD--the commonwealth of 30 of the worlds's most developed nations.

4. **Difficulties with translation:** Evidently, performing the entire K-12 educational process in a foreign language is almost impossible. Very few courses do not intensive textual support. The last choice is translation of the courses.

Thus, one can only expect wider applications of e-learning at the higher educational levels when the taught material is general enough and student's foreign language skills are adequate. At the same time, high schools and universities in all countries are better equipped by powerful technology. Seemingly, there is a much higher chance to overcome the above obstacles. In this paper we demonstrate another reason why delivering successful and well-designed courses is unlikely even in this cases. Crossing the digital divide is equal to crossing an economic barrier.

Security Problems

Korba (2003) states that security examines ways and means for implementing data integrity and protection policies for organizations involved with e-learning. He recommends that security in e-learning need to be taken serious, security have to-date been largely ignored. At best, they have been accommodated in an ad-hoc, patchwork fashion.

Gender, Race, and Age

Tanner (1981) notes that sexual selection in the hominid divergence also could have increased the capacity of males for relaxed social interaction. What may have been selected for among the transitional hominid males was the capacity to be extremely social but yet sufficiently aggressive when required and an ability to make fine discriminations as to situational necessity. Thus, the males of the transitional population would come to more closely resemble the females than had the males

Table 1. Spread of age of respondents

16 to 24	78%
24 to 44	72%
45 to 54	59%
55 to 64	41%
65+	16%

of the ancestral population. Much of the selection pressure engendered by female choice of sexual partners was directed toward male social and communicatory behaviour, reinforcing the potential and capacity for sociability, social learning, and intelligence.

Morris (2004) states that research from the National Statistics Omnibus Survey 2003 estimates that 54% of adults in Britain had used e-learning in the past three months. This represents a 5% point increase in April 2002. Over the period January to March 2003, an estimated 11.7 million households in the UK (47%) can now access the Internet from home.

The statistics claim:

*   85% of adults had used the Internet to e-mail.
*   80% to find information on goods and services.
*   69% to search for information about travel and accommodation.

Research for adults using the Internet, for personal and private use, shows the most popular purchases were travel, accommodation or holidays (54%), tickets for events (41%), books, magazines, e-learning, or training material (40%) and music or CDs (38%). However, younger adults use the Internet far more. Seventy eight percent of people aged 16-24 to only 16% for adults aged 65 and over.

There were nearly 60% of men in the sample. This was not by intention but because the sample was by assembled by chance.

Advantage and Disadvantages of E-Learning

There are many advantages to online and computer-based learning when compared to traditional face-to-face courses and lectures.

- Class work can be scheduled around work and family.
- Reduces travel time and travel costs for off-campus students.
- Students can study anywhere they have access to a computer and Internet connection.
- Self-paced learning modules allow students to work at their own pace.
- Instructors and students both report e-learning fosters more interaction among students and instructors than in large lecture courses.
- Develops knowledge of the Internet and computers skills that will help learners throughout their lives and careers.
- Successfully completing online or computer-based courses builds self-knowledge and self-confidence and encourages students to take responsibility for their learning.

Advantages of Web-Based Learning

Kruse (2001) notes that the general benefits of Web-based training when compared to traditional *instructor-led training* include all those shared by other types of technology-based training. When compared to *CD-ROM training,* the benefits of Web-based training stem from the fact that access to the content is easy and requires no distribution of physical materials. This means that Web-based training yields additional benefits, among them:

- Access is available anytime, anywhere, around the globe.
- Per-student equipment costs are affordable.
- Student tracking is made easy.
- Possible "learning object" architecture supports on demand, personalized learning.
- Content is easily updated (Kruse, 2001).

Disadvantages of Online or Computer-Based Learning

Kruse (2001) lists some of the disadvantages of e-learning as follows:

- Learners with low motivation or bad study habits may fall behind.
- Without the routine structures of a traditional class, students may get lost or confused about course activities and deadlines.
- Instructor may not always be available when students are studying or need help.

- Slow Internet connections or older computers may make accessing course materials frustrating.

Conclusion

E-learning is gaining a foothold in school districts across South Africa. Most universities are responding to new technologies, e-learning. Universities have a proud tradition of combining learning, research, teaching, and professional development. Although e-learning is growing fast it still has many problems in South Africa one of them being the fact that in South Africa most of the population are poor they can't even afford basic education. The next section will discuss the research methodology.

Why This Research Study is Important

Most institutions are looking at investing into ICT as a tool for e-learning as a method of providing learning and research. Although some South African universities may have resisted some e-learning, they are all turning to e-learning. Interest in the area has grown over the last couple of years. It is clear from previous research, El-Khatib (2003), who stated that the major benefits of online distance education are an improved quality of learning, an improved productivity of learning, an improved access to learning, and an improved student attitude to learning. Another advantage of the new online distance education model is the opportunity available for students to interact with others internationally and gain a more sophisticated and global understanding of complex international political issues, while gaining information technology literacy in the process.

Online delivery, if designed correctly, will improve distance education in the way that it will allow an increased level of interaction between students and teachers. The Internet has therefore provided many ways in which students can communicate in real time, which had previously missing from distance education courses. Students of online distance education need to be more motivated in order to keep on track and this will lead to a better level of education for all involved.

The survey was drafted after the first phase of literature review and interviews, which formed the scope and direction of the survey, as well as supporting questions. The population were Information Systems and technology students from the University of KwaZulu Natal (Westville campus) and the sample were 105 students.

The instrument is compiled in such a way it will help answer the research questions:

- Q1-Q5 race, age, gender, and year of study
- Q7-Q14 online services and computer literacy
- Q15-Q 19 e-learning and securities

Students will be given questions with option of choosing the answer from supplied answers. One of the main disadvantages of surveys, according to Dunn (2003), is finding a representative sample of respondents. Items that were covered include:

- What is e-learning?
- Race, age, and gender of students?
- Can e-learning be supportive?
- When should you use e-learning and when should you not use it?
- What competition or risk will the institution put itself in if they get involved in e-learning?
- How do you select the right tool? How do these tools work?
- How do student feel about e-learning?
- Is e-learning real?
- Securities in e-learning?
- How do you prove that the right candidate is doing the assignment?
- What are the best-practices for rapid development processes and rapid instructional design?
- How do you organize your team for e-learning?
- How can you avoid "rapid development" of poor content?
- How do you build instructional templates for reuse and efficiency?

The data was collated on a spreadsheet, and imported into SPSS for processing.

Presentation and Discussion of Result

Gender

From a sample of 105 students, 52% were females and 48% were male. One of the reasons of having more females than males is because females were more willing to answer questionnaires than males, who complained about lack of time. The aim of this question was to see whether there is a difference in student reaction to e-learning based on gender. Tanner (1981) argues that female cooperation is essential for the maintenance of special relationships and they thus present an opportunity for females to exercise choice. If female choice is involved, it is of interest to note that the selection criteria appear to be social and care should be taken to obtain the abilities of the males and not their dominance status into account.

Racial Composition

The question on race was aimed at determining whether there is a difference in the way students view e-learning based on race. The questionnaires stated that the purpose of stating race was for research purposes. This was to ease the sensitivity in students when asked to specify their race. The race listed in questionnaires covered all races found in South Africa and the rest of the world with an option of other if you did not belong to any of the race listed in the questionnaires. The racial composition of the research is 58% were African, Indian (35%), coloured (6%), and other (1%). Also, racism requires real or imagined differences and might affect e-learning applications.

Age

Age is important in research as different age groups react different to situations. The aim of this questionnaire was to see if different age groups have differing views about e-learning as it can be seen as follows.

Table 1. Respondents' gender

Male	50
Female	55

Table 2. Age of students

Age	No. of Students
16-19	44
20-23	44
24+	7

Table 3. Composition of age and reaction to e-learning

Age	How they feel about e-learning	No. of Students
16-19	excited	22
	will not mind	21
	uncomfortable	1
20-23	excited	15
	will not mind	15
	uncomfortable	14
24+	excited	17

Age does have influence on e-learning if one compare the age group of 24 and above, which are older people ready to start their own families and they are matured enough to know what they want, they turn to like e-learning. This can be a result of many influences they can be under pressure to support their families. It can be that they want to work and study at the same time so e-learning will enable them to do both at the same time.

If one takes the age group of 16 to 19 years, you will see that out of 44 students, only one student is not comfortable with e-learning. This can be because many young people like to experience new things without knowing the outcome of it. Another factor can be that if the students grow up playing computer games, they can be influenced by this and turn to technology-based learning.

From the 20 to 23 age group, 15 students will like to see UKZN engaging in e-learning, while 15 will not mind whether they are involved in e-learning or not. The other 14 don't support the idea of e-learning. Some of their reasons for not supporting e-learning was that they enjoy being around campus and they believe in traditional ways of learning

Morris (2004) states that research from the National Statistics Omnibus Survey 2003 estimates that 54% of adults had used e-learning in the past three months.

This represents a 5% point increase on April 2002. However, younger adults use the Internet far more.

Composition of Student View About E-Learning

The aim of the questionnaire was to see if student from different geographical areas have different views on e-learning. Table 4 compares students and their views about e-learning.

From the table, it can be seen that students from the suburbs would like to use e-learning, as 17 of them will like to use e-learning and the other five would not mind e-learning. This can be a result of those students from suburbs or developed places using technology so they are unlikely to reject technology-based form of education.

There were 34 respondents from urban areas, 20 of them will like to use e-learning, while six would not mind e-learning, and the other six will feel uncomfortable if they were to use e-learning for their study purposes. More than 30 (36) respondents from township answered questionnaires, where 17 will love to study through e-learning, 18 will not mind, and one will feel uncomfortable. Fifteen respondents from rural areas were given the questionnaires (seven of them will not mind to study through e-learning and eight will feel uncomfortable if UKZN were to offer courses through e-learning). The reason may be because many students from rural areas are technological disadvantaged when they come to the university. A lot of them have never used a computer before, so it can be difficult for them to support e-learning as they have to adjust to this technology base form of education while they are used to traditional based education. For one to be involved or study through e-learning, one needs to learn the programs and software being used.

Table 4. How students feel about e-learning

townships	17
urban	20
suburb	17
townships	18
urban	6
rural area	7
suburb	5
townships	1
urban	6
rural area	8

It can be concluded that students from rural area are less computer literate compared to students from other places. Though all the students who answered the question-naire were from the information systems and technology department, some of them can not print while others can't use Microsoft Excel, so they ended up failing the computer literacy test. Many of the students from rural areas who are not computer literate have deregistered IS&T course. They said it gave them problems as they did not know how to use a computer before or during the time they attended the IS&T course, they were not given time to adjust, and they were taken as if they know how to operate a computer. They have decided to reregister the course next year.

Hudson (1994) advocates that the following be made available in rural and remote regions to ensure equitable access:

- Universal single-party touchtone service (digital switching)
- Service quality sufficient for voice, fax, and data
- Rates based on community of interest (i.e., flat rate plans such as extended area service)
- Universal enhanced 911 (emergency services)
- Access to optional information services (local or toll-free calls for gateways to e-mail and databases in rural and remote areas)
- Mobile services

Just as salient, however, is ensuring that urban environments where a majority of the new, visible, and minority immigrants tend to congregate, are able to get con-nected. A 1995 report by the U.S. Office of Technology Assessment (OTA) discussed the complex problems faced by urban cores with the increasing digitization of our knowledge sector. Given that much of the technological growth is taking place in the outer suburbs, edge cities, and high-tech parks, where there are often tax incen-tives and a congruence of higher amenities, central and inner city urban areas are facing population losses and a lack of serviceable amenities.

Online Information

The 105 respondents noted as follows: (1) 55 students use online information more often, (2) 43 sometimes depending on the need, and (3) seven students don't use online information. It can be concluded that IS&T students have the capability of adjusting to e-learning as they are used in using online information, accounts, and libraries. From a sample of 105 students, 28 students would not mind if the course was to be offered online only, while 35 students would love to see their course being

100% online, and 42 in total disagree with the course being 100% online. There are many advantages to online and computer-based learning when compared to traditional face-to-face courses and lectures. There are a few disadvantages as well.

Advantages and Disadvantages of E-Learning

As noted in a previous section, some advantages of online or computer-based learning are:

- Class work can be scheduled around work and family.
- Travel time and travel costs are reduced for off-campus students.
- Students may have the option to select learning materials that meets their level of knowledge and interest.
- Students can study anywhere they have access to a computer and Internet connection.
- Self-paced learning modules allow students to work at their own pace.
- There is flexibility to join discussions in the bulletin board threaded discussion areas at any hour, or visit with classmates and instructors remotely in chat rooms.
- Instructors and students both report e-learning fosters more interaction among students and instructors than in large lecture courses.
- E-learning can accommodate different learning styles and facilitate learning through a variety of activities.
- Knowledge of the Internet and computers skills are developed that will help learners throughout their lives and careers.
- Learners can test out of or skim over materials already mastered and concentrate efforts in mastering areas containing new information and/or skills.

The disadvantages of e-learning are:

- Learners with low motivation or bad study habits may fall behind.
- Students may feel isolated from the instructor and classmates.
- Instructors may not always be available when students are studying or need help.
- Slow Internet connections or older computers may make accessing course materials frustrating.

- Hands-on or lab work is difficult to simulate in a virtual classroom (Iowa State University).

Students Impression of E-Learning

Fifty-six students think UKZN has the right resources to offer e-learning, students believe that the institution does not have what it take to offer e-learning, while 35 students were not sure. Some students think that e-learning degrees are not such good value as classroom learning or traditional learning. Seventy-seven respondents believe that e-learning can be supportive and 28 students believe e-learning can not be supportive

Hvorecky (2004) argues that one of the big expectations tied to e-learning speaks about its ability to introduce equal education to everyone. Authors of this claim assert that the possibility of e-courses to reach any corner of our planet will lead to the opportunity of delivering the same high-quality education everywhere. The biggest optimists have a vision of top-ranking universities acting over the Internet using ready-made courses for huge amounts of students in third world countries. In accordance to well-known practices of e-learning, the students would study on their own pace by self-learning. Despite the author's conviction that that e-learning has this potential, it is not difficult to express several counterarguments against such overoptimistic conclusions (Hvorecky, 2004):

1. **Language barrier:** The world's population speaks several thousand different languages. Teaching and learning must reflect social and cultural specifics so it can hardly cover more than the particular region. Consequently, most of materials have to be produced locally. Such geographical limitations minimize chances for applications of e-learning.

2. **Absence of prerequisites:** At all education levels in countries behind the digital divide, the total absence of qualified teachers is a much bigger problem than the distance from them. There are not enough human resources for preparing appropriate courses in any form—regardless whether on-ground or online. For that reasons, student's lack "standard volume of knowledge" requested for university enrolment and might struggle with problems during their study.

3. **Technology hurdles:** Some teaching materials can be exploited as they do not require any knowledge of the foreign language or can be understood using limited language abilities. Another question arises: Is if there is technology capable of presenting them in a relevant form and quality? Broadband connection, high-resolution screens, and other course producers' expectations are

often difficult to achieve in many countries. Slovakia for example belongs to OECD—the commonwealth of 30 of the world's most developed nations. Yet, a few days ago, who have watched a physician working with a 386 machine in one of the biggest Bratislava hospitals. What can one expect in remote cities of less developed countries?

Thus, one can only expect wider applications of e-learning at the higher educational levels when the taught material is general enough and student's foreign language skills are adequate. At the same time, high schools and universities in all countries are better equipped by powerful technology. Seemingly, there is a much higher chance to overcome the above obstacles. In this paper we demonstrate another reason why delivering successful and well-designed courses is unlikely even in this cases. Crossing the digital divide is equal to crossing an economic barrier (Hvorecky, 2004)

Plagiarism and E-Learning

In Figure 1, respondents were asked whether you can prove in e-learning that the right student is doing the work and does plagiarism occur in e-learning. From Figure 1, 28 respondents believe that you can prove who is doing the work, 35 think you cannot prove, and 42 are not sure.

Figure 1. Plagiarism

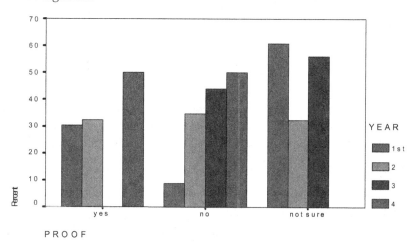

Hi-Tech Answer to Student Cheats

Measures to help detect cheating students are being demonstrated at a conference in Newcastle. A survey of around 350 undergraduates found nearly 25% had copied text from another source at least once. A service that can scan 4.5 billion Web pages is now online so that lecturers can check the originality of the work submitted by students. The software is being demonstrated at a Plagiarism Advisory Service conference at St James's Park (BBC News, 2002). Student Tom Lenham said of the statistics: That's a pretty modest interpretation of the situation at the moment. "From my own experience and that of fellow students, it's a lot higher than that because it is not drummed into the heads from the start. Only more recently one has been told how to use the Internet for referencing. The Plagiarism Advisory Service note that cheating is not a new phenomenon but the Internet has led to concerns within the academic community that the problem is set to increase dramatically. Service manager Fiona Duggan said:

The software has four databases that it checks students' work against and produces an originality report, which highlights where it has found matches. It demonstrates where the student has lifted text from, and it also takes you to the source where the match was found.

The software has been developed in the USA and the Plagiarism Advisory Service hopes it will go some way to stamping out the practice. Ms. Duggan said:

There are other things that can be done, like the way you set assignments so each student has something individual to put into the assignment so it is not so easy to copy. (BBC News, 2002)

Ownership of Personal Computer

Table 5 shows that 59 respondents own a computer or can have access to a computer at any time they want to use it, 46 respondents do not own one and have limited access to a computer. From Table 5, it can be concluded that the geographic place where a student comes from does not have any influence for a student to own a computer. Thirty-nine respondents have full access to the Internet at any time, 62 can access the Internet at any time when there is a need, and only four students have difficulty to access the net.

From Table 6 it can be concluded that all UKZN IS&T students have equal access to the Internet.

Table 5. Students that have access to a PC

townships		urban		rural area		suburb	
yes	no	yes	no	yes	no	yes	no
19	17	16	16	9	6	15	7

Table 6. Student access to the Net by race

	yes	no	sometimes
African	19	1	41
coloured	4		2
Indian	16	3	18
other			1

Computer Literacy and
Place Where Students come From

The researcher correlated computer literacy and the place where students are from. The purpose was to find out how strong the relationship is between computer literacy and the geographic place where a student comes from. In Table 8, the researcher observed that there is a weak correlation between the place a student comes from and computer literacy. In Table 7, it appears that students from townships, urban and suburbs, are more computer literate than students that come from rural areas. The study also shows that there are more than 50% of the respondents from rural areas are computer literacy. The correlation is weak which suggest that there might not be causality.

Table 7. Computer literacy and place

yes				no
townships	urban	rural area	suburb	rural area
36	32	8	22	7

Table 8. Correlation table between computer literacy and place

		PLACE	LITERACY
PLACE	Pearson Correlation	1	.185
	Sig. (2-tailed)	.	.059
	N	105	105
LITERACY	Pearson Correlation	.185	1
	Sig. (2-tailed)	.059	.
	N	105	105

Correlation Between Race and Accessing the Internet

Table 9 shows that race does not have affect on ones accessing the Internet as all 105 respondents have access to the Internet. Some of them can access the Internet at any time they want and others have limited access to the Internet. There is no student that does not have access to the Internet. Table 10 shows that there is a weak negative correlation between the two variables of -.143.

Table 9. Race and accessing the Internet

African		Coloured		Indian		other
yes	sometimes	yes	sometimes	yes	sometimes	sometimes
29	32	5	1	21	16	1

Table 10. Correlation table between race and accessing the Internet

	RACE	ACCESS the Internet
Pearson Correlation	1	-.143
Sig. (2-tailed)	.	.146
N	105	105
Pearson Correlation	-.143	1
Sig. (2-tailed)	.146	.
N	105	105

Table 11. Place and accessing the Internet

townships	yes	10
	sometimes	26
urban	yes	9
	no	3
	sometimes	20
rural area	yes	6
	no	1
	sometimes	8
suburb	yes	14
	sometimes	8

Table 12. Correlation table between place and accessing the Internet

	PLACE	ACCESSIN
Pearson Correlation	1	-.274**
Sig. (2-tailed)	.	.005
N	105	105
Pearson Correlation	-.274**	1
Sig. (2-tailed)	.005	.
N	105	105

*Note: ** Correlation is significant at the 0.01 level (2-tailed).*

Accessing the Internet and Places Where Students Live

Table 11 shows that a negative relationship between accessing the Internet and the place where student live.

There is a strong positive relationship between age and the way students will feel if their course was 100% online. From Table 13, one can see that most of the young people (age 16 to 19) want to do their course online. This can be a result of the fact that most young people want to experience new things and that during their days, most of the things are done technological. From turning a TV on to playing computer

Table 13. Online and age

16-19	you will not mind	14
	you will be exited	21
	total disagree	9
20-23	you will not mind	14
	you will be exited	7
	total disagree	23
24+	you will be exited	7
	total disagree	10

Table 14. Correlation table between online and age

	FULONLIN	AGE
Pearson Correlation	1	.306**
Sig. (2-tailed)	.	.001
N	105	105
Pearson Correlation	.306**	1
Sig. (2-tailed)	.001	.
N	105	105

*Note: ** Correlation is significant at the 0.01 level (2-tailed)*

games and one of the reason that might cause old people to reject e-learning is that old people are not flexible in terms of adjusting for new things they tend to prefer traditional class room compared to e-learning.

Year of Study and E-Learning

There is a weak positive relationship between year of study students are in and the reaction towards e-learning meaning there is no causality.

Table 15. Year of study and e-learning

1st	you will not mind	7
	you will be exited	7
	total disagree	9
2	you will not mind	14
	you will be exited	14
	total disagree	15
3	you will not mind	7
	you will be exited	7
	total disagree	11
4	you will be exited	7
	total disagree	7

Table 16. Year of study

	YEAR	FULONLIN
Pearson Correlation	1	.149
Sig. (2-tailed)	.	.130
N	105	105
Pearson Correlation	.149	1
Sig. (2-tailed)	.130	.
N	105	105

Recommendations and Conclusion

In this section, the researcher will draw recommendations and conclusion based on the findings. The research questions, which were designed previously, will be answered and recommendations for future studies will be made. It can be argued that e-learning can potentially transform education at every level. It can make high-quality educational experiences available to those whose location, economic, and personal constraints have prevented them from pursuing their educational goals. These learners also represent a wider student market for universities and other education establishments.

Recommendations

Privacy

The researcher recommended that keeping information privacy in e-learning is very important. If your information is not private, someone else may steal your work and submit it before you do and when you submit it later, you may be charged for plagiarism. One way of ensuring privacy in e-learning is encryption. Universities are resorting to e-learning to provide instruction online. While many advances have been made in the mechanics of providing online instruction, the needs for privacy and security have to-date been largely ignored. At best, they have been accommodated in an ad-hoc, patchwork fashion. Privacy can be described as a learner's ability to maintain a "personal space" within which the learner can control the conditions under which personal information is shared with others.

Security examines ways and means for implementing data integrity and protection policies for organizations involved with e-learning. This chapter examines privacy and security issues associated with e-learning. It presents the basic principles behind privacy practices and legislation. It investigates the more popular e-learning standards to determine their provisions and limitations for privacy and security. Privacy requirements for e-learning systems are explored with respect to the "Privacy Principles." The capabilities of a number of existing privacy enhancing technologies, including methods for network privacy, policy-based privacy/security management, and trust systems, are reviewed and assessed.

Student Training

The researcher suggested that students must be taught about e-learning benefits and disadvantages so that they can decide whether to study using e-learning or use classroom learning. Further more, universities and the government should introduce projects that will teach students in primary and secondary school about this technological ways of studying so that when they reach tertiary they already know about this things.

Securing E-Learning

El-Khatib (2003) states that security examines ways and means for implementing data integrity and protection policies for organizations involved with e-learning. The researcher recommended that security in e-learning be taken serious. At best, they have been accommodated in an ad-hoc, patchwork fashion.

Infrastructure

The researcher suggests that for a university to offer e-learning it has to upgrades its resources.

Verification

The researcher recommends that universities need to come up with special tools and techniques that can ensure user verification. So that one can be sure that the right candidates is doing the work. In the case where it is not possible to verify whether the right candidate is doing the work, Universities can set exams centres around the country to ensure that the right candidates is writing the exams.

User Accounts and Passwords

The study show that many students they use the same passwords for different accounts, the password they were given by the university for their log in at the university they also use it in other accounts.

Government Involvement

The government must set rules, standards, and policies that institutions must meet before they can be allowed to offer e-learning.

Research Questions

How Will Students Benefit from E-Learning?

Students leave universities with degrees but with no working experience, these leads to a high percentage of unemployed graduates. With e-learning students can study and work at the same time so by the time they have finished studying they will be having work experience and qualification. There are many other ways students can benefit from e-learning and they are listed next:

- Class work can be scheduled around work and family.
- Travel time and travel costs are reduced for off-campus students.
- Students may have the option to select learning materials that meets their level of knowledge and interest.

- Students can study anywhere they have access to a computer and Internet connection.

- Self-paced learning modules allow students to work at their own pace.

- There is flexibility to join discussions in the bulletin board threaded discussion areas at any hour, or visit with classmates and instructors remotely in chat rooms.

- Instructors and students both report e-learning fosters more interaction among students and instructors than in large lecture courses.

- E-learning can accommodate different learning styles and facilitate learning through a variety of activities.

- Knowledge of the Internet and computers skills are developed that will help learners throughout their lives and careers.

What can be Done to Make Students Feel Comfortable with E-Learning?

According to the findings of this study student from technological disadvantaged places turn to reject e-learning. They prefer traditional way of learning one of the reasons that make student to reject e-learning is that they come to universities with out any computer skills yet e-learning require one to have certain computer skills. Secondary schools need to teach computer courses so that student can .

Is Government Involvement Necessary in the Implementation of E-Learning?

The government can play an important role in e-learning by setting rules, standards, and policies universities need to follow before they can engage in e-learning. This will improve the standard of e-learning as universities will have to meet certain standards before they can be allowed to offer e-learning.

Conclusion

Context may be the most important element that can help one to determine the success of an e-learning initiative. An in-depth analysis of the context should be the departure point of every e-learning design effort. To consider the context, take into account learner characteristics, including:

- **Physical features:** Age, gender, disabilities
- **Education:** Fields of study, degrees earned, computer literacy

- **Cultural background:** Language, place of origin, traditions, sensitive subjects
- **Employment background:** Experience, time in current job, relationships with other participants
- **Expectations:** Reasons for attending the course, expected results

More than 85% of students will love to see UKZN (Westville campus) engaging in e-learning. Sixty percent of the students will love to see their course being 100% online. From the previous information, one can conclude that there is a need for e-learning at the University of KwaZulu-Natal (Westville campus) in the department of information systems and technology.

References

Callaghan, G. (2001). *Collections of work on e-learning.* Retrieved September 25, 2004, from http://www.gocallaghan.com

Dunn, S. (2003). *Return to SENDA? Implementing accessibility for disabled students in virtual learning environments in UK further and higher education.* Retrieved September 25, 2004, from http://www.saradunn.net/VLEreport/index.html

El-Khatib, K. (2003). *International Journal of Distance Education, 1.* Retrieved June 30, 2004, from http://iit-iti.nrc.gc.ca

Hudson, H. E. (1994). *Universal service: The rural challenge—changing requirements and policy options.* Benton Foundation Communications Policy Working Paper #2. Washington DC: Benton Foundation.

Hvorecky, D. (2004). *Can e-learning break the digital divide?* Retrieved August 20, 2004, from www.eurodl.org/materials/contrib/2004/hvorecky.htm

Kruse, O. (2001). *Beyond Kirkpatric.* Retrieved October 24, 2004, from http://www.elearning.com/articles/art5_1.htm

Iowa State University. (2004). Press release. Retrieved August 15, 2004, from http://www.dso.iastate.edu/dept/asc/elearner/advantage/html

Major, J. (2002). *Plagiarism.* Retrieved June 25, 2004, from http://education.guardian.co.uk

Morris, D. (2004). *Help is at hand.* Retrieved June 15, 2004, from www.helpisathand.gov.uk/news

Tanner, N. (1981). *On becoming human.* Cambridge: Cambridge University Press.

The survey system. (2004). *Correlation*. Retrieved June 15, 2004, from www.sur-veysystem.com/correlation.htm

Wood, R. (2003). *Minorities more likely to use IT for education*. Retrieved June 15, 2004, from http://education.guardian.co.uk

Chapter XV

The Nearest Some of Us Will Ever Come to Information Heaven

Buyile Ngubane, TransNET, South Africa

Abstract

This study addresses the needs for a community computer centre (telecentre) for the community of Emkhambathini. This study was part of the information systems research exercise that was conducted by students. The problem that the researcher experienced was that Emkhambathini has no access to information and a need exists to ensure that this community joins the 21st century. The telecentre will also serve as a community upliftment tool. The data was collected using a questionnaire, it was collated and analysed using SPSS. The conclusion was that gender or employment does not play a role when there is a real need to access information.

Introduction

Advancements in information technology (IT) throughout the world have had an impact on the way people live their lives, communicate, and even on the way they do business. These developments have become part of people's daily lives and it has become important for everyone to embrace technology and all that comes with it. Unfortunately for rural communities, the advantages of using technology have not been utilized to their best advantage. This has encouraged researchers (i.e., Campbell, 1995; Etta, 2004; Sayed, 2003) in many parts of the world to focus their attention in finding ways in which technology can be used in the development of rural areas.

The Problem Statement

Although there has been some progress on the use of information and communication technologies (ICT) as previously mentioned, rural people are still falling behind in these developments. The lack of progress is due to the lack of infrastructure and finance that has led to a situation where there are not enough computers in rural areas. Rural people do not have computer skills and the cost of computer equipment is high for people in rural communities. Previous studies (e.g., Benjamin, 2000; Fuchs, 2000; Richardson, 1998) have focused on the use of computers neglecting the benefits that can be obtained in the use of other technologies. This caused the government and private sector to intervene by providing shared facilities such as telecentres. The study will uncover other services that can be offered to rural areas in addition to computing.

The spread of ICTs in the last few decades has had an impact on work, leisure, culture, and social interaction (Sayed, 2003). The modern world is undergoing a fundamental transformation as the industrial society of the 20th century rapidly gives way to the information society of the 21st century. This dynamic process promises a fundamental change in all aspects of people's lives, including knowledge dissemination, social interaction, business practices, political engagement, media, education, health, leisure, and entertainment. The speed of global technological and economic transformation demands urgent action to turn the present digital divide into digital opportunities for all (Ryan, 2004).

ICTs can be used as tools to provide access to information to the underprivileged people in the rural areas. Given the characteristics of rural women and men, such as having little or no schooling, speaking only the local language, among others, they are among the last to reap any benefits. This calls for more creative and innovative ways to enable the use of ICTs in rural environments (Epodoi, 2002).

There have been many examples in recent years of the applications of distance-shrinking effects of ICT. These technologies have been used in the United States and other parts of the world as an aid to economic or community development in rural areas (Campbell, 1995). The fact that more than 2.5 billion people (over 40% of the planet's population) live in rural and remote areas of developing countries has encouraged researchers to look into ways that telecommunications can help improve the lives of these communities (ITU, 2003). In Africa alone, over 70% of people live in rural areas, and there is limited access to telephony outside of cities. Telecentre projects have strung up throughout Africa in an effort to provide access to telephony and other ICTs in the content with the lowest access to these systems (Castells, 1998). Telecentres offer a promising route for rural communities of the developing world to break out of their isolation (Fuchs, 2000).

Definitions

Benjamin (2000) defines a telecentre as an organization offering telecommunication and other information services to a disadvantaged community. Etta (2004) defines a telecentre as a place whose primary goal is the public provision of tools to enhance communication and the sharing of information.

Chapman and Slaymaker (2003) define ICTs as those technologies that can be used to interlink IT devices such as personal computers with communication technologies such as telephones and their telecommunication networks. Campbell (1995) defines a telecentre as a central location within a rural community or region equipped with computer and telecommunication equipment and services shared by users from a variety of sectors; the services are usually superior to those that the users often have themselves. It provides hardware, software, and support to a group of individuals and organizations that alone might find them unavailable, difficult to understand, or more expensive.

This study will use the first definition because it also covers the issue of users and the kind of services available at telecentres. For the purpose of this study, a telecentre and a computer centre will have one meaning.

Telecentres as a Business Centre

In the work and debate around telecentres, some key themes have become clear, one is the business model. This can help answer the question of whether community centres should be economically self-sufficient, or rely on external funding of one kind or another (Benjamin, 2000).

A full telecentre costs around R20000. This buys around five phones, four computers, a photocopier, fax machine, printer, scanner, overhead projector, TV, video, and modem. The building is renovated with furniture and security being added. A mini-telecentre follows a model developed by the CSIR, a computer in a movable cabinet with a 3-in-1 (printer, copier, scanner) with phone lines and a modem, costing around R15,000. The turnover is usually around R8000 per month with a sizeable profit (Benjamin, 2000).

Fuchs (1998) argues for public funding of centres as a public facility similar to libraries and schools. However, Richardson (1998) notes that in developing countries, there is not enough money for such things and these projects should be run by self-sustaining entrepreneurs, anything else encourages incompetence and dependency. Benjamin (2000) further states that the rural telecommunications network must be operated as a commercial, entrepreneurial, profit-focused, and profitable enterprise as this will motivate the service provider to continually seek to maximize revenues and minimize costs. Their sustainability depends on them being run on business lines and charging enough money to users to keep the operation sustainable.

Fuchs (1998) argues that to create a tech boom in Africa will require African developers and entrepreneurs to join together in virtual, multinational companies to focus on developing African solutions to African problems. Balancing Act (2004) states that the central idea is that the public sector with donor support provides at a cost or low cost service for communities that are too poor to pay more. It is however important to ensure that the telecentre doesn't die when the donor moves on. And this can only be achieved because the local communities find that it serves their real needs and will continue supporting it (CINSA, 2004).

Policy

The advantages of rural communications and information technology collaboration may be becoming clearer to national policy makers (Campbell, 1995). Issues relating to policy about telecentres have generated interest in South Africa and the government is committed to addressing the inequalities of the past. This was seen in the reconstruction and development programme, which states that, "The aim of the telecommunications sector will be to provide universal, affordable access to all as rapidly as possible within a suitable and affordable telecoms system" (Benjamin, 2000). In South Africa, all telecentres are established in line with the Telecommunications Act of 1996, aimed at ensuring the supply of low-cost, local communication services to South Africa's townships and rural areas (Matsepe-Casaburi, 2003). She argues that guaranteeing the communications access rights are a state obligation as public security or education especially when market driven initiatives can't do it.

Sound and effective policy is the key to making sure that ICTs bring solutions that connect to real problems, otherwise it is likely that initiatives will be small scale and have little impact on the system (Sayed, 2003). According to Sayed (2003), policy makers will also need to consider the following:

1. Who will pay for ICTs in schools and how?
2. What is the role the private sector should play?
3. What is the appropriate balance between investing in training and infrastructure, such as software and hardware?
4. What kind of software will be used?
5. How schools that obtain ICTs and infrastructure will cover recurrent costs (e.g., Internet access and maintenance)?

Festa (2003) further states that government involvement is a crucial point in the establishment of telecentres, for example if computers are to be installed in a certain area and there is no electricity, the government has to act fast to connect the area.

More policies concerning software and hardware have been adopted by governments. South Africa has adopted an official policy promoting the use of open-source software but stopped short of jettisoning proprietary applications (Festa, 2003). The new policy by Africa's wealthiest nation expresses a preference for open-source applications when proprietary alternatives don't offer a compelling advantage. The policy reads in part, "The primary criteria for selecting software solutions will remain the improvement of efficiency, effectiveness, and economy of service delivery by the government to its citizens," which was drafted and published in a final version. Open-source software (OSS) offers indirect advantages. Where the direct advantages and disadvantages of OSS and proprietary software are strong and where circumstances in the specific situation do not render it inappropriate, opting for OSS will be preferable. "Elsewhere in the policy, the government pledged to promote 'fair and impartial treatment' of open-source software in procurement, create 'opportunities for trial use,' and take advantage of 'the opportunities presented by the OSS movement to promote access to information for citizens'" (Festa, 2003).

The State Information Technology Agency (SITA) has already helped the government save millions of rands by implementing open source in the public sector. According to Moseki (2003), the Northern Cape provincial government is the largest user of open source software, while the Western Cape government also uses an OSS-based document management solution and bases its portal on the system's platform. The department of land affairs uses Linux and is about to implement Oracle on Linux. Open source software is as good if not better than commercially available software. In many cases, it's more stable and more reliable. Unlike most proprietary software, OSS is available at little or no cost. Festa (2003) argues that South Africa and Africa will not be able to afford the investments in imported technology that are required to be a participant in the global information society if conventional approaches are followed. The government expects that OSS, by contrast, will provide flexibility (Festa, 2003).

Services

There is no magic formula for a successful local ICT's appropriation process. It depends on local specifications, and the designs should be relevant to local needs. There is no single successful model applicable to all; success depends on the capacity of adapting the model to best of local opportunities and synergies. No local plan or solution should be designed far away from the community. Top down solutions tend to be big failures.

Telecentres can also provide services in areas such as education, health care, local democracy, and small business support (Benjamin, 2000). The Mogalakwena Hewlett Packard project provides lessons daily for both adults and youngsters ranging from computer literacy to call centre training, computer repairs, business, and science and technology training. In the past year, the i-Community has trained more than 1,000 people, including municipal councilors and staff, traditional healers, health officials, students, and members of the wider public (BuaNews, 2003).

Distance learning is also an area that can be enhanced by the use of telecentres, it is much easier for rural people to study through distance learning close to their homes than going to city universities, a privilege many of them can't afford (Eggers, 2000). The term telecentre has been used to describe a range of services that include call centres and facilities offering fax. Among the services offered will be videoconferencing and telehealth communications so that patients can avoid, for example, a helicopter ride to a hospital when a teleconference with a physician attended locally by a nurse might instead render the diagnosis and treatment plans (Romberg, 1999). According to Eggers (2000), ICTs can help improve the level of governance in rural areas by allowing the public to access government services like grant application, marriage applications, and business support.

Etta (2004) argues that in addition to all these points, services should be designed in accordance with public needs. Time and space should be allocated for different user types like women and younger users. Booths for privacy in addition to sensitivity to human functions and functioning e.g. availability of toilets, fans should also be cared for. Etta (2004) also argues that efforts should be made to develop subsidised services and group rates (e.g., for women, students, or members). Time banding where cheaper rates can be given for off peak periods and differential pricing must be implemented.

Training and Skills

Fuchs (2000) states that a first step in training is often to demonstrate how the equipment and facilities available in a telecentre can work for the communities they are located in. Secondly, time must be spent helping locals, teachers, or entrepreneurs understand the value of information and the tools that can be used to access it.

According to CINSA (2004), the processes that need to be redefined and implemented are:

1.   Grow accurate awareness as to what is possible.
2.   Establish a shared vision around measurable goals.
3.   Establish a widespread skills development and citizen engagement strategy.
4.   Establish a sustainable process for encouraging ongoing learning, skills sharing and innovation.

The need for basic literacy, computer skills, and training in the use of ICT applications remains a challenge for rural areas. Language barriers and the complexity of personal computer operation have been shown to hinder Internet diffusion (ITU, 2003). Matsepe-Casaburi (2003) agrees that in South Africa, there is limited capacity to operate affordable and sustainable ICT facilities, and there is also low utilization of ICT services due to limited training and skills.

Gaster (2003) adds that management and technical training and ongoing backup need to be built in because if the managers do not have the imagination or skills to search the internet, he or she won't be able to transmit them to others. Managers should also be able to handle money, organize, plan, mobilize, and teach. He states that centre managers are not only facility managers, they are trainers, facilitators, and motivators. It is essential that they receive special attention and training so they can develop a strategic vision of their role, raise community awareness, train for a productive ICT use, and facilitate the appropriation process.

Problems

Excitement about new ICTs is tempered by long-standing problems in development (Hafkin & Odame, 2002). Parkinson (2004) states that the reason is a combination of lack of resources and because a commitment does not generally exist at the policy level. A striking observation is the absence of old and disabled people at the telecentres. Fewer women than men use telecentre services in practically all of the countries and facilities (Etta, 2004).

The problems of gender inequality are, in most areas women are marginalized with respect to ICTs. Their needs are often different from those of males and this need to be addressed at planning phases of these centres. Etta argues that addressing the gender issue goes beyond promoting equal access and use of the facilities.

In other countries, an inferior level of service from the existing telephone system, the lack of organizational capacity to coordinate such projects, and the lack of leadership to make it happen (Campbell, 1995). Ryan (2004) found that the Kgautswane computer centre in the Northern Province, South Africa succeeded against all odds such as no power, telephones, funds, or trained personnel. They only had power from a generator. Etta (2004) states that examples of more sustainable community telecentres were found in Phalala (South Africa) and Guédiawaye (Senegal).

Benjamin (2000) argues that major telecentres are an overkill to provide basic telephony. They use too much capital for the services they deliver, have difficulty in recovering running costs, and can not be reproduced in the numbers required to provide widespread access. One problem is competition, which has reduced the turnover of the telecentre in Thembisa. Etta (2004) notes that most of the telecentres experienced management problems, ranging from poor attitudes, to weak management, and the absence of adequate technical skills, inadequate equipment and high cost of equipment maintenance and services

Parkinson (2004) adds that fragmented and isolated initiatives often lack knowledge, resources, and expertise. They may not know even about things like open source software, or depth of their understanding of its relative advantages and disadvantages compared to proprietary software may be limited. Staff at these centres often has fairly limited technical expertise, and they often do not know how to implement open source or have access to relevant technical support. Further, because so many of these centres are struggling to get by financially, they cannot afford the luxury of experimentation with solutions that may cost them in the short term but benefit them in the long term. If investment in ICTs for development is to be sustainable, it needs a proper long-term plan that considers these ongoing costs. Hafkin et al. (2002) states that as a result of all these problems in Africa, most of the population remains unable to afford access to computers and the Internet, and reliance on imported software and a closed IP regime slows local development of technology.

Rural areas are low dense and this means ground based telecommunications networks are costly per user (Campbell, 1995). Telecentres are therefore facing technical and infrastructure problems in all countries. These include power failures or interruptions, poor connectivity, computer failures, printer breakdowns, non-functioning software, obsolete or unusable equipment, complex management arrangements, security failure, and policy failures (e.g., import duties or taxes on equipment (Etta, 2004)).

The power problems in Malawi have made the implementation of ICTs impossible and as a result of this, a project that involves laying high voltage cables over a distance of 220 kilometres from the Matambo power station in Mozambique's north-western Tete province to Phalula, 60 kilometres north of Malawi's commercial capital, Blantyre has been started. The project is aimed at ending the frequent power failures in Malawi that are caused by prolonged environmental degradation along the Shire river-site of the hydro-electric plants that form Malawi's main source of power (Etta, 2004).

Existing Infrastructure

Infrastructure has proven to be the first thing that demands attention before any project can be started. Matsepe-Casaburi (2003) proposes that the same cables that are being laid to bring electricity to rural areas should have the capacity to be used for ICT services. Benjamin (2000) agrees that existing institutions must be used where possible. BuaNews (2003) notes that the Mogalakwena Hewlett Packard project has succeeded by placing computers in libraries, schools, community centres, municipal offices, clinics, and traditional authority halls across the municipality

The Kgautswane Computer Centre has been used more than initially expected and as a result, there is pressure to add more computers (Ryan, 2004). According to Parkinson (2004), local schools can also play a role by introducing younger generations to computers, e-mail, and Internet. School computer labs are increasingly offering public use after-hours. But low Internet penetration rates and limited infrastructure outside of the major urban hubs indicate universal access is an ambitious goal. Etta (2004) argues that cheaper hardware and software should be developed (e.g., thin client solutions and telecentres should be used to pilot them).

Sayed (2003) argues that the debate over which technologies are appropriate and relevant in development has received little attention in the developing world context. One further cause for concern is the difficulty in obtaining good quality software at a reasonable price. Software is not only expensive initially but even if free in the first instance, as with Microsoft's recent promise to South Africa's public institutions, the cost of renewing the license prohibits many institutions from using it One target of private sector involvement should therefore be ensuring that developing countries have access to sustainable software that is tailored to their needs (Sayed, 2003).

Research Questions

Although the literature attempted to solve all the problems as described, certain issues still need attention. These are:

1. Why does the South African government take such a long time to create computer centres?

2.   How will the community benefit from such a computer centre?

3.   What other benefits are there for the community?

4.   Can this help in other terrains?

Conclusion of the Literature

There is evidence that important support for the MDGs can be achieved with the use of ICTs. The Internet offers extensive development opportunities, particularly for people in rural areas and living in poverty. Wireless Internet technologies can allow developing countries to leapfrog generations of telecommunications. Connecting local communities in developing regions to the Internet will have a positive impact on education and their health system The Internet complements locally available information, improves and accelerates knowledge flows, and can be used to deliver innovative education models to remote areas (Eggers, 2000).

Support should therefore be given to start, maintain, and run telecentres because they perform a primary development function for information and education, which is considered a basic and important human right. telecentres are to information what schools are to education and health centres to health and bodily well being (Etta, 2004).

Telecentres still appear to be a good idea. Market-based mechanisms may be penetrating, but it is questionable that they are sufficient to address social inequities and maximize the potential of ICTs for rural development. While current research hasn't produced any easy-to-follow instructions on how telecentres are done, it has found broad support and validation for the idea amongst rural and other disadvantaged populations. Amongst these communities, access to communication tools is highly valued. However, implementing telecentres successfully in Africa remains a rare art mastered to-date only by a very few skilful social entrepreneurs. Creating access for all through telecentres remains a distant goal and the passage to reach it, a mystery (Balancing Act, 2004). The next section will discuss the research methodology.

Research Methodology

In this section, the researchers discuss the choice of methodology that was used in this study. It will also cover issues like sampling, questionnaire administering and data analysis.

How This Study Will Be Conducted

A quantitative research approach has been adopted for this study because the aim of the study is to come up with solutions relevant to the rural people in rural areas. This approach will help in the understanding of rural areas in their context (Ihde, 1977).

The motivation for doing quantitative research, as opposed to qualitative research, comes from the observation that, if there is one thing that distinguishes humans from the natural world, it is our ability to talk! Quantitative research methods are designed to help researchers understand people and the social and cultural contexts within which they live. Kaplan and Maxwell (1994) argue that the goal of understanding a phenomenon from the point of view of the participants and its particular social and institutional context is an important feature of research. For this study, the need to collect quality data from different people and the fact that reliable results should be found before any telecentre project can be started has necessitated this choice of approach.

The Questionnaire

A questionnaire was designed to accomplish two main objectives: the first one was to maximise the proportion of subjects answering the questionnaire—that is, the response rate; and the second one was to obtain accurate relevant information for the survey. The questions were also divided into personal questions like age and gender, and knowledge questions like "How would you rate your level of computer competency?"

The researchers first explained to respondents that the questionnaire was anonymous and that the information they gave was intended for the research purposes only. A detailed explanation of the purpose of the study was given. The questionnaire was also made available in IsiZulu, as most rural people do not speak English fluently.

Sampling

The research was conducted from a sample of 125 randomly selected rural people residing in a rural area of Emkhambathini (Camperdown) outside Pietermaritzburg. This sample is taken from one district with the population of about 180 people according to municipal records. Respondents were chosen in no particular order to allow diversity in their responses. This was done by visiting them in their homes and in other public places such the tribal authority offices and clinics. Random sampling was adopted for its ability to allow every member of the community to get an equal opportunity of being selected for participation.

After completion of this process, all questionnaires were analyzed using SPSS and graph plotters to derive possible conclusions from answers given by users. Graphs and charts were used for the purpose of presenting the findings in a user friendly and understandable format. The relationships between the different variables measured will be determined by computing correlations based on the Stockburger (1996) model.

This information and all data gathered from other sources such as popular press articles will lead to the finalization of the research results. The literature review also formed part of the data analysis process. Upon completion of the data analysis, the researchers derived answers to the research questions.

Discussion of Results

The aim of this section is to provide a detailed explanation on all responses gathered by using questionnaires. The analysis also utilises other existing literature to support (validate) the findings of this research study. One hundred twenty-five questionnaires were distributed to the Emkhambathini community. Of the 125 questionnaires, 123 questionnaires were collected and two questionnaires were never returned to the researcher. Of the 123 questionnaires returned, one was considered unusable, as the respondent had ticked more than one response and in some cases left the response blank. The following analysis is therefore based on the 122 responses that the researcher considers usable. The return rate is therefore 98%.

Fifty-nine percent of the participants were females and this is attributed to the nature of rural life as women are still expected to remain at home and take care of the house and children while men go to the cities to find employment. This is supported by a study conducted by Ryan (2004) in African countries. He argues that old traditions have led men to believe that it is their duty to be responsible for income generating while women look after children. Lack of employment opportunities in the rural areas is a problem.

Nearly all (97%) of the population studied is African, 2% is coloured, and only 1% is white. The Emkhambathini area is a deep rural area and the researcher could not find people of other races in the area except for those who came to work on government projects. Rural people still live in the ways their forefathers lived. Their need for farming has made them to occupy these rural areas. ITU (2003) states that agriculture is probably the mainstay of the economy in rural areas. It is further cheaper for them to survive outside the cities. They found that about 58% Africans are living in impoverished rural areas of South Africa.

Table 1. Age distribution

	Respondents	Percentage
0-19	36	29
20-29	36	30
30-39	27	22
40-49	18	15
50+	5	4

Age of Respondents Who Participation in the Study

Table 1 reflects the age groups of the respondents. The biggest age group is 20 years to 29 years (30%), followed closely by the 0 years to 19 years group (29%). A further explanation of these figures would be the fact that older rural people are mostly uneducated and usually avoid participating in things they perceive to concern education (Etta, 2004). They referred the researchers to their children who attend school.

The results show that of the 122 responses gathered, 60 went to secondary school and that 45 respondents had gone to tertiary institutions. The educational level measured was taken as the highest level of education reached which means that it also took into account the people who have dropped out of school. The pass rate at matric level in rural schools is low which has led to rural students not being able to go beyond secondary education. Another problem facing rural students is that tertiary education is expensive for them. Six respondents ignored this question possibly because they had no formal education to select.

Employment

Of the 122 responses, 57 (47%) respondents answered that they were employed. This consists mostly of teachers and people working as unskilled workers (like construction). Epodoi (2002) made a similar finding that more employed people in rural KwaZulu-Natal were engaged in the teaching profession than in any other type

Table 2. Employment

	Respondents	Percentage
Yes	57	47
No	65	53

of paid employment. In bringing ICTs to this community, people will benefit, as this will provide them with tools to gather new knowledge. Also, the integration of services like youth portals and government information give them the opportunity to access services like internships and skills development initiatives. Telecentres also provide them with the opportunity to learn new skills that they could have not afforded to go to educational centres to learn. They access information to help them start businesses through government grants. All respondents answered this question showing interest in issues of employment.

Only 37% of the respondents have reached tertiary levels of education, which presently is the only level a rural student can learn computing, as rural schools do not offer these facilities. Due to the complexity of computers, most people in Africa will never own a computer (Ryan, 2004). Campbell (1995) states that by their very nature, rural communities do not produce economies of scale that make it less expensive to provide an advanced telecommunications infrastructure, powerful computers, and well developed networks. Etta (2004) agrees that the need for basic literacy, computer skills, and training in the use of ICT applications remains a challenge for rural areas. The low level of computer literacy presents a challenge in the implementation of telecentre projects as it requires that expertise be imported from urban areas, which might increase the cost of implementation. This was also supported by Sayed (2003) who states that because technicians were not obtainable locally many technology projects have failed to realize their goals.

Training to Use the Computer

Of the 25% of respondents who stated that they could use a computer 21% have received formal training at a university, technikon, or college. None of the respondents indicated that they have obtained an IT related Diploma or degree, but stated that they have learned the basics of computing as part of their studies. Others have taken computer courses at private colleges but these institutions are not available in rural areas. The results agree with the statement made by Campbell (1995) which states that in urban areas, single organizations such as large corporations, school systems, and city government can operate systems that are beyond the reach of any single entity in any rural community. Access remains an obstacle to rural participation in the ICT arena. Only three respondents had access to computers at school.

The Level of Computer Literacy

More than 50% of respondents indicated that they are completely illiterate and six respondents ignored this question. Only 41% of the respondents indicated that they have some knowledge of computers. Twenty-one percent specified they their

Table 3. Computer literacy level

	Respondents	Percentage
Beginner	35	21
Medium	12	10
Expert	3	2
None	66	54
No response	6	5

knowledge is limited. Most of them only know word processing and are not able to use tools like the Internet effectively. Rural people have not been able to access these tools because of the disadvantaged background and due to the lack of infrastructure. Benjamin (2000) argues therefore that the legacy of apartheid is as strong in the telecommunications as other parts of life.

Money Available for Computer Training

It appears from Table 4 that rural people think it is important to get a certain level of computer training. Twenty-five percent of the respondents indicated they are prepared to up to R150.00 for their training. These people chose the minimum amount and there are several reasons for this. Firstly, most rural people don't know how much computer training is worth in practice. Adverts usually promise free training with participants required to pay around R75.00 for administrative costs. This has led these rural people to believe that computer training is cheap. Not having enough information on service fees is a concern in the deployment of ICT solutions and the need to grow awareness arises (CINSA, 2004). Secondly, they might believe that computer training is for the rich and they don't have enough money to afford

Table 4. Money for training

	Respondents	Percentage
100.00-150.00	31	25
150.00-250.00	24	20
250.00-350.00	16	13
350.00+	20	16
Nothing	30	25
No response	1	10

it or they do not see its importance in a rural setting. This is supported by Campbell (1995), who states that when payment is involved to access information, people at rural information centres are less likely to have disposable income to spend. They hesitate to use family food, education, and clothing money for information. Twenty percent might pay up to R250.00, which is enough money in many cases to cover essentials of basic computing like word processing, spreadsheets, e-mail, and Internet.

More than 15% of the respondents are prepared to pay more than R350.00 to receive computer training. This number probably consists of people who have already received basic training and feel they need advanced training like programming. They have been exposed to computer training and know it can be an expensive exercise. Telecentres can help them in areas such as education, health care, local democracy, and small business support (Benjamin, 2000). On the other side these people might be coming from the group that has never used a computer before and have always regarded computers as expensive equipment that are only available to the urban communities. This has made them believe it is more expensive to learn anything about computers. This is an area that must be addressed in the establishment of telecentres in rural areas. There is a need to develop subsidised services and group rates (e.g., for women, students, or members) (Etta, 2004).

The last group of respondents is not willing to pay anything for training. Their reasons can range from the fact that the unemployment rate in rural areas is very high and people do not have money to use on training. Others are old people who see no value in learning new tools like computing. There is also a belief that telecentres are for the elite educated (Etta, 2004).

The results confirm the fact that rural people are falling behind in the advances in technology. Only nine respondents own a computer at home indicating that rural people do not know about computers or cannot afford computers. Ryan (2004) agrees that most people in Africa will never own a computer in their lifetimes. Telecentres provide a solution to introduce them to the information society and bridge the digital divide and will enable the community to share resources and information. This will allow the people who already have a certain understanding of computers to help the community members who do not know how to use computers. Rural people and organizations must be organized to work together and pool resources and demand (Campbell, 1995). Telecentres also provide an alternative to buying a computer and refrain from spending maintenance costs allowing this to become the responsibility of the centre authorities. Ninety percent of the respondents would like to own a computer. This figure corresponds to the previous discussion of people who do not have a computer at home. People show an interest in owning their own computers and believe that having computers will improve their standard of life in terms of skills. It enables them to access the Internet. They want to use the Internet for job searching and learning about opportunities on the Internet. It shows they understand that ICT are a condition for freedom in the modern world (Eggers, 2000).

Amount of Money to Spend to Own a Computer

A number of respondents are prepared to pay amounts above R4000.00 to buy computers. This confirms that some rural people understand the value of computers and the contribution they have in development. More than 85% of the respondents are prepared to buy computers for their personal use. Computers have the potential to help leapfrog the development process and empower communities (Epodoi, 2002).

Lack of infrastructure has been the biggest threat to the implementation of telecentres in rural areas. Nearly 60% of the respondents do not have an alternative place to access computers. This number indicates that rural people are still living outside the information society. Telecommunications connectivity in developing countries is usually available only within the capital and in major centres. Yet the majority of the population lives outside these cities (Ryan, 2004).

To find out the kind of alternative places available to this community the researchers asked them to explain where they can alternatively access computers. Nearly 40% responded to the question.

Most respondents only use computers at work (Sayed, 2003). Second largest is that of users at a local school with 17 responses. The people who have access to a computer at the local school are teachers and other people doing administrative work at these schools. If the schools can be used in the establishment of telecentres, more people will be able to access computers. This view was supported by Benjamin (2000) who proposes that existing institutions be used to establish telecentres. In the Northern Province, a secondary school has been used to establish a telecentre and they are control of this facility (Ryan, 2004). Matsepe-Casaburi (2003) made a similar proposal about the use of normal community institutions to speed ICT implementation in rural areas.

The majority of the people do not have an alternative place to access computers, which confirms that the alternative places previously mentioned are not available to the whole community. Sayed (2003) argues that there are two views in the public about telecentres and ICTs in general. In this community of Emkhambathini the

Table 5. Monetary value spent on PCs

	Respondents	Percentage
500.00-1000.00	28	23
1001.00-2000.00	15	12
2001.00-4000.00	21	17
4000.00+	40	33
No response	18	15

Table 6. Access to PC

	Respondents	Percentage
Local school	17	14
Public library	3	2
Internet café	5	4
At work	19	16
Other	5	4
No response	73	60

optimistic view is that the establishment of a community computer centre will bring advantages to the community. It will bring development and open up opportunities that never existed before. This is particularly encouraging to the researchers as it indicates community readiness for ICT implementation. According to CINSA (2004), establishing a shared vision around measurable goals is an important part of the implementation process. Fuchs (2000) agrees that the first step is often to demonstrate how the facilities in a telecentres can be made to work for community. In this community, this task looks simpler as most people support the establishment of a telecentre.

The responsibility of who will finance community initiatives like computer centres has been a key theme in the debate around telecentres (Benjamin, 2000). The majority of the people (84%) thought it is the government's responsibility to build community computer centres. This was influenced by the background that rural people come from, which has made them dependent on the government for their needs. These people often think the government is the only institution that can afford these services. Their view is supported by Fuchs (1998) who argues for public funding of centres just like the funding given to schools and public libraries. About 10% of the respondents suggested that business people are the ones who should finance this initiative. Although there are no big businesses in the rural areas, the new movement of popular government officials to the business sector has made rural people to think these people are rich and can finance any project in the community. Benjamin (2000) also supports that telecentres must be run by profit-focused organizations to encourage quality service.

Use of the Computer Centre

Responses were collected into four categories. The first was community empowerment where 30% of the respondents indicated that they would use the computer

Table 7. Uses of telecentres

	Respondents	Percentage
Community empowerment	37	30
Computing business	9	7
Education	53	44
Internet and e-mail	13	11
No response	10	8

centre to teach youth life-skills and starting community projects. The projects mentioned ranged from HIV/AIDS awareness, adult basic education, and youth empowerment. This can go a long way in improving lives and governance in the rural community (Eggers, 2000)

Only nine respondents wanted to start their own businesses in the computer centre (e.g., typing assignments and curriculum vitas). Some respondents already had businesses and believe the telecentre would give them added advantages. Also, access to government information like business registration records and tax records will be of benefit to small rural businesspeople. More than 40% of the respondents view the establishment of the computer centre as an opportunity for them to im-

Table 8. (a) Gender and employment, (b) correlation between gender and employment

	Yes	No
Female	30	42
Male	27	23

(a)

		GENDER	PC USAGE
GENDER	Pearson Correlation	1	-.011
	Sig. (2-tailed)	.	.902
	N	122	122
PC USAGE	Pearson Correlation	-.011	1
	Sig. (2-tailed)	.902	.
	N	122	122

(b)

prove their education, learn skills like computer literacy skills, e-mailing, and also to take courses online. ICTs are known to bring about distance shrinking possibilities (Campbell, 1995). The computer centre is therefore seen as a tool to promote information literacy and provide access to information.

Correlation Between Gender and Employment

The correlation between gender and employment in the community was calculated and reflects that more males are employed than are females. Sixty percent of the males in the study are employed. In Table 8a and 8b, the correlation between gender and employment is presented. The correlation is -0.122 indicating a weak negative correlation. The researchers find that gender and employment are independent of each other. This means that whether a person is male or female that will not influence his or her chances of employment. Gender equality is an important issue in the establishment of telecentres as women have needs that are different from males (Campbell, 1995). As a result, women find themselves marginalised in the implementation of ICTs.

Correlation Between Gender and the Ability to Use Computers

Table 9a shows that more males can use computers as compared to females. Table 9b reflects a correlation of -0.011 indicating a weak negative correlation between

Table 9. Gender and the ability to use computers, (b) correlation between gender and the ability to use computers

	Yes	No
Female	18	54
Male	13	37

(a)

		GENDER	PC USAGE
GENDER	Pearson Correlation	1	-.011
	Sig. (2-tailed)	.	.902
	N	122	122
PC USAGE	Pearson Correlation	-.011	1
	Sig. (2-tailed)	.902	.
	N	122	122

(b)

the variables. This correlation is very close to 0.00 and indicates that there is no linear dependence between a person's gender and the ability to use a computer. It implies anyone can learn to use a computer and gender plays no part in determining that. For this study this information is necessary as it tells the researchers that the services must be designed to the same standards for both males and females. It shows that women also have the potential to learn computers. In other countries, it has been discovered that fewer women use telecentres than men (Etta, 2004).

Correlation Between Gender and Educational Level

Table 10a indicates that females are more educated than males. This might be as a result of the fact that males are more likely to drop out of school and seek employment to support their families while females continue with their studies. Table 10b shows that the correlation between these variables is -0.03 which is a weak negative correlation. The variables are not dependent and an increase on one variable does not necessary imply a decrease on the other or vice-versa. Education plays an important role in the establishment of telecentres as the services must be developed to meet the educational level of the public. The fact that females are more educated as compared to males indicates that females will be more suitable to lead the development of a telecentre. It will also allow them to play a constructive role in the process leading to the establishment so that their needs are taken care of (Etta, 2004).

Table 10. (a) Gender and the level of education, (b) correlation between gender and the level of education

	Primary	Secondary	Tertiary	Other	No response
Female	5	34	30		3
Male	5	26	15	1	3

(a)

		GENDER	EDUCATION
GENDER	Pearson Correlation	1	-.030
	Sig. (2-tailed)	.	.741
	N	122	122
EDUCATION	Pearson Correlation	-.030	1
	Sig. (2-tailed)	.741	.
	N	122	122

(b)

Table 11. (a) Education and the computer literacy, (b) correlation between education and computer literacy

	Beginner	Medium	Expert	None	No response
Primary	2	1		5	2
Secondary	17			41	2
Tertiary	15	10	3	17	
Other				1	
No response	1	1		2	2

(a)

		EDUCATION	COMPUTER LITERACY
EDUCATION	Pearson Correlation	1	-.097
	Sig. (2-tailed)	.	.287
	N	122	122
COMPUTER LITERACY	Pearson Correlation	-.097	1
	Sig. (2-tailed)	.287	.
	N	122	122

(b)

Correlation Between Education and Computer Literacy

In order to determine whether the level of education of respondents had any influence on whether they have learned a certain level of computing, a correlation was calculated between the two variables. Table 11a shows that people who have tertiary education are more computer literate followed by those who have secondary education. The study had found that most people have received formal training in computers and also the number of people who had access to a computer at work was larger.

Table 11b shows the correlation between the two variables to be -0.097. This weak negative correlation indicates the absence of a linear relationship between the two variables. This supports the researchers claim that people might have taken computer courses at institutions that do not require any level of prior learning like matric. This result is a reflection of the availability of people who can be trained to work as trainers and managers in the telecentre. Sayed (2003) notes that technology projects have failed because technicians were unobtainable locally and staff were not sufficiently trained to make the most of the technology.

Table 12. (a) Gender and willingness to pay for training, (b) correlation between gender and the willingness to pay for computer training

	100-150	150-250	250- 350	350+	Nothing	No response
Female	19	10	10	14	18	1
Male	12	14	6	6	12	

(a)

		GENDER	PAY FOR TRAINING
GENDER	Pearson Correlation	1	-.072
	Sig. (2-tailed)	.	.429
	N	122	122
PAY FOR TRAINING	Pearson Correlation	-.072	1
	Sig. (2-tailed)	.429	.
	N	122	122

(b)

Correlation Between Gender and the Willingness to Pay for Computer Training

Table 12a shows that females are more willing to pay for computer training. The reason for this can be that males are responsible for supporting the family and feel that the money they have must not be diverted to buying things like computers. The study also found that more males are employed as compared to females. Table 12b shows a weak negative correlation of -0.072, which implies that there is no significant correlation between the measured variables. From this table it can be said that the gender of respondents has no influence on the decision to pay for computer training but factors like employment and level of income have an indirect influence on this decision.

Correlation Between Gender and Ownership of a Computer

The researchers wanted to know if there is any relationship between gender and the ownership of computers. Using Table 13a and 13b, it appears that only five females and four males have computers at home. Although more males do not own computers, the difference is too small to suggest that females have more access to computers than males. The correlation coefficient is -0.064, the result indicates that for both males and females the number of people owning computers in this rural

Table 13. (a) Gender and ownership of a computer, (b) correlation between gender and ownership of a computer

	Yes	No	No response
Female	5	65	2
Male	4	46	

(a)

		GENDER	OWN COMPUTER
GENDER	Pearson Correlation	1	-.064
	Sig. (2-tailed)	.	.484
	N	122	122
OWN COMPUTER	Pearson Correlation	-.064	1
	Sig. (2-tailed)	.484	.
	N	122	122

(b)

area is very low. This further indicates that more training will be required in order to get the people used to computers. Fuchs (2000) agrees that the first step is training, to demonstrate how the equipment and facilities available in a telecentre can be made to work for the communities where they are located.

Correlation Between Gender and View on the Establishment of a Computer Centre

Table 14a shows that the majority of male and female respondents are in support of the establishment of a computer centre for their community. Table 14b shows that the relationship between the two variables has a correlation of only 0.001, a weak positive correlation. This coefficient is too close to 0.0 to suggest any linear dependence between the variables. This means that whether the respondent was a female or a male they all felt a computer centre would improve the conditions of life in the community. This is because all rural people suffer the same problems of underdevelopment regardless of their gender. The result means that the whole rural community will welcome the establishment of a computer centre which is very important in order for the project to be sustainable (Sayed, 2003).

Table 14. (a) Gender and the view on the establishment of a computer centre, (b) correlation between gender and a person's view on the establishment of a computer centre

	Yes	No	No response
Female	64	6	2
Male	44	5	1

(a)

		GENDER	COMPUTER CENTRE
GENDER	Pearson Correlation	1	.001
	Sig. (2-tailed)	.	.988
	N	122	122
COMPUTER CENTRE	Pearson Correlation	.001	1
	Sig. (2-tailed)	.988	.
	N	122	122

(b)

Correlation Between Education and Employment

Table 15a is a reflection that more than 70% of the people with tertiary education are employed, while 26% with secondary education are employed. Table 15b shows a significant correlation of -0.315. This means that the services offered at the telecentre must focus on improving the education level of the people, which will in turn improve their chances of getting employment or starting their businesses (Eggers, 2000).

Employment and Who Should Finance Computer Centre Projects

In this study, the researchers looked at a model for community computer centres. This is important in determining whether computer centres should be economically self-sufficient, or rely on external funding of one kind or another (Benjamin, 2000).

Table 16a shows the relationship between people's employment status and their view on who should take responsibility to establish the computer centre. Among the people who indicated they were employed, 75% states that it is the government's responsibility to finance the establishment of a computer centre. These people take the government as the only source of finance for developmental projects like schools

Table 15. (a) Education and employment, (b) correlation between education and employment

	Yes	No
Primary	4	6
Secondary	16	44
Tertiary	32	13
Other	1	
No response	4	2

(a)

		EDUCATION	EMPLOYED
EDUCATION	Pearson Correlation	1	-.315**
	Sig. (2-tailed)	.	.000
	N	122	122
EMPLOYED	Pearson Correlation	-.315**	1
	Sig. (2-tailed)	.000	.
	N	122	122

(b)

*Note: ** Correlation is significant at the 0.01 level (2-tailed)*

and clinics. They believe that this is part of government initiatives the RDP, GEAR and the Black Economic empowerment. Although these people are employed, they are not prepared to finance this project as the community. Nearly 90% of the unemployed people also see it as the government's responsibility to provide finance for the project. Their opinion is shared by Fuchs (1998) who argues for public funding of centres, as a public facility similar to libraries and schools. It is worth noting that the South African government passed the Telecommunications Act of 1996 to speed up the supply of ICTs to rural areas. More than 20% of the employed people stated that self-sustaining entrepreneurs must finance this project. The reason that can be given is that these people are working for big businesses and have been exposed to the way these projects are handled. A good example is that of the Mogalakwena HP i-Community (BuaNews, 2003)

Table 16b displays the correlations between the variables. A significant positive correlation coefficient of 0.236 was found. Although a positive correlation exists, it is not strong enough to suggest that there is linear dependency. There are obviously other factors that might have led to people's opinion on the issue. The past political

Table 16. (a) Employment and views on who should finance the computer centre, (b) correlation between employment and views on who should finance the computer centre

	The Community	Businesses	Government	No response
Yes	2	12	43	
No	2	2	58	3

(a)

		EMPLOYED	FINANCIER
EMPLOYED	Pearson Correlation	1	.236**
	Sig. (2-tailed)	.	.009
	N	122	122
FINANCIER	Pearson Correlation	.236**	1
	Sig. (2-tailed)	.009	.
	N	122	122

(b)

*Note: ** Correlation is significant at the 0.01 level (2-tailed)*

system left rural areas out of the developments in the country and they now feel that because there is a new system, the government must correct past imbalances.

Conclusion

In this section, a discussion of the results collected from the respondents was presented by means of tables and charts. In examining the results of this study, it was found that the majority of the population of Emkhambathini is characterised by high illiteracy rate, high unemployment, high level of male absenteeism, and poverty. The results indicate a negative level of readiness in the community for ICT initiatives. More programmes aimed at the reduction of poverty and unemployment must be started to address the problems faced by rural people in accessing ICTs. Government and private sector programmes must also be focused in the provision of necessary infrastructure like electricity, water and roads as these might hinder the supply of ICTs to rural areas. Festa (2003) made similar remarks in his study.

Conclusion and Recommendations

Information access in the lives of rural people around the world has become important and this study focused on their use for rural development. The advancements in technology must be used to help rural communities take advantage of the digital opportunities. The need to bridge the digital divide between the urban and rural communities has encouraged many researchers to investigate the implementation of ICTs in rural communities. This study makes a contribution by investigating the establishment of a computer centre for a rural community of Emkhambathini (Camperdown).

Summary of the Study

The lack of proper infrastructure and finance in rural areas has prevented rural people from accessing the new opportunities that come with ICTs. The high costs of computers, low levels of education, unemployment, and poverty are some of the many things affecting rural development. This has made the government and the private sector start initiatives aimed at speeding rural development. The communities now have the task of ensuring that these initiatives contribute to their development by participating in their planning and implementation.

The study was carried out in the rural area of Emkhambathini to make a contribution in the resolving of these problems. The researchers randomly distributed 125 questionnaires to the community. The questionnaires were then collected and analysed using SPSS, which gave the results that were discussed. The findings are based on these results.

The Main Findings

The study wanted to investigate the feasibility of establishing a community telecentre for a rural community and the overall result of this study found to be that the centre can be established in this community. The area studied had access to electricity, which plays an important role in the implementation of ICTs in rural areas.

The study also wanted to establish if any rural people have computer knowledge and what they would best use the computers for. The finding was that the level of computer literacy in the community was very low in that only 31 respondents knew how to use computers. This indicates that the project must focus on the training of the community to use computers and other services that do not require computer knowledge must be offered. These projects include a government information centre where leaflets can be given to the community to read. This will improve government understanding in the community. The community was interested in using the telecentre for educational purposes. These include distance learning, adult basic education, and computer studies. The community computer centre must also address issues of community empowerment like life skills, youth development, and small business development. This can be achieved by the provision of information to the community and connecting them to government departments and other organisations offering help to small businesses.

Business Model

The study focused on the question of a business model that should be adopted for telecentres. The popular view on the business model for telecentres is that the government in partnership with the private sector must be responsible for establishing telecentres. For this study, the researchers find that the community of Emkhambathini would like the government to take responsibility for telecentres. Taking into account that this rural community is poor and cannot afford the costs of running a telecentre, the researcher agrees with this view. The fact that more than 80% of the community stated that the government must provide support similar to that given to public schools and libraries helped to make this conclusion.

Policy

Realising the importance of the role played by policy makers in the establishment of community computer centres, the researcher reviewed literature by other authors in the theory. This study has found that South Africa already has a policy on telecentres which is the Telecommunications Act of 1996 (this act specifies guidelines on the how to establish telecentres). The reconstruction and development programme also addressed the issue of telecentres but unfortunately, both of these policies still fail to achieve their goals because of a lack of funds and information on the part of the local governments who are the ones to drive these initiatives. The researchers conclude that local councilors who are in daily contact with the people do not understand the different policy documents of the government.

Government involvement must also contribute to other projects like electricity, water, and sanitation, as these are important infrastructural requirements for telecentres. This means that the South African government must start drafting other policy documents to address the rural telecentre situation.

These policies must consider the following:

1. The role of the private sector.
2. What kind of software and hardware will be used.
3. How will the running costs be recovered?

Services

The research found that people would most use the telecentre for educational pur-poses. It was discovered that the level of education in the community was low and people wanted to improve their education and acquire more knowledge through the telecentre. Services that are aimed at improving the conditions of living for the community must be provided. These include Telehealth, distance education facili-ties, youth portals to house organisations like Umsobomvu Youth Fund, and the Youth Commission for the people to get information that can help address the high levels of unemployment and illiteracy. The telecentre should also be used to provide information for small businesses as this is an alternative to unemployment. For the success of these services, the Internet plays a crucial role to provide a platform for communication and information sharing. It must also be used to help schoolchil-dren in their assignments, as there is no local library in the community. This will improve the quality of assignments the students complete, as they normally have limited information for this purpose.

Training and Skills

In any rural community, computer literacy levels are low because of limited resources to learn these skills. Training is therefore needed in this community, as 75% of the community cannot use computers. The study found that the rural community of Emkhambathini would need training before the telecentre project can succeed.

Infrastructure

The findings supported the fact that the infrastructure in this community is not as bad as in most other communities studied before. The community already has access to electricity, water, and tar roads. Although only a few individuals have access to their own telephone lines, the community has access to phone shops, which means providing Internet is possible.

Research Questions

Why Does the South African Government Take Such a Long Time to Create Computer Centres?

According to the findings of this study, the South African government does have a programme at the national level to create computer centres but slow delivery shows the lack of commitment by the provincial and local governments. This can be a result of a lack of information and funds for these projects. The rural communities are facing other problems such as limited electricity, clean water, health facilities, education facilities, and limited tar roads. The local governments prioritise these neglecting the telecentre projects, which are viewed as a luxury.

How Will the Community Benefit from Such a Computer Centre?

As discussed previously, the community will use the computer centre to improve their education and acquire new knowledge. Information about child nutrition, agriculture and tertiary institutions application procedures will be provided by use of leaflets or through the Internet. For a rural community this information is important as they do not have access to experts like the urban communities. For local business, the computer centre will enable them to obtain information on stock prices and free business training on the Internet. The government departments will find a place to make available information about grants, bursaries and other useful services.

Computer literacy in the community will be improved through the provision of computer classes at cheaper rates. This will also help in creating employment opportunities for the local trainers who have an understanding of computers.

What Other Benefits are There for the Community?

The telecentre can be used as an incubator for small business and youth will have a chance to form co-operatives and take advantage of the governments youth empowerment programme. For teachers and health workers in the community this centre will give them a chance to improve their knowledge, which will in turn ensure that the quality of service is kept in line with developments in their fields.

Can This Help in Other Terrains?

The study did not only focus on the use of computers in the telecentre but also looked at other fields that might benefit from the telecentre. Apart from the fields of education, business, and health, which have been discussed in the previous pages, the telecentre can be used by government to train municipal councilors and staff on local government policies and update them on the policies being adopted at national level. This will help speed government service delivery and address the slow creation of computer centres as the information will easily get to the local government. Training on computer repairs, call centres, and science and technology are other terrains that will benefit.

Recommendations

Training

The researchers recommend that computer skills training be incorporated into the normal school curriculum to address the problem of high illiteracy in the community. The telecentre must, as its first priority, offer training to the community at low rates so that they are able to use the services offered effectively.

Infrastructure

As rural schools do not have modern facilities to house a computer centre, the telecentre must be built as a separate building that is reachable and accessible to the whole community. This involves taking into consideration disabled people, children, and female needs.

Government Involvement

The government must, in addition to drafting policy documents, set up a formal committee to lead the establishment of telecentres. The committee must be allocated a budget similar to that given to other departments for this purpose. The government must also embark on a fundraising programme to attract big businesses to sponsor telecentres. This has been achieved in the Mogalakwena Hewlett i-Community project. Government supported companies like Telkom, Transnet, and others must also be encouraged to sponsor telecentres.

Staff Requirements

The researcher recommends that the governments SETA learnership project be used to recruit information technology graduates to work at the telecentres while they receive experiential training. This will decrease staff costs and help give unemployed graduates work experience, which will help them in applying for employment.

Conclusion

The advantages that come with the use of ICTs in the lives of ordinary people have started to show in South Africa. Although the South African government is determined to improve the lives of rural people, more support is still needed from the communities, the private sector, and international investors to address the imbalances of the past.

This research study has shown that the rural communities are disadvantaged in terms of accessing technology and information. The digital divide that exists between the urban and rural communities has played a contributory factor in deepening the crisis of poverty, malnutrition, high unemployment, high illiteracy, and other social ills in these communities. The lack of information can be easily addressed through the establishment of telecentres that will provide a single point of information and its sharing. It has been shown that information is an important part of a human's life and its unavailability isolates one from the progresses in real life. Telecentres are possibly a cheaper way of speeding rural development. It is the conclusion of this study that it is possible to establish a telecentre for the rural community of Emkhambathini.

References

Balancing Act. (2004). *The road to telecentre success remains mysterious*. Retrieved May 11, 2004, from http://www.cinsa.info/portal

Benjamin, P. (2000). *Telecentre 2000*. Retrieved May 14, 2004, from www.communitysa.org.za/docs/intafrica.doc

BuaNews. (2003). *Limpompo's rural i-Community*. Retrieved September 28, 2004, from http://www.southafrica.info/pls/procs/iac.page?p_t1=690&p_t2=1823&p_t3=2717&p...

Campbell, C. (1995). *Community technology centres: Exploring a tool for rural community development*. Retrieved July 2, 2004, from http://www-unix.oit.umass.edu/~ruralma/CTC_ToC.html

Castells, M. (1998). *The information age 3: End of millennium*. Retrieved September 28, 2004, from http://www.communitysa.org.za/africaict/report_intro.htm

Chapman, R., & Slaymaker, T. (2003). *Beyond the digital divide: Harnessing ICTs for rural development*. Retrieved March 29, 2004, from http://www.cinsa.info/portal/index.php?option=articles&task=viewarticle&artid=54#

CINSA. (2004). *Lessons on sustainability from Alaskan villages*. Retrieved May 4, 2004, from http://www.cinsa.info/portal/index2.php?option=content&task=view&id=129&pop=1&pag

Eggers, I. (2000). *Mali's centres of information*. Retrieved May 4, 2004, from http://www.findarticles.com/p/articles/mi_m1309/is_2_37/ai_66579838

Epodoi, R. (2002). *Bridging the gender gap: Women in the information society*. Retrieved March 20, 2004, from http://www.findarticles.com/p/articles/mi_m1309/is_4_40/ai_114007090

Etta, F. (2004). *The experience with community telecentres*. Retrieved September 28, 2004, from http://www.acacia.org.za/telecentres.htm

Festa. (2003). *South Africa embraces open source*. Retrieved September 28, 2004, from http://www.zdnet.co.uk/print/?TYPE=story&AT=2129893-39020381t-10000002c

Fuchs, R. (1998). *Literature review for the telecentre 2000 study*. Retrieved June 28, 2004, from http://www.communitysa.org.za/T2000LitRev.htm

Fuchs, R. (2000). *If you have a lemon make lemonade*. Retrieved August 4, 2004, from http://web.ask.com / www.idrc.org.sg/en/ev-8785-201...

Gaster, P. (2003). *Piloting telecentres in Mozambique: Learning the hard-won lessons*. Retrieved March 29, 2004, from http://www.cinsa.info/portal/index.php?option=articles&task=viewarticle&artid=111

Hafkin, N. J., Odame, H. H. (2002). *Gender, ICTs, and agriculture*. Retrieved March 29, 2004, from http://www.cinsa.info/portal/index.php?option=articles&task=viewarticle&artid=16#

Ihde, D. (1977). *Experimental phenomelogy: An introduction*. New York: State University of New York.

ITU. (2003). *New technologies for rural applications*. Retrieved August 15, 2004, from http://www.eldis.org/static/DOC10547.htm

ITU. (2004). *New technologies for rural applications*. Retrieved March 16, 2004, from http://www.cinsa.info/portal/index.php?option=articles&task=viewarticle&artid =45

Kaplan, B., & Maxwell, J. (1994). *Qualitative research in information systems*. Retrieved October 14, 2004, from http://www.qual.auckland.ac.nz/

Matsepe-Casaburi, I. (2003). *South African community telecentres face problems*. Retrieved September 28, 2004, from http://www.info.gov.za/speeches/

Moseki, M. (2003). *South Africa launches open source centre*. Retrieved September 28, 2004, from http://www.southafrica.info/pls/procs/iac.page?p_t1=690&p_t2=1823&p_t3=3376&p...

Parkinson, S. (2004). *Open source and public access*. Retrieved September 27, 2004, from http://www.cinsa.info

Richardson, D. (1998). Rural telecentre in a box. Retrieved August 24, 2004, from http://www.telecommons.com/uploaddocuments/Telecentreinabox.htm

Romberg, D. (1999). *Wireless links remote regions—satellite technology brings wireless communications to Newfoundland: Technology Information*. Retrieved May 20, 2004, from http://www.findarticles.com/p/articles/mi_m0CGC/is_18_25/ai_54593952

Ryan, M. (2004). *Computer centre lets impoverished village take first step into digital era*. Retrieved August 20, 2004, from http://www.govtech.net/magazine/gt/2000/sept/poverty/computercenter.php

Sayed, Y. (2003). *Missing the connection? Using ICTs in education*. Retrieved June 15, 2004, from http://www.id21.org/insights-ed01/insights-issed01-art001.html

Stockburger, D. (1996). *Introductory statistics: Concepts, models, and applications*. Southwest Missouri State University Sehrt.

About the Authors

Sam Lubbe is an associate professor in the School of Information Systems and Technology at the University of KwaZulu-Natal, Durban South Africa. He has a PhD in information systems and has taught many years in the field of IS. He has attended and presented many papers locally and overseas. He has also published articles in refereed journals and has written and edited four books. His field of expertise is IS strategic management, e-commerce, digital divide, accounting information systems, and database management. He has also published papers and a book on research.

* * *

Udo Richard Averweg is employed as an information analyst at eThekwini Municipality, Durban, South Africa. He entered the IT industry during 1979 and holds master's degrees in IT (*cum laude*) and science. He is a professional member of the Computer Society of South Africa and has delivered IT research papers locally and internationally.

Maxwell Mdumiseni Buthelezi is an IT and Webmaster specialist in profession, engaging in projects related to the uplifting of ICT standards and proper usage in a workplace environment. He has been involved in research projects focusing on the information resources usage at tertiary institutions and within educational departments. During the past year, he has been a core author under the supervision of his appointed supervisors working on an article looking at services within the previous discipline.

Geoff Erwin has worked in government (state and federal), private industry, and higher education in Australia, UK, USA, and South Africa. He has been an ICT team member, project manager, and senior manager/researcher for many years. He has written and co-authored several ICT books and textbooks, published and reviewed for international conferences and research journals, and represented organizations in international projects and committees. In universities, he has recently become Dean of a large business faculty and is currently director of an international research centre focusing on information society themes at the Cape Peninsula University of Technology (CPUT) in Cape Town, South Africa. CPUT has adopted the information society as a major theme and is positioning itself to approach e-service delivery and the social appropriation of ICT within the context of newly democratic South Africa. He is a founding and institutional member of The Information Society Institute (TISI) established in South Africa as a multi-stakeholder partnership with three levels of government, using the community informatics discipline and membership of CIRN (Community Informatics Research Network) as platforms.

Rembrandt Klopper is a trans-disciplinary specialist engaging in and publishing the results of research focusing on interrelated aspects of informatics, communication science, and linguistics, either as sole author or as co-author. Over the past decade, he has supervised scores of master's and doctoral students working in the previous disciplines. He is a special issues editor of the South African scholarly journal, *Alternation*, for which he has recently edited two cognitive science and three informatics issues.

Solitaire Maherry-Lubbe is a successful researcher and a qualified chef. She has the ability to negotiate with respondents to enable her to complete and participate in complicated situations. She has 10 years experience in the IT and business industry. She has helped in numerous other research projects and hopes to get more publications behind her name.

Mike Moncrieff is a freelance computer consultant who is completing a masters degree in information technology at the Cape Peninsula University of Technology in Cape Town, South Africa. He holds a masters in business administration (MBA). His research interest is trust and privacy issues for small business in e-commerce. He has presented papers on his research topic at several international conferences.

Inban Naicker is a young academic who completed his BCom degree at UDW in 2001. He has been recognized in the media for his paper on plagiarism and his selfless efforts in community building. Currently the chairperson of ESO, an N.P.O dealing with skills development, he believes hard work brings success.

Karna Naidoo has qualifications in each of the sub areas of information technology (computer science, information systems, and software engineering), a diploma in datametrics (information systems), a BSc (software engineering), and a BSc (Hons., computer science). Further to this, he has a diploma in education. His industry experience involved the technical support (both hardware and software), supervision, and management of technical and human resources. His industry experience in information systems and technology is as a result of holding various senior positions at IT companies over the past 10 years. This experience has provided him with the requisite insight and skills essential for the smooth running of an organization. His duties as a consultant were in an outsourcing department. Outsourcing is heavily dependent on strong management skills in order to deliver on customer service level agreements. Further, he developed essential communication and administration skills in a highly competitive and professional environment. As an information systems industry manager, the main challenge was to provide solutions that were cost effective and long lasting.

Johan Nel is a successful senior manager with substantial experience in strategic and performance management in a customer-focused service delivery environment, including the ability to negotiate with and influence the stakeholders. He has 31 years experience in the IT and business industry. Strong management experience in strategic, financial and change management, feasibility, methodologies, planning, development, and implementation. Extensive experience in methodologies and metrics with thorough knowledge of performance modelling. He has excellent project management abilities as well as group leadership.

Buyile Ngubane is a BCom (Hons., information systems) graduate from the University of KwaZulu Natal. He completed a research project focusing on telecentres for rural development under the supervision of Professor Sam Lubbe. He has spent some time teaching in the information technology field at a college in Pietermaritzburg before joining a major IT company in Johannesburg as an Oracle technical developer.

Hakikur Rahman is the project coordinator of SDNP in Bangladesh. Before joining SDNP, he worked as the director of the computer division at Bangladesh Open University. He has written and edited several books on computer education and research. He is the secretary of the South Asia Foundation Bangladesh, founder-chairperson of Internet Society Bangladesh, editor of Monthly Computer Bichitra, founder-principal of ICMS Computer College, head examiner (computer) of the Technical Education Board, and executive director of the BAERIN Foundation

Marcus Sikhakhane is a graduate from the University of KwaZulu-Natal, South Africa. He is working for an IT company in Johannesburg as an IT consultant. He was born in Melmoth where he started his primary education. He went to Impumelelo High School in Mahlabathini for secondary education. After finishing his Matric, he went to University of KwaZulu-Natal to study BSc computer science. He then enrolled for BCom (Hons.) in IS&T. His Honours project was focusing on poor information access in rural areas using ICTs, from which his chapter is extracted.

Pieter van Staaden is a database administrator at Media24 Ltd., a subsidiary of Naspers Ltd. He is also involved in application development, enhancement, and installation for both the financial and personnel systems.

Index

S

T

U

V

W